JESUS NEVER WASTES PAIN

All inquiries should be addressed to:

Book Domain LLC.
543 E Louise Dr Phoenix, Az 85050

Ordering Information:
Amount Deals. Special rebates are accessible on the amount bought by corporations, associations, and others. For points of interest, contact the distributor at the address above.

Printed in the United States of America.

ISBN-13   Paperback   978-1-964100-37-1
            eBook   978-1-964100-36-4

Library of Congress Control Number: 2025902290

Revision Date: March 1, 2025

JESUS NEVER WASTES PAIN

But Can Bring Eternal Gain

Keturah C. Martin

BOOK DOMAIN LLC

Dedication

Jesus Never Wastes Pain was written and dedicated first of all to Jesus Christ and His glory, the One Who so graciously preserved my life amid repeated abuses, destructions, horrors, and imminent death, in addition to affliction and being taken a prisoner to unfathomed depths and irons against my will and choice.

This book is also dedicated to my sons—Jarrett, James, and Elijah—and to my daughter, Zanthia. My love for them is so great that my life was laid down on their behalf countless times, unknown and unseen by all but Jesus my Preserver.

It is also dedicated to every other survivor of abuse as a beacon of hope to all, encouraging them to hang on and to press toward Light one breath at a time. My prayer is that all who seek to be used to minister to the broken-hearted as representatives of Jesus may also benefit from this book.

Acknowledgments

First and foremost, I want to acknowledge Jesus Christ, the Son of God. Without His sustenance and preservation, I wouldn't be alive to share hope, for it was the angel of His presence that saved and carried me through what was worse than death throughout a time span of thirty-six years. He was also the One Who performed several miracles in the time prior to and during the writing of this book.

There are three specific ambassadors of God who need to be acknowledged for their willing openness to be channels of divine love in the hand of God. It was through them He could work to touch the broken shatters of the ash pile of my agonized life with the unconditional love of Jesus. If God had not stepped in through the three invaluable agents who never gave up on me, my life would have diminished to nothing. May Jesus be glorified!

There are several angels behind the scenes whom I need to acknowledge as part of the miracle that this book was written.

This acknowledgment includes an angelic Weber cousin and her brilliant husband who gave me a quiet upper chamber in their home where I wrote a large portion of this book.

I want to recognize my mother, who was an angel in disguise, flying in from the far north to care for my children and manage my house in the last weeks of writing. She is an example of hearing and obeying the voice of God in a sacrificial way.

Also, I want to acknowledge the prayer warriors whom God miraculously put into my life right at the onset of writing this book. The loving sacrifice and time which these angels of prayer were willing to commit to amid severe warfare launched against them was truly the love of God in action.

Also to be acknowledged is Wendell Glick, who is the composer of the song printed in this book. He has graciously composed music for some of my poems, one of which is included in this book. It may be freely sung to the praise and glory of God, although permission must be gained for including them in albums.

Recognition is due to my son Elijah who was instrumental in creating the book covers.

Preface

Before this book was ever initiated or formulated to my awareness by God, I was under extreme warfare and attack from the enemy for no perceivable reason. At the worst, every ten minutes for seventy-two hours around the clock, I experienced horrendous attack and oppression from Satan, which rendered my body inoperable, though I cried out for the blood of Jesus to cover me. On the last day, God used a fellow Christian to pray and claim the blood of Jesus on my behalf. After praying, she suggested that we need to pray that God will make a way that the poems I've written and also my experiences could be published. Ten minutes after hanging up the phone, I was overcome with inspiration to write. As soon as the ink hit the paper, the terrible oppression of two weeks was 100 percent diminished! Praise God!

This was a strong indicator that the previous war was between Satan and the Lord regarding the work God wanted to be done. Subsequent to the Lord winning this battle, the inspiration came so rapidly that my hand could hardly keep up.

In the late summer and autumn of 2014, there was a series of miracles that God performed, resulting in the writing, completion, and publication of this book.

At 12:29 a.m., when my daughter was sleeping for the night, I was busy claiming the blood of Jesus to choose to forgive someone in a particular situation of lack of understanding. During this time, the Lord chose to show Himself strong on my behalf. Suddenly I heard beautiful singing in the corner of my room, which sounded like a male octet. The angels sang clearly the song "Each Step I Take, My Savior Goes before Me." At the end of the chorus, the music died away, but the presence of the Lord remained. I sensed Jesus right beside me, giving the assurance that He would walk beside me each step of the way!

Then while an anonymous, wingless angel gave me an upper chamber in which to just get away from life's bustle and write, another wingless angel unknown to me had filled my heating oil tank to overflowing in my absence. This covered a sizable chunk of my heating expense for the coming winter. I had not known previously how we would pay for our heating this year.

Unexpectedly I was invited to a ladies' seminar in another country. While I was there, the Lord arranged that I stay with a couple I had never met before.

However, through this arrangement, God set in place a powerful and committed prayer support during the writing of this book. I praise God for seeing to this detail so thoroughly and give Him all the glory for answering before I even called.

Finally, I must share that the spiritual warfare and the fight of Satan against this book have been tremendous! There were many times that my body would nearly give out physically and be on the verge of collapsing in dizziness, weakness, and deadly oppression. Praise God that the power of the blood of Jesus is far greater! Then I understood why God had initiated a team of prayer warriors who would daily and repeatedly pray and cry out to God on my behalf. May the Lord Himself abundantly bless their rich contribution and sacrificial living of love!

Last, but not least, I received an unexpected call from my mother a few weeks before the deadline and was informed that God had told her that she was supposed to come to care for my children and manage the house while I write!

This is His work, and I am but a scribe to write down what was dictated. Praise God!

PRAYER: *Lord, could You please send Your Spirit to help me understand whatever You want to teach me through this book. I choose to open my heart and mind to Your divine love and living hope. Lord, help me to connect to You on a heart to heart level, and experience Your healing and love through Jesus Christ for His glory. Amen*

"Ah Lord God! Behold Thou hast created

the heaven and earth by Thy great power and

stretched out arm, and there is nothing

too hard for Thee."

Jeremiah 32:17

"Lord, Take This New Year"

This New Year dawns untarnished, clear
To some brings sighs, new hopes, a tear:
Some souls its unknown paths may fear,
But God assures us He is near.

Christ walked before the path we tread,
Escorts us on the path ahead;
He only leads where grace will feed,
And He supplies our every need!

"Lord, take this year—unscathed as yet—
Take full control, that we not fret;
Lord, guide us on, each step, each day:
For You already know the way.

You know the trials up ahead,
And ev'ry blessing we'll be fed—
True grace and strength for us You hold,
To pour on us—refine as gold.

We trust the future to Your hand—
Glad we don't know the whole that's planned:
For anxious fears may then arrest—
Cause us to doubt that You know best.

Lord, lead and guide us, hold our hand,
Renew each day our inner man;
Each day, week, month this whole year through,
Help our resolve to walk with You!"

Amen.

Crying Out In A Barren Land

Most of Susan's life was barren, dry, and indeed, she was as a walking corpse, just existing in survival mode due to a lifetime of abuse, rejection, and life-threatening trauma.

Longingly, she cried out to God, for more than anything she yearned to have a close relationship with Him. However, due to the abuses, rejections, and consequent broken relationships, she did not know how to connect to God on a heart level, though at that time she did not know why she could not trust.

Sometimes in our life, we may face devastating circumstances that we cannot even begin to understand. It is so important to cry out to God our Father and cling to Him amid every storm and trial. He is the only true source of hope and help. Often the flesh and the enemy would try to sell us a lie that God does not love us or He would change our circumstance. However, the truth of the matter is that "He loves you so much He has called you through or allowed some hardship to refine you and draw you closer to Himself, and thus is taking additional interest in your eternal well-being!" Praise God!

If the Lord leads you to it, He will also guide you through it in His strength. His promise of being with us is a very strong indication that He has a divine plan and purpose for us that we cannot see or fully understand.

PRAYER: Lord Jesus, everything in my life feels so barren, dry, and destitute. Could You please come and lead me to Your well of living water? I desire to have a future that glorifies You; so can You please make it possible to find complete healing from all the pain, abuse, and destruction that most people want to ignore? I choose Your love, healing, and forgiveness and ask that Your Spirit begin His work in me to bring life, hope, and healing. Amen.

How We Choose To Take It

It's not what has happened to you in your life—
Though it may be heartache, deep anguish, or strife;
The circumstance, outward, will not make or break—
What matters is how we will choose each to take.

So sad you may feel about what came your way—
You're tempted to think you can't live one more day:
Or else you can search for a person or place
Where someone needs love and be shown God's great grace.

To crawl in a shell, so depressed, one may choose,
Believing that they were created to lose;
Or else count the blessings that still you possess—
Assured there are others in deeper distress.

Some say life's not fair, and that it can't be borne,
Neglecting to see fragrant roses midst thorns;
Or good we can seek and endeavor to share
God's love with the needy, to show them His care.

The pain of the past need not dictate the pace,
Nor shall it determine just who wins the race:
For through Jesus Christ we can conquer and win,
Despite what we've been through—what pain we've been in!

The winning or losing can never be based
Upon all the things God allowed one to face,
But strictly in choosing the Lord as our Guide,
As Lord of our life—to walk close by His side.

Is Life Always Fair?

"For I know the thoughts that I think toward you, saith the Lord, thoughts of peace, and not of evil, to give you an expected end" (Jeremiah 29:11).

Life is not necessarily fair, but living in a fallen world, one cannot expect a sin-plagued earth to hand out everything fair, for the father of sin is definitely not fair.

It is so easy for our human nature to blame God for all the pain, sorrow, abuse, hardship, or destruction and loss we may be faced with. We may tend to think that "a God of love would shield me from all these adverse experiences," and we fail to remember that a "shielded" Christian is not necessarily a very strong or stable one. We forget, however, that the enemy of our soul is the one who is out to steal, kill, and destroy, and it is our merciful God Who will not allow him to go beyond the bounds that are placed around us by the hand of the Lord. How wonderful to have the confidence that we are safe in the hand and control of God, Who protects us from the enemy of our soul when we come and cry out to Him!

It is our loving Heavenly Father Who can defeat all the devil's schemes if we but choose to surrender our pain, tatters, loss, and/or despair on Him to take control of completely. He then will use the most agonizing and hopeless circumstances as tools to foil the enemy and reverse all the impossibilities into that which builds us in Christ, draws us closer to Himself, and glorifies His Son Jesus Christ! Satan has already been defeated by Jesus, but is nonetheless out to relentlessly destroy as many as possible.

PRAYER: Lord, I choose to place all the adverse and painful circumstances of my life into Your all-knowing hand. Can You please take everything that was meant for evil and use it in a positive way in my life to glorify You? Help me not to stand in the way of the healing work You want to do in my life. Amen.

KETURAH C. MARTIN

The Underground System Of Abused

There is in the underground system of use,
By Satan's trained agents, a world of abuse,
Where innocent victims are downtrod and trapped—
Are broken and bleeding, and in fetters wrapped.
Through violence and horrors, abuse and dread threats,
Where words of dark cruelty all the stage sets,
Here, vile degradations destroy to the core,
It seems hope and worth will be seen nevermore.
Here innocent victims, which few understand,
Are brutally caught in the enemy's hand:
For Satan's trained agents seek total control
Of their victim's body, heart, mind, and the soul.
Through scheming and plotting deliberate abuse,
They throw out, midst terror, their spine-chilling noose,
Which captures their prey in a yet tighter grip
While crushing the spirit and sealing the lip.
The threats and stark brainwashing few souls do know
Set stakes in the captive which outward don't show—
Invisible walls round the innocent stand,
And fences internal ensure freedom's banned.
Their spirit is broken—so crushed—brought to naught,
And just as a robot they're programmed and taught
That "fences internal can never be crossed,
Lest horrors increase, or some lives may be lost!"
The innocent cry out, "Lord, where have You been?
My Jesus, please save me from violence obscene!"
The agents have lied, saying, "God does not care!"
But victims would die if the Lord was not there!
He tenderly holds them within His embrace,
Infilling each breath with divine strength and grace;
Midst horror and squalor and dark, endless pain,
'Tis Jesus alone Who doth fully sustain!
He longs that you bring Him the rags of vile shame,
With heart-shreds of anguish, so bleeding and maimed—
When ALL to Him's yielded He'll make you brand-new:
For things thought "impossible" Jesus can do!

Victims, Survivors, And Victors

When people have experienced abuse, there are usually two stages that are unavoidable, unless they die in their victimization, which then is called murder. The first stage is that of being a victim.

A victim is somebody who is trapped in a situation of danger, threat, harm, traumata, and/or abuse. Victims are helpless to escape or stop the damage and pain being perpetrated against them, whether it is physical, emotional, mental, spiritual, sexual, or verbal. In some abuse situations, people are victims for years only because the abuse is repetitious for that length of time and they cannot escape. People can remain victims long after the abuse stops if they refuse to seek appropriate help to address the aftermath of abuse or insist on keeping everything buried. The healing that Jesus can bring to all types of abuse is the only healing that is 100 percent complete.

The second stage is that of a survivor. When it pertains to abuse, survivors are those who outlive the abuse. This means that they continue to exist after the initial abuse has stopped. They have also continued to live despite the unfathomed demolitions left behind, although their existence may be very crippled, especially emotionally. A survivor of abuse may continue to live and breathe after multiple abuses, yet the more this life-shattering process is repeated, the greater the damage sustained in body, spirit, and emotions. There are cases where survivors, when found or rescued by someone willing to be used by God to help, are only existing as walking corpses. But I am alive to tell you that even as a walking corpse and being made dead emotionally, there is abundant hope and healing through Jesus, Who is the resurrection and the life!

There is a third stage that is available to all survivors of abuse, but is not possible for those who choose to remain victims after the abuse has stopped. This stage is that of the victor.

The victor is one who has chosen to expose the enemy (Satan), forgive the perpetrator, face the reality of what was done, and who is willing to bring all the pain and destruction of the abuse to Jesus for healing. Victors are those who choose to empty out all the consequent baggage and effects onto Jesus and accept from Him the boundless healing and restoration He can bring. Healing from abuse is not like instant mashed potatoes, but is a long arduous journey. It is, however, 100 percent worth the effort, agony, and time when healing and

Cont.

KETURAH C. MARTIN

freedom spell out the victory over all the evil that the enemy meant to use to destroy!

PRAYER: Jesus, I choose to advance from victim and survivor to victor, with You to lead out and bring me to healing. I choose to place in Your hand the one who hurt me, so that my journey will not be hindered by bitterness and unforgiveness. Amen.

Defiling Filth To Feel

To be abused in sexual ways will leave one's mind in jumbled maze;
It seems the hurt will never end—heart, body, mind it breaks and bends.
This road, abused, few understand, unless abuse gives them a hand:
That filthy hand is dreadful fate and leaves one in a horrible state.
Defilement's muck so constant streams, while fearful guilt seems always screams;
At every turn there's something new to bring the haunting past to view.
This road yields brambles, hurting sore, and one feels worthless to the core;
The victims feel they are to blame—are overwhelmed with guilt and shame.
The stones that others may find small, in agony makes victims fall—
A look, a touch, or just a word, brings back past horror—filth unheard.
The flashbacks are so very real—defiling filth e'en more to feel:
It seems the perpetrator's near and one knows panic's dirty fear.
The insecurity to face seems always walks at just your pace;
Mistrust and terror oft sneak near—at victim's fate to laugh and jeer.
Words can't express the hurt that's there—the ceaseless hurting one must bear:
The filth they live with day and night and nothing in their life seems right.
The victim feels there is no hope: escape defilement—learn to cope,
To rise above that inner pain and happy freedom feel again.
Friend, be assured the guilt you feel is not your shame—its hurt must heal;
The pain you bear with all its grime will heal, but it takes Christ divine!
And He is there right at your side—without Him near you would have died—
He longs to mend your broken heart and give to you a clean, fresh start.
Renounce the lies which Satan brings that "filth to you forever clings,"
That "you are dirty, bad, and vile:" for he's a liar all the while;
But rather to God's truth do cling, "My Child, 'tis over thee I sing,
The darkened tatters of your heart I long to take and then impart
My robes of righteousness for thee once I have cleansed you full and free:
For I the Lord your life do hold and bring you forth as purest gold.

PRAYER: Jesus, I choose to give You all the filth, shame, terror and agony, for You to take care of. Cleanse me and clothe me with Your robes of righteousness. Thank You Jesus. Amen.

Truth Amid The Shatters

Shattered, filthy, and alone, Michelle walked for years in a maze that was filled with terror, shame, self-hate, filthy horror, and unlimited agony. It was all buried down so deep in a dissociated state that only the ghastly effects could be seen or known, though not understood. By age nine, she had been sexually molested by three different men, some repeatedly, and was just trying to survive. It is in the writhing excruciation of survival, both during and after the horror, that the enemy attempts to get his lies in on the victims at their most vulnerable time. To the survivor, the following are lies:

- "I am too bad and yucky to be loved or cared for."
- "I do not deserve to be protected."
- "God was not there to help me when I was being hurt."
- "The bad man will kill me if I tell, because I am the bad one."
- "I am too filthy to qualify for God's love and help."

God's Truths are as follows:
- "I have loved thee with an everlasting love."
- "The Eternal God is thy refuge and underneath are the everlasting arms."
- "In all their affliction He was afflicted, and the angel of His presence saved them; in His love and in His pity He redeemed them."
- "There is in the damsel no sin worthy of death: I am her shield and exceeding great reward."
- "He [or she] that cometh to Me, I will in no wise cast out."

With the help of Jesus, these lies must be renounced and replaced with truth, or the enemy will use them to obstruct our healing journey. Lies are the absence of truth, and it is the truth that shall make us free when we embrace it with Christ, Who is the Truth.

No matter how shattered one may be, I am alive to share that there is abundant hope and healing through Jesus!

PRAYER: Lord, I choose to renounce every lie with which Satan has attempted my destruction. I claim the blood of Jesus over the lies and embrace the truth of what You have to say. Amen.

A Broken Trust

Trust in no way can stay alive—
It cannot bloom, expand, or thrive,
When it is shattered and deceived—
Condemned and broken, disbelieved.
Trust shrivels up in speedy haste—
Retreats in anguish and distaste
When misinterpreted and judged,
It fast decays to darkened sludge.
With broken trust comes bitter grief,
An aching heart with no relief:
The salty rivers ceaseless flow,
From ragged depths of pain and woe.
Again I cannot dare to trust:
For then, alas, it turns to rust,
As "trusted friends" strive to assist,
But think "tough love" can clear pain's mist.
Trust dwindles down till it's all gone
When judgments darken all hope's dawn,
When pain's depth one can't validate—
Its deepest root won't estimate.
With broken trust, midst anguished fate,
One no more can communicate—
The inner struggles dark and deep
Cannot bring out, but in must keep:
For misinterpreted are they,
Boxed up and labelled in their way.
"It seems impossible to trust,
Yet, Lord, I know it is a "must"
To fully trust You every day,
So please help me in this hard way."

KETURAH C. MARTIN

Trusting is the most difficult thing for those who have been shattered, trafficked, abused, and/or betrayed by another person. God is not forceful like men may be, but is a perfect gentleman. He will step in to help you bear your pain as soon as you are willing to invite Him to be a part of your healing journey. He will never desert you when the load you carry seems too complex for Him; and He will never fail or betray you. He is waiting to embrace you in the arms of His love.

PRAYER: Lord, it is impossible to trust. But please show Yourself to me and teach me to learn to at least trust You. It hurts so bad, so please help me, Jesus! Amen.

He's Master Of The Billows

Though the waves may dash against me in the darkness of the night,
Yet the Lord is my Salvation, my Deliverance and Light;
He grants joy amid the thunder and gives peace throughout the storm:
For when He the wave rides with me, I am safe, secure and warm.

When the stormy waves come crashing, in His truth He doth enfold,
While assurance then sweeps o'er me and protects me from the cold:
For despite one's painful circumstance the Lord is in control,
And He'll not forsake His children, but protects their heart and soul.

Though the clouds of doubt may scuttle all across the twilight sky,
We must fix our eyes on Jesus and believe His hand is nigh—
Look beyond the lies of Satan to the cross of our dear Lord:
For His blood is all-triumphant, and we have His living Sword!

And regardless of the enemy, his tactics and attacks,
We have all of heaven for us, and through Christ no power lack:
For our Lord has won the victory which we must daily claim—
We are conquerors through Jesus and the power of His name!

Though dark pain and heartache threaten our frail bark on life's wild sea,
Yet no wave can ever hit us, except Christ says it shall be:
For He's Master of the billows and holds all within His hand—
Your eternal best He's working, though you may not understand.

So each day do come before Him and there offer up anew
A true song of deep thanksgiving for your pain and storms that brew:
For each trial signifieth that on you the Lord's hand rests—
Though the enemy then rages, yet your Captain plans the best!

With sufficient grace and power Christ in-fills you ev'ry step,
Though your circumstance would shake you, by His hand, divine, you're kept;
In Gethsemane draw near Him, and there say "Thy will be done:"
For the Master walked before you and the victory He's won!

KETURAH C. MARTIN

JANUARY 12
READING: PSALM 107:23-31

The Finger Of God

What kind of waves are beating at your ship today? Do you ever feel like crying out, "Lord, save me, I perish"? Have you ever felt that you are sinking on the sea of life and will soon go under forever?

In my experience, there were many days and years of being heaved about on the foaming waves and then being completely swallowed up in the dark, briny depths of hopeless horror, ceaseless agony, filthy terror, writhing loneliness, and excruciating worthlessness. It very often felt as if I would never again come up to the light, and sometimes there were sharks or perpetrators that held me down in the agonizing pressure and painful turbulence.

With absolutely no place to turn, how was preservation of life and sanity even possible? I am positively assured without any shadow of doubt that while in the very deepest depths it was the finger of God Himself that reached down to the lowest abyss to bring sustaining hope and help when all else was completely zero.

God is Master of life's sea and raging billows, and we can be assured He is constantly watching over His children. He sees the SOS signals even when we are too lost, pained, nonfunctional, and trapped to send the signal of our crying, bleeding heart. Our Captain is out searching for those floundering amid the waves, and His life-boat will never sink: for He is the Giver and Sustainer of life! He is there to save each one when we call out, accept His saving grace, and grab His sustaining hand, which holds bountiful love, hope, and restoration!

PRAYER: Lord Jesus, please save me and help me out of the endless hopelessness and excruciating inner agony. Please deliver me from all the darkness of these horrible depths where there is nothing and no one but the unspeakable past which nobody understands. Please show me Your truth, Jesus. Amen.

My Shepherd Of Love

My Savior, the Shepherd, is guiding each day—
No want do I know when I follow alway;
In lush and green pastures He makes me to lie,
As cool, sparkling waters flow silently by.
My Shepherd of love always guides me aright,
Although the whole future may look black as night:
For He walked before all the paths I must tread,
And thus by His grace I'm sufficiently fed!
My soul He restores as I walk by His side,
And for His name's sake He so near doth abide,
As down paths of righteousness we daily walk
And have sweet communion as we share and talk.
So often my Shepherd will search through the night
For lost and pained lambs who may roam without sight;
He lovingly rescues from enemy snares,
And carries them home amid tears, love, and prayers.

He binds up their wounds with the tenderest care,
And each heavy burden so kindly doth share;
He lovingly holds them within His embrace,
While giving assurance of undying grace.
Sometimes through the valley my Shepherd doth lead,
Where shadows of death amid anguish do feed:
Yet He never leads through a chasm so wide,
Except that He always will walk by my side!
With my hand in His, I no evil shall fear:
For my loving Shepherd remains ever near—
His staff and His rod offer comfort so true,
As each darkened valley He guides me safe through!
My Shepherd, a table, prepares midst my foes—
Anointing my head as my cup overflows;
His mercy and goodness pursue all my days—
And in God's bright house I'll forever sing praise!

KETURAH C. MARTIN

Jesus, My Shepherd Of Love

There is only one Shepherd Who died in the place of all His sheep and then arose from the dead in triumphant life so that He could lead His flock and walk beside each one in their life journey! Had Jesus not sacrificed His life on our behalf, we would be subjected without hope to the roaring lion's deadly bondage and relentless torments forever.

What a wonderful Shepherd Who would choose to walk in our shoes before dying so He can understand our human limitations and struggles. He was tempted in every way as we are, including being abused, yet He lived a sinless life of example and now intercedes daily on our behalf.

The Shepherd's heart yearns and bleeds over each of His hurting lambs wherever they may be, as He seeks to carry them through dangerous waters and over the agonizing terrain they may encounter. He sees the enemy crouching in hidden shadows waiting to spring and wreak havoc on His wounded lamb and He takes action. Many battles are fought between the enemy and our Shepherd that we may not always be aware of: for Christ is ever faithful. He is always there to sustain the wounded, invigorate the dying, and seek out the lost or wandering ones as He binds up all the brokenhearted wounds He comes across. The Shepherd also puts limitations on the enemy of our soul, who is crafty in his desire to consume the Shepherd's flock, and Christ does not allow him to go beyond that set boundary. He sees and understands the needs of His sheep and will often use the hardships and pain that come to refine His lambs as He tenderly guides, carries, and succors them through each trial. His rod and staff are very comforting: for they depict safety to the sheep who then know that the Shepherd is near.

Being clasped to the Shepherd's breast during intolerable torture and inutterable anguish when all alone was often the Source of survival in my darkest nights! He carried me safely in His arms of love through agony, warfare and abuse aftermath that often felt worse than death as the enemy fought against my freedom and healing. Thank You, Jesus my Shepherd!

How Precious God's Thoughts

Before the foundations of earth were e'er laid,
For you in His plan had the Lord a place made;
He knew all about you before you were formed,
And near to His heart, there His thoughts of you warmed!

He sees the full path that He's laid out for you,
And just how He'll use all the things you go through;
His plan for your life is all woven in love,
And He will sustain you with grace from above.

How precious each day are God's thoughts unto thee—
Which number far more than the sands of the sea;
Although you're asleep or awake this you'll find:
Around you His thoughts and His love always wind!

Although dark adversity darkens your path,
Don't ever assume it is part of God's wrath,
But be most assured it is God's divine hand,
Who uses pained trial we don't understand.

For trials are tools we can welcome with joy,
Designed to build up and to never destroy:
For when to the Lord we yield all of our pain
He transforms it all into undying gain.

Our God specializes in taking your heart,
Which may be so wounded or broken apart;
The dark, bleeding shreds He will take in His hand—
Creating a vessel to use as He's planned!

He carries you close to His bosom of love
And longs to bring healing and peace like a dove;
He never can fail you—His child you remain,
And He, ev'ry step of your life will sustain!

KETURAH C. MARTIN

More Than The Sands Of The Sea

In the daily routine of life (especially when that routine may include just getting through a day of agony and staying safe), we may forget that God is right there beside us and thinking about us. The time He spends in protecting, providing, and also defending us from the attempts of the enemy is far more than we could ever realize.

His thoughts for you are more in number than the sands of the seashore! What a great and loving God whom we can serve and pledge our allegiance to! He Who holds all the universe in His hand and knows all about our life, past, sufferings, and losses—Who better to put in control of our tatters, sorrows, and dark-looking future? He is always thinking about us and longing to bind up any wounds we have if we but let Him. Besides that, He knows us better than we know ourselves: for He is our Eternal Creator and Everlasting Father.

When it may feel as if the raging sea is washing all God's thoughts of you out into the foaming ocean of life and you start to believe that you don't count with Him anymore, just stop and renounce the lie of the enemy and cry out to the only One Who can put the tatters of your life together. It is in these most agonizing moments when Satan is attempting to side-track you that God is not only thinking about you, but holding you to His bosom as He is intricately preparing you for some job He wants to accomplish through you, as He carries you beyond the current pain. The Lord can see your entire life and future from start to finish. He has a special plan for you that no one else can fill, which is why He oversees your painful healing journey. Rest in His embrace of love as He carries you through by grace divine!

PRAYER: Lord, I just cry out to You in the darkness and pain, asking that You would bring Your light and help me! I choose to put You in charge of my tattered life and the healing I need. Please help me, Lord Jesus, and teach me truth. Amen.

HE WILL KEEP YOU AS THE APPLE OF HIS EYE

JANUARY 17
READING: NUMBERS 23:19 AND PSALM 103

"I Know Your Pained Plight"

Lord, how can I trust You amid all this pain?
Where barriers loom and the doubts always rain?
I can't comprehend why abuse You've allowed,
Which ravaged through me like a field that is ploughed;
To You I can't come when I'm angry and pained:
For life, help and hope with great fear is disdained,
Yet deep in my heart how I long to be loved,
But I'm so afraid that from You I'd be shoved.

My Child, though you're fearful, do hark to My voice,
And understand fully that trust is a choice;
And this be assured, that I know your pained plight,
Yet I, your Redeemer, for you do now fight.
I still see the little girl shattered in woe,
With no earthly father to whom she could go;
I see shame and anguish projected on you,
Until you now feel that you're vile through and through.
My power is greater than massive-sized walls,
My ears always hear all My broken child's calls;
The chains of vast terror My love can subdue,
And I'll never leave or give up, Child, on you!
I'm waiting, dear Child, with My arms open wide,
For you to dare trust, then to step right inside
My loving embrace where true healing abounds,
Where love is divine and no limit it sounds.
For I'm not a man that to you I should lie,
Nor do I reject any soul which doth cry;
How precious, My Child, are My thoughts unto thee,
And long that enfolded to My breast you be!

KETURAH C. MARTIN

JANUARY 18
READING: PSALM 27

Trusting The Heavenly Father

It is not uncommon for survivors of abuse to struggle greatly with trusting others, including God. When one's father was the perpetrator, it can feel impossible to ever view God as our Heavenly Father and trust is out of the question—we think. How could a perfect God ever allow such a horrendously imperfect happening to impact my life and completely shatter my future? Often anger at the abusing father is directed at God.

Is a Heavenly Father safe to trust if He lets me get hurt and destroyed, or is He just like the one who shattered me? "I'm afraid He will hurt me if I let Him be a father to me."`

In spite of our insurmountable agony, devastating ashes, and the dirty ruins left behind, there are a few basic facts we need to acknowledge:

- God is not a man that He should lie or prove unfaithful.
- God's ways and thoughts are higher than I can even begin to comprehend and He sees the full picture.
- Man is given freedom of choice; so even though God allows the perpetrator to follow through on perverse choices, it still is not God's perfect will.
- When the wrong choices are made and the innocent suffer because of it, that is when the Lord picks up His children and carries them through the unspeakable pain, filth, rejection, and/or terror, etc., holding them to His bosom.

By this time the excruciating shatters and dirty fear is so extreme that the victims may not even discern the Lord's empathizing presence there sustaining them. There was many a time in my darkest nights of agony and horror that I couldn't say or pray anything more than "Lord Jesus, please help me!" Despite the confusion and pain of how we feel, Jesus is right there to help see us through! He will never desert us, and we have to choose whether or not we will desert Him Who holds all our future and healing.

PRAYER: Lord, it is so hard and scary to ever trust again, but I choose to trust You, and I ask that You please help me. I choose to accept You for the loving Heavenly Father that You are. Amen.

Lord, You Know The Pain

You know the pain, Lord, in my heart,
And how the teardrops often start
When anguished memories scream at me—
At every turn they seem to be.
Lord, take the pain of this abuse,
And every second of misuse
My body, mind and soul endured,
When help and hope were all obscured.
My heart feels naked and alone,
To filthy flashbacks always prone,
When dirty rivers flood my soul—
Defiling grime upon me rolls.
You know the shame and agony
That rages on, though none can see:
How torturous filth seems shreds my heart,
And hopeless guilt strikes like a dart.
Lord Jesus, You're my only hope:
For without You I cannot cope—
I only sink in deep despair
Midst dirty worthlessness that's there.
Lord, I surrender in Your hand:
The filthy shame You never planned,
The fearful guilt which is not mine—
The painful anguish and its grime.
My Jesus, at Thy cross I bow,
Requesting cleansing from thee now:
Please wash me fully with Thy blood,
And purify me in that flood.
Lord Jesus, cleanse, restore, and heal:
My body, heart, and mind to seal—
A vessel that pours out Thy love—
And clothed by Jesus Christ above!

KETURAH C. MARTIN

A Survivor's Cry To God

There may be times in the healing journey when almost every minute of each day one is engulfed in the excruciations of flashbacks and all their subsequents effects of filth, terror, hopelessness, trapped sensations, and extreme post-traumatic stress disorder. Very often for Carol it was so great in severity that her mind would dissociate, and there would be time losses from ten minutes to two or three weeks in length. The extreme pain was so far beyond the deepest depth that she literally could only humanly feel a small fraction of it. Truly it was God in His great mercy and all-knowing wisdom that did not allow her emotions to feel the full load of anguish because He knew she could never bear it. How faithful God always remains, even when life is so dark that we cannot discern His loving care or know that He is actually there!

Although the future was completely black from Carol's point of view, yet in great longing she conveyed her heartrending cry of desperation and yearning to God. How she longed for some kind of response from Him so she could at least discern if He was anywhere close.

In the best of times God is our only hope and help, but in the midst of unspeakable anguish, filth, darkness, and hopelessness, He becomes the only sure, safe, and imperatively necessary anchor for us to cling to and cry out to. He will never abandon us and even in the darkness is right there beside us, helping us to get through moment by moment.

PRAYER: Lord Jesus, can You please help me get free from the grimy filth, endless pain, and shameful worthlessness? It is so hard to trust, but please help me to trust You, even though it is so dark I cannot feel You near. I acknowledge that I cannot help myself and that You, Jesus, are my only hope to ever be free. I choose You, though I can't feel You; I choose Life though I feel it is easier to die. I choose to accept Your love, life, and salvation, and ask You to work a healing transformation in me, Jesus. Please take charge of the ruins and shameful tatters and send me some light. Amen.

Despite What Came, I Love Thee

"My precious Child, come near to Me:
For I thy God shall ever be,
I know thy pain, the filth, and shame—
Yet I have called thee by thy name.
I suffered with thee through the pain,
And longed to spare thee of the stain:
I loved thee, Child, despite what came,
And will yet glorify My name.

My ways are higher, Child, than thine:
For I have planned thee—thou art Mine,
And I allow no grief or pain,
Except that it should bring true gain.
Child, come surrender to My hand
All pain which you don't understand,
The guilty filth, the naked shame,
The agony which none can tame.

The cleansing blood of My dear Son
Suffices fully for each one
Who comes to Me just as a child—
It matters not how sore defiled.
So meet Me, Child, beside the cross,
That all you suffered won't be loss:
For if you give it all to Me,
I fully cleanse and set you free.

The tattered rags of filth's despair,
I will exchange because I care:
Will clothe thee, Child, in raiment white—
With purity dispel thy night!
Though called through fire, naught is loss:
For fire rids thee of all dross;
Trust all to Me—thy hand I hold,
Then you'll come forth as purest gold!"

KETURAH C. MARTIN

God's Response To My Cry

The response from the Lord through the words of yesterday's poem could have come only from God Himself: for that time of my life was over-flowing with filth, shame, just surviving, untold excruciations, unlimited self-hate, and desperate hopelessness.

It started a rejuvenation of hope that was only a wispy, tangled thread that I tried to grasp. It seemed, however, that it broke and disappeared so often, especially when I surveyed the seemingly insurmountable mountains of defilement, nestled among the looming boulders of degradation and self-hate. How could God's hand ever be big enough to hold such loathsome things as my experiences contained? How could I be sure He would not reject me as so many of His people had and count me as nothing?

Could the cleansing and the white raiment He promised actually suffice for one who had been so trashed, defiled, terrorized, and robbed of everything but life itself?

The hand of the Lord is, indeed, big enough, not only to hold everything I had to bring to Him for healing and cleansing, but also for every other suvivor of any and all types of abuse suffered! God will never cast off His people, nor will He forsake the work of His hands that He has begun in you! Whoever comes to Him He will in no wise cast out: for He Who has a full picture of our life also has a full understanding of every detail about our experience and all the horrific aftereffects. Though humans cannot always empathize, understand, and assist us, yet the Great Physician, Jesus, can fill all these areas of need if we but come to Him: for He walked the road before us!

PRAYER: Lord Jesus, I feel like a dirty pile of worthless rags fit only for the dunghill, but if You can detect any value left after the degradations, will You please help me and save me from the unlimited filth and endless shame? Please help me to be clean again through Your blood, Jesus. Amen.

Choose By Grace To Pay

I loved thee, Child, before thy birth—sent Jesus to this sin-cursed earth:
He tasted death for every man—and finished My redemption plan.
So sinless, yet He chose to give His life and blood that you may live:
He paid your ransom debt so high, as on the cross He chose to die.

I chose to give you pardon, free, through Jesus Christ—His death for thee:
Forgiving all your sin and past—behind My back, it all do cast!
Yet, Child, in order to be free, true love, divine, must come from thee,
Toward your fellowmen expressed, who have caused hurt—your life have
messed.

From off yourself now take your eyes, renouncing Satan's bitter lies,
And choose to go right to the cross in place of him who caused your loss.
There die to self and choose by grace to pay pain's debt for all you faced:
Forgiving the offender's sin—all painful damage wrought within.

As you release him to be free—assume his debts he brought on thee,
Then freedom full returns to you, allowing Me to heal anew!
But if you think you can't forgive, then freedom, full, I cannot give,
But chains of bitterness will bind your spirit, body, heart, and mind.

So yield your "rights" into God's hand with all that you can't understand;
Give Him the strands of throbbing pain: for He alone turns all to gain!
Oh glorious freedom, joy and peace, to choose forgiveness, to release
All pain and past into God's hand, Who has for me a perfect plan!

The chains will snap and fetters fly when you call to the Lord on high,
From heaven He'll reach down in love and lift you up to heights above
Where His true love He'll show to you as He restores and makes life new—
His Child He never will forsake, but with you every step will take!

KETURAH C. MARTIN

Choose To Pay

The Lord brought me a second response that I had absolutely no idea how to perform. For my flesh and all the anguishing destruction contained therein was screaming out for revenge on all the many perpetrators who had shattered my broken life in every way. "It is impossible to ever forgive any one of them or to personally assume upon myself their horrendous debts against me. They deserve to be severely punished."

Our Father in heaven is so patient and kind toward His broken children who often cannot understand all He is trying to teach and help them with in the journey of healing, which He longs to lead them on. God used some of His instruments to show me very clearly in my darkest night some fundamental truths.

- "We will *never* be free from pain, filth, and shame unless we choose to forgive those who had been used by the enemy to hurt and destroy us."
- "If we choose to *not* forgive, we are automatically choosing to place ourselves as slaves to unforgiveness, our abuser and ultimately Satan."
- "If I do not forgive those who have wronged me, God cannot forgive me to any greater extent."
- "To *not* forgive is choosing a life in prison where bitterness and hatred would be my guards and ultimately lead to a self-chosen death-row."
- "Jesus was the most perfect example of choosing to forgive His abusers even while they were murdering Him."
- "To *not* forgive is placing our life and future in the control of our abuser."

With all these facts before me, in my anguish and desiring to do that which is right, I knew I must choose with God's help to forgive.

PRAYER: Jesus, I choose to forgive _____ and release him into Your hand for _____, which made me feel _____. I am willing with Your help to pay the emotional pain and after effects that _____ has caused me, and I ask You, Lord, to take back all the ground Satan gained in me through my bitterness and ask You to take full control of those grounds. Lord, please show me if I have wronged in any way the one who hurt me. Amen.

Real Gains Of Forgiveness

Because of my Jesus, I never could dare
To walk on the road of dark pitfalls and snares,
Where gulches of hatred would trip many feet,
And quicksands of bitterness one often meets.
This road leading downward, breathes anger, its air,
While fires of vengeance at passers may stare;
Here travellers dragging in burdens and chains,
Trudge wearily on with no hope of real gains:
For fetters have bound them in hopeless despair—
Beginning the moment they blindly did dare
To taste of the venomous, life-sucking bait,
Where dark unforgiveness fueled up fatal hate.
That first taste grew wildly, which none could abate—
Its flourishing poison spelled out deadly fate
As spiritual life was then deadened in gloom,
And freedom was vanquished beneath hatred's doom.
The Lord Jesus Christ is our hope and our stay—
Through His love, divine, we can choose the straight Way,
Avoiding the road of hate's fiery breath—
Escaping the pitfalls and snares of sure death.
Despite what one's been through, though treated so wrong,
In Christ and His love we can still have a song:
For there's no excuse to be bound in hate's chains,
When Christ shed His blood to forgive every stain!
We must decide fully "to choose to forgive"
Our every offender that we then can live:
Through Jesus "to choose to release them complete,"
And pay for pain's damage as God with us meets.
"To choose to forgive," we cannot do alone,
But need love, divine, for the flesh is so prone;
The Lord will then meet us partway in our choice—
Give strength to proceed as love helps us rejoice.
When we have forgiven, released them to God,
Surrendered to Christ the pained paths we have trod—
Unspeakable freedom and joy He then gives—
When we "choose forgiveness," our soul freely lives!

KETURAH C. MARTIN

JANUARY 26
READING: GENESIS 45:1-11

How To Choose Forgiveness

Forgiving one's abuser or offender goes directly against the human nature and is not possible in the truest sense without the divine assistance of Jesus. The flesh cries out for revenge when one becomes an innocent victim of life-shattering abuse or destruction. The more prolonged or intense one's suffering may be, the greater is the attempt of the enemy to implant his poisonous seeds of malicious anger and bitter hatred within the tattered depths of the victim's heart. Once he gains that foothold, the downward spiral of destruction gains momentum with each step taken in that direction of hateful unforgiveness. One of the most liberating experiences is to renounce and reject every bitter thought and hateful intent that one may harbor against anyone who has hurt or even shattered them. Once we have chosen, with God's help, to reject the bitter seeds of Satan's sowing, we then reach a distinguished crossroads. Here we will have to make a conscious choice of following our feelings and traveling the dark road of anger, revenge, and bitterness, or going against our will, feelings, and natural inclinations to take the steep, impossible-looking ascent on the rocky unbeaten path that leads to forgiveness. The moment we decide to choose the path of forgiveness, even though "we don't feel like it," Jesus, the Master Forgiver, steps right beside each soul and enables us to proceed against all other argument or obstacle. With Jesus at our side, He freely pours out His divine love, abundant strength, and Spirit-led direction. With His divine assistance, we can then make a choice that overrules the will, mind, pain, and all the bitter lies and interference of Satan. At the cross of Jesus and kneeling at His feet, He aids us in love as we completely release into His hand all the agony of our abuse or hurt, the perpetrator of that pain, all the resulting damage, consequences, and everything spoken or enacted against us. He then gives the abundance of grace, love, and power to pay for the damage done as we surrender it all to His nail-pierced hand to take full charge over. Jesus then replaces every poison seed of unforgiveness or hatred with a deep compassion and love for the soul of the abuser or offender, and the freed individual is filled with a longing that this person who ravaged so much destruction in his life would experience Jesus and join him in eternity's bliss!

PRAYER: I choose to forgive and release _____ to You, Lord, for _____ , causing me to feel _____ . I am willing to pay the emotional pain and consequences _____ caused me, and I ask You to take back all the ground Satan gained through my bitterness. Jesus, I choose Your love. Amen.

Why Does God Let It Happen?

Just why does the Lord allow tragedy's pain?
How could it be possible that there's a gain?
Does God really see the dark anguished despair?
Amid crushing pain, will He show me His care?
Do not lose your courage—take heart and look up:
For God's in control of each thing in your cup;
He sees the full picture of life as a whole,
And works it all out for the best of your soul!

When heartache and anguish is dished on my plate,
I must praise my God for His all-knowing trait:
For He will allow only that which is best,
And gives grace sufficient for each painful test.
Although it is tragedy, pain, or abuse—
Commit it to God for His infinite use:
For He has a plan of eternal design,
And say, "Lord, not my will be done, but just Thine."

An attitude, meek, with God's help do maintain—
Assured amid heartache thy Lord will sustain:
For when you commit all the pain to His hand,
He works it all out for the best that He's planned.
God uses each circumstance, painful and grim
To spill out His power right over the brim:
For when we are weak then our God becomes strong,
And midst ceaseless anguish creates a new song.

The enemy seeks to destroy us through pain,
But God supervises the Devil's disdain;
The Lord always writes the last chapter, you see—
And He shows His power to you and to me!
So yield all your rights and your life to His hand—
Each dark situation you don't understand;
When given to Him, He your life fully holds,
And He for His praise brings you forth as pure gold!

God Will Never Waste Pain

After years of suffering the aftereffects of countless abuses and destructions God made me aware that the pain of what I endured and survived with His help need not be a despicable thorn or abhorrent blotch to my life and future. Grasping eagerly at this concept, I began to hear the Heavenly Father instruct me into His higher way of thinking about the excruciations and demolitions of the past.

- To adopt the thought pattern that "I am a victim" and focus solely on the pain will give Satan greater leverage in my life, just as he plotted to do through the abuse that he alone instigated.
- The pain, filth, and/or destructions must be brought to Jesus, Who is the only One capable of bearing such an agonizing load.
- When the pain, perpetrator, and past is surrendered to the hand of Jesus for cleansing or healing, along with "choosing to forgive," then God steps in and turns the whole mess into divine tools within His divine hand to shape and refine His surrendered child to fit His plan more perfectly.
- To remain bitter or attempt to cling to "my rights" will actually feed right into the roaring lion's game plan to steal, kill, and destroy me.
- Satan's schemes against me are defeated, and God can reverse all his attempts when the pain and past are put under the complete control and Lordship of Jesus and His blood while being turned into divine tools.

Jesus will never waste our pain and circumstances if we just choose to commit them 100 percent to Him and leave them there for Him to use in the eternal building of our lives. Because our Heavenly Father sees our life from start to finish, He is most qualified to be in full charge, as He uses even the most agonizing pain and dirty degradations to build eternal gains and glorify the name of Jesus Christ Who is the Source of our healing!

PRAYER: Lord Jesus, You know how the pain is so extreme that sometimes I cannot take another step as it engulfs me. I choose to surrender to You all this agony, and I ask that You take all the tangled anguish, dark horror, and dirty shame and turn these impossibles into tools by which You can build my life and defeat the purposes of the enemy. Thank You, Jesus! Amen.

The Enemy's Dark Ditches

How goeth the travel in your life today?
What obstacles, friend, do you find in your way?
Do boulders and brambles loom harshly and grim?
Obscuring your vision as all grows so dim.
Do dark lies and unbelief come from all sides?
Attempting to hide the dear Savior Who died;
The enemy's seeking to camouflage Truth
And laying dark ditches of doubt so uncouth.

By faith cling to Jesus, despite what befall,
And hold to His hand, Who has power o'er all;
He'll bear you above all the lies at your feet,
As near to His bosom your rest is complete!
For Satan's defeated in all that he tries,
Despite his deceptions, his traps, and his lies,
But if he can get you to doubt just a bit,
He'll get a dread toe-hold where doom will soon sit.

Renounce ev'ry lie and the doubt that he brings
Keep focused on Jesus—to all His truth cling;
The winning is yours only as you keep on:
And joys are awaiting just inside the dawn!
For Christ paid the price to redeem you from death
And bids you to bring Him each dark, painful breath—
Through Him we shall conquer all sin, death, and hell,
So press on in Jesus and let His truth swell!

PRAYER: Lord Jesus, I choose to renounce every lie, deception and pitfall the enemy has launched against me, and I yield that all into Your control to destroy. Preserve me by Your power and stretched out arm, and please guide me daily in Your truth and paths of righteousness. Thank You Jesus! Amen.

KETURAH C. MARTIN

The Ditch Of Doubt

When children are subjected all their lives to various and repeated abuses, rejection, and/or abandonment right into adulthood, the enemy is overactive in more ways than one. At every agonizing turn, he is attempting to weave lies into the very core of his suffering prey, which in their vulnerable and pained plight they often absorb—sometimes without even knowing it.

In my situation, there were life-shattering lies absorbed so deep within and repeatedly re-enforced throughout thirty-three years of abuse that I did not know of them. When godly counsellors pointed the lies out years later, I could in no way perceive them as lies, but sincerely believed they were the absolute truth. Such beliefs as "I am too bad to be loved and accepted," "I do not deserve to be saved," "God cannot love such a bad, dirty girl," "I deserve to die;" plus many more lies were ingrained deeper than I knew anything about.

Years later, during an urgent heart-cry when God sent a specific messenger to me through whom Christ ministered to the very core of my heart's need, it became very clear that I had been chained in fetters of doubt and unbelief. These fetters were so massively binding that when the blood of Jesus rent them in twain the freedom was life-altering, and for the first time in my life, I could begin to connect directly to God. I had never perceived how bound I was until the freedom became vibrantly apparent and most of the obstructions to healing were abolished, leaving a path more clear to pursue to find healing in Jesus. Now I could freely bring anything and everything to Jesus to cleanse, heal, and restore as I realized that with the fetters broken the enemy had lost massive holds on me and I could combat him through the blood and power of Jesus without any outside assistance!

There is no chain or fetter that is too massive for the power of Jesus' blood to break and completely obliterate, shattering enemy strongholds! He can dissolve mountains of doubt, lies, and deception with one drop of His blood, causing truth to come in like a flood of power and eternal light!

PRAYER: Lord, I choose to renounce every lie and deception of the enemy against my soul. I claim the blood of Jesus over him and every doubt and deception he attempts, and I ask You to reveal to me Your truth. Amen.

Rejection He Faced

When Jesus was here and He walked among men,
Rejection's dark wave He faced time and again:
For He was despised and by many cast out,
As dark unbelief had in-filled them with doubt.

Our Lord was acquainted with sorrow's pained grief,
But prayed to His Father for strength and relief:
All night on the mountain, alone, He would pray,
Well knowing that He is the Life, Truth, and Way.

The self-righteous leaders had mocked Him to scorn,
Yet inwardly they were like dead bones forlorn,
But Jesus yearned over their hearts and their life,
And longed to deliver from bondage and strife.

He never turned back from the cause He was sent,
But hung on the cross 'til His life was all spent;
He died for the skeptics, the Council, and Guard:
For me He died too, when my heart was so hard.

Rejection's dark waters, so frigid may flow,
Submerging one's heart in a pain none doth know,
But we have a Friend, an Example, and Guide
Who bore it before us and walks by our side!

Commit every detail to His divine hands,
Who knows what is true and in full, understands;
Let Him take the pain and the source whence it came—
When fully released, one is never the same!

PRAYER: Lord, I choose to surrender to You every pang of rejection and pain for You to deal with. Thank You for understanding the painful rejection, and for walking with me each step. Amen.

KETURAH C. MARTIN

FEBRUARY 1
READING: PSALM 63:1-7

Rejection And Acceptance

Stepping into the large dairy barn, Ramona made her way in heart-throbbing agony to the calf barn and gave a specific whistle. Her heart was nearly bursting in pain after another day at school where she had been mocked, abhorred, and shunned by all, due to the many seizures she experienced every day and the subsequent depression that the scar tissue on her mood center produced with each seizure.

In response to the whistle, fifty calves began bawling out their welcome to her, and she went around patting their heads or letting the small ones suck on her fingers. After ensuring they had hay and water, she climbed into a small pen and snuggled up to a baby calf, feeling accepted by this warm creature and basked there for quite some time.

Years later, medical doctors and counsellors declared that the calves actually helped to save Ramona's life when the pain, abuse, aloneness, and rejection were too great to bear.

Jesus was well acquainted with rejection and the anguish of it all: for He was despised and rejected of men, a man of sorrows and acquainted with grief. He was also a supreme example of how to handle it as He chose to forgive and stood firmly on truth no matter what accusations, shunning, or attempts against Him were made. It is so comforting to know that because Jesus experienced it all before us, He can understand perfectly what anguish we are faced with and can identify with us in the agony of being misunderstood. When it feels as if we are all alone, that is when Jesus is right there carrying us through our darkest night of excruciating rejection, misunderstanding, and/or condemnation, which may be projected upon us by the enemy through some person. He understands the torn, shredded, and bleeding agony that results from rejection and abandonment, and His tender presence is our only hope. It is His nature of love that teaches us to forgive and release those whom Satan worked through in an attempt to destroy us. We have the power in our hand to choose whether the painful circumstance will make us bitter or better—Jesus makes the difference.

PRAYER: Jesus, I choose to forgive and release every man, woman and leader who rejected, judged, and abused me. Bless them today and fill me with Your divine love. Amen.

Designed For A Purpose

Forlorn and forsaken, abandoned I lay,
Just thrown in a heap with junk's rubble and clay:
A write-off of "trash" branded "useless" by man—
Devoid of all worth, as an empty tin can.

Smashed flat and all mangled for thirty some years—
Rejected and sinking in oceans of tears,
Until at the depth of the ocean's pained floor,
"All hope, worth, and value are seen nevermore."

Forgotten old garbage, condemned to "just die,"
A broken heart bleeding, which always must cry
Out rivers of anguish, no mind comprehends:
For valueless trash has no one to defend.

But hark, hear the footsteps now wending their way
Past mountains of rubble; I thus hear one say:
"This battered old scrap in such agony bent—
Designed for a purpose, and I have been sent

To quickly retrieve what is precious to Me:
For pain's tools have shaped it for Me perfectly;
A valuable place of great use I have planned
For this worthy scrap branded *useless* by man.

I'll thoroughly wash her in My blood, divine—
Rejection's rust fades as true value will shine:
For I am the Lord and no junk ever make,
But long to restore all that evil may break."

My Jesus delights in impossible things,
Turns oceans of tears into valleys that sing;
From broken, trashed rubble makes vessels all new—
For all transformations my Jesus can do!

KETURAH C. MARTIN

Jesus Specializes In The Impossible

When the mountains seem insurmountible and the rivers are uncrossible, that is when my Jesus delights to specialize in doing the impossible!

Jesus is just as capable of performing miracles today as He was when He walked on earth. Often our lack of faith is the biggest obstacle to Him working freely in His supernatural way in our life.

My entire life has been filled with many impossibles to which Jesus Christ has responded in miraculous intervention. This includes survival assistance, hand-writing on the wall, saving me from death by the angel of His presence, rescuing me from the lowest pit of hell, breaking the chains of occultic bondage, and bringing complete healing for a life of dirty shatters and unsounded depths of agony! Praise be to Jesus for His unlimited love and miraculous power! Just His preserving of my life repeatedly was indeed a miracle that contributed to believing that God had created me for some specific purpose after all, even though the enemy had induced me to believe for years that "I was just a destroyed garbage bin worthy of death." This lie and all its companions had to be renounced and replaced with truth before I could advance in the healing journey.

I am over-awed with the boundless love of Jesus, just thinking how He took the time to look for my ragged ruins and agonized tatters. When He found them, He not only picked up each broken piece, but also brought miraculous cleansing and healing, creating a whole vessel through which to pour His love and hope.

PRAYER: Lord Jesus, I choose to bring You all the shreds, agony, and filth of my past that so drastically affect my current living. I ask You, Jesus, to please begin a work of healing and restoration in my life by the power of Your blood. Please show me what the next step is that You want me to take in my healing journey. Thank You, Jesus. Amen.

Christ Stands By Your Side

My friend, do you feel you've been cast out to die?
In heart-broken anguish, do you cry out "Why?"
It may seem you're shunned with the lepers of old—
The pain and rejection in words can't be told.
Though family disown you—pain pierces your soul,
And you feel encompassed by death as a whole,
Don't ever lose hope: for the Lord passes by,
And Jesus the Savior won't leave you to die.

Christ came for the downtrod, the lepers and blind:
He loves the rejected with love none can find;
He came for the heart-broken, sick, and the sad—
In mercy He gathers the bruised and ill-clad.
The Savior well knows you right down to the core,
He understands fully the pain you have bore:
He too knows the heartache of being cast out—
Christ stands by your side—is a Shield 'round about!

Though powers of darkness may stalk you each day,
There's no cause for fear when he roars at his prey:
For Jesus has conquered the devil and death,
And God's power shields you each step and each breath.
Come lay all your burdens within Jesus' arms:
For He loves you dearly and guards from all harms;
He paid your full ransom and He holds your soul—
There's naught comes to you but which He doth control.

The love of the Savior no limit doth know—
He gently embraces His child amidst woe;
He tenderly wipes away heartache and tears
And draws you still closer, dissolving your fears.
Our Lord Jesus Christ is the Healer of pain,
Who brings balmy sunshine out after the rain;
From ruins and rubbles He heals and makes new:
For all things impossible Jesus can do!

KETURAH C. MARTIN

Angry At God?

Have you ever faced abuse, rejection, or losses of some nature that make you want to scream out against God for allowing your difficult and possibly very agonizing circumstances? Does the excrucitation or dirty shame become a contributor to your vulnerability of accepting the enemy's lies that "if God loved me, He would have stopped this from happening" and "I will never serve a God Who doesn't care any more than that"? Do you inwardly rant at God for apparently standing by while your life was literally shattered?

Satan is thrilled when we angrily blame God for the painful atrocities that he himself subtly instigated against us. Most often in our anguishing experiences, God gets more blame than the enemy who was the one attempting to steal, kill, and destroy some innocent prey he got his talons on. Sometimes when the pain and loss are so severe, we become blinded to the reality that God is the One Who stopped the enemy from doing any greater damage. It is God Who stands guard over our souls. In our limited understanding of the full picture, it is okay to feel that initial anger at God. However, we dare not allow it to remain, or Satan will use that in his deceptions wherein he attempts to destroy us eternally. Anger, bitterness, and unforgiveness will destroy from the inside out those who wallow in it. It also makes life far more miserable than what the original trial, abuse, or situation had already produced. Anger and bitterness are literally nooses by which people hang themselves in deadly destruction and shut the door on healing.

PRAYER: Lord, I feel so angry at You for allowing _____, and I don't understand how a loving God can permit such devasting things to happen. I choose to forgive You for allowing _____ and I am willing to pay the emotional pain and consequences You have seemingly caused me. I ask that You would take back all the grounds and footholds Satan gained in me through my anger and bitterness toward You, and I yield that ground to Your control. I ask You, Lord, in the name of Jesus, to teach me truth and unmask every lie and deception of the enemy so I can see You for Who You really are. I renounce in the name of Jesus every lie and attempt of Satan against my soul, and I claim the blood of Jesus over him. I choose to believe that You love and care for me, Lord, and I ask You to continue to bring me healing through Jesus. Amen.

"You Are A Treasure"

You are, My Child, a treasure rare,
Whose priceless worth cannot compare
With anything in all the earth:
For you were planned before your birth.

I planned you for a special role:
For you are Mine—I've saved your soul;
No other human can perform
The job for which just you were born!

When storms and trials come your way,
Hold to My hand each step each day:
For trials never come to you,
But that My grace will see you through!

Consider, Child, midst tears or pain,
That through affliction there is gain:
For in My strength you are made strong—
I hold your hand and give a song!

Whoever touches you, My Child,
Or wreaks some havoc pained and wild,
Has touched the apple of My eye,
And I beside you still stand by.

The trials, Child, are tools of use
Yes, even pain and stark abuse
Which you must yield and I will hold,
To bring you forth as purest gold!

KETURAH C. MARTIN

A Specific Plan

Each individual that is born was created by God for a specific plan He has in mind. Every soul, regardless of what they have suffered, is worth more than all the world to the Lord. It is not uncommon for survivors to truly believe that "they are a born mistake, undeserving of life, and ultimately a used piece of worthless trash." However, these are lies that the enemy has subtly ingrained into the minds of his suffering prey during their most vulnerable times of severe agony and survival attempts. These lies must be replaced with the truth of God's Word if healing is to proceed.

God never creates junk despite the fact that a survivor of abuse will always feel like "junk" after the devil has wreaked destruction and pain through some pawn he has mastered. The enemy of our soul uses every form of abuse and all the boundless aftereffects in attempt to destroy and tarnish the jewels or souls God has created in His image and for His glory.

The self-hatred I experienced for decades was so intense that it nearly consumed me, as it all coincided with the lies that the enemy had ingrained within me too deeply for me to identify. I was in complete denial of being any type of treasure to God, believing rather that "I was the most detestable scum of the earth and far beyond hope." However, after Jesus burst the lies to pieces by the power of His blood He began to teach me the truths of Romans 12:1.

TRUTH #1: "My body is acceptable to God through Jesus regardless of what type of horrors and agony it was put through."

TRUTH #2: "Because of the cleansing and healing available through Jesus' blood, my body can become a holy and living sacrifice to God for His glory."

TRUTH #3: "Satan wants you to hate your body because it is created in the image of God and he hates God."

TRUTH #4: "Though Satan attempted to destroy you through abuse on your body, yet I the Lord can pour My love and hope through it to others if you yield it completely to Me for the glory of the Father."

TRUTH #5: "Your body is created to be the temple of the Holy Spirit and to hate God's living temple is counter-productive to Me working in and through you for My eternal purposes."

"Neither Do I Condemn Thee"

The scribes and the Pharisees shoved her along,
While railing her actions amid the great throng;
To Jesus they brought her, condemning her sore,
Explaining to Him what for her was in store.
Her action so sinful is all they could see,
And wanted to let the stones fly along free;
They had her all labelled "an outcast" each breath,
And wanted to be there to put her to death.

But they could not see to the core of her heart—
Knew not what she'd suffered in life from the start,
Yet there in dread anger and bitter control
To death they condemned her—no love for her soul.
She shrank in deep anguish, stark terror, and shame,
Engulfed too in guilt for the sin she must claim—
Oh, just for some mercy, true love, and a chance
To start life anew and with hope to advance.

And then she looked up into eyes so divine—
The face of the Master with love-light did shine
She sensed He could see to the pain of her heart,
And knew of the stain that caused teardrops to start.
He wrote on the ground—then the Savior did speak,
"Whoever is sinless a stone he may seek
To cast at this woman, whom here ye have brought,"
But then in deep shame each accuser was caught.

From eldest to youngest they silently left—
Of all deadly stones in their sins were bereft;
"Hath no man condemned thee?" then came His kind word,
To which she responded to Him, "No man, Lord."
Oh beautiful words from the Lord did then pour,
"Nor do I condemn thee—Child, go sin no more;"
He cares for the broken, the outcast, and sad,
And brings full salvation to make each heart glad!

KETURAH C. MARTIN

Lover Of The Unlovely

The love of Jesus supercedes our most in-depth evaluation of what love actually is. The very closest we can come to understanding the unlimited mercy and power of Jesus' love is by accepting His love sacrifice in which He died in a sinless state a criminal's death in order to purchase our ransom as He suffered for our sins on our behalf.

Jesus was a perfect example of separating the sin from the sinner: for He loved the sinners so much He died for them all to save them from all sin that He abhors. In His great love, He could look beyond the adultery that the woman in John 8 had committed and see right into her wounded, depraved soul to the need and cry of her heart, which none understood.

As humans we cannot see to the depth that Jesus did, but we must none-the-less live His love to even the person who in our eyes may appear to be most sinful or unlovely. Who are we to judge any soul's heart need based on what we see rather than looking through the eyes of Jesus?

Often those who have suffered severely or survived abuse of any degree may live and respond in pain until their heart issues of anguish and destruction are addressed by Jesus and His healing touch. It is not our job to diagnose, doctor, or judge them, but to walk beside them offering safety, no condemnation, a true friend, empathy (never pity), and Christ-like love in action. We are the hands, feet, and mouth of Jesus whom He seeks to use to represent His undying love, abundant provisions, unlimited power, divine salvation, and miraculous healing to the downtrodden and brokenhearted. If His own children cannot be the vessels through whom His impartial love flows to these shattered, dying individuals, there is no one else to represent Him and all He is waiting and yearning to do for each destroyed or hurting life. We are all on equal ground needing Jesus, so no matter what we have been through or how destroyed we may be, we all have the same amount of value to Jesus: for He died for one and all and is no respecter of persons!

PRAYER: Jesus, I bring You all the condemnation and judgments I have received from others. Show me what is true according to Your records and bring me cleansing. Everything else I surrender into Your hands to deal with and I release the condemning individual and their words to You, Jesus. Amen.

By Thy Grace I Will Pay

Lord Jesus, please search all my torn, ragged heart,
To know all Your findings, my Jesus, I yearn;
Dear Lord, from my side, please don't ever depart:
For all of Your will for my life I'd discern.
I can't understand all the arrows that fly,
Nor why misconceptions on my head are piled,
But, Jesus, please search my torn heart and pained cry,
To see if some wicked way in me is filed.
Am I, Lord, condemned within Your Book, divine
Because of abuse, I survived midst death's pain?
So wretched and wanting, have I crossed a line,
Which bars from Your people, obscures from Your gain?
Through Your blood and righteousness, Savior, wilt Thou
Accept me as Thine, though from others I'm barred?
My life, past, and pain I surrender just now—
Impossible messes for You aren't too hard.

My Lord, calm the tempest that rages about,
Which dash at the comfort zones where many wait:
Make manifest, Lord, without limit or doubt,
That Your love exceeds ev'ry comfort zone's gate.
I choose to release ev'ry soul to Your hand,
Who cannot accept or love one so defiled:
For my life and theirs, You in full understand,
And oft You've confirmed, Lord, that I am Your child.
I plead, Lord, that You would a blessing impart,
Where minds have been closed, that they won't understand;
Lord, pour out a blessing within each cold heart—
These pained situations I place in Your hand.
I choose to forgive them and leave them with You,
And, Lord, by Thy grace I will pay the pained price,
For all the harsh damage, though words lash anew:
For Thou art my Refuge, Whose grace doth suffice!

KETURAH C. MARTIN

Just To Be Accepted

Very often the survivors of abuse are longing desperately to be accepted, loved, and cared about just as they are, but are susceptible to slander and misunderstanding, many times to severe degrees. Also these shattered individuals are very prone to believing that others see them as they themselves do—"filthy, worthless, detestable, unlovable, and bad." Therefore outsiders are often not given a chance to attempt to understand, although if one has not walked in the boots of the abused, it is not fully possible to understand them.

In all fairness, we do well to consider that those who have not been unfortunate enough to experience what we have are likely very scared and unsure how to relate considering that they have no experience. It may well be that they would love to reach out and try to understand, but lack of experience and knowledge can often be a huge barrier. It can be overcome to a major degree when Jesus Christ Himself is fully personified in the one seeking to understand the broken and downtrodden. Jesus Christ experienced various abuses to extreme degree, especially at the trial and crucifixion.

It is very important for the survivor who feels misunderstood, rejected, or condemned by those around to bring all these things to Jesus, whether real or imagined. He is the only One Who is capable of taking care of it all and helping us avoid the bitter road. Christ is the One Who teaches us the following truths:

- "Since I too walked this road while on earth, I will walk it with you even though all others should forsake you or not understand."
- "Because of My provisions for your healing and cleansing, there is hope for you regardless of what humans say or perceive."
- "It is not so important what others say or think about you as much as My Father in heaven. If you are clean before Him, that is all that matters."
- "There is no respect of persons with God, and through My blood applied to your life and past you are acceptable to Him in the beloved."
- "When you are clothed in the robes of My righteousness, that is what can be seen as you remain hidden in your Savior."
- "In order to maintain the freedom I give, you must forgive and release to Me all those who hurt you or cannot understand from whence you came."

Come Forth As Gold

My precious Child, come near to Me:
For I thy God shall ever be,
I know thy pain, the filth, and shame—
Yet I have called thee by thy name.
I suffered with thee through the pain,
And longed to spare thee of the stain:
I loved thee, Child, despite what came,
And will yet glorify My name.
My ways are higher, Child, than thine:
For I have planned thee—thou art Mine,
And I allow no grief or pain,
Except that it should bring true gain.
Child, come surrender to My hand
All pain which you don't understand,
The guilty filth, the naked shame,
The agony which none can tame.
The cleansing blood of My dear Son
Suffices fully for each one
Who comes to Me just as a child—
It matters not how sore defiled.
So meet Me, Child, beside the cross,
That all you suffered won't be loss:
For if you give it all to Me,
I fully cleanse and set you free.
The tattered rags of filth's despair,
I will exchange because I care:
Will clothe thee, Child, in raiment, white—
With purity dispel thy night!
Though called through fire, naught is loss:
For fire rids thee of all dross;
Trust all to Me—thy hand I hold,
Then you'll come forth as purest gold!"

KETURAH C. MARTIN

No matter what one has been through, there is nothing too hard for Jesus to address and totally fix it. Though it may look hopeless to one who is writhing in shatters, yet Jesus can view it all from a different perspective and He can see the full picture. Even though we sometimes feel like giving up on ourselves, the Lord never feels that way about us. He is in it for the long haul and will stick it out with us to the end.

PRAYER: Jesus, I choose to believe that You are able to fix all the broken pieces, and I want to give them to You. Amen.

The Cracked Cup's Beauty

Perhaps, friend, your life like a tea cup has been,
So jaggedly cracked midst adversity's din;
Life's pained situations have chipped the cup's rim,
As clouds of affliction may rise up so grim.

Your life is still beautiful, friend, despite all,
Although your cup's broken, with chipped or cracked wall:
Because of God's grace you have value to Him—
With hope, faith, and love He can fill to the brim!

A crack in your cup, friend, depicts not a flaw,
But shows God is faithful, whom we hold in awe;
Your cup He has held through life's tempests so wild,
Preserving in love the cracked life of His child!

The tea cup so fragile has strength none can see,
Though damaged and chipped, yet so useful can be:
For it bears the beauty of hope kept alive—
Preserved by God's love, which through Christ did arrive!

Your life may be broken or cracked by life's pain,
But yet to the Lord it bears beauty and gain;
He paid to preserve you for His praise above—
Your life He has rescued by His matchless love!

PRAYER: Father in heaven, I want to surrender to Your loving hands all the cracks and broken pieces of my life. Please bring me complete healing and unfettered freedom through Jesus. And Lord, I ask You to shine Your love and light through the cracks of my broken life for Your glory. Please restore me and make me a vessel of honor for Your service. Amen.

Value Of A Broken Life

Very often when we come across a broken, jagged cup, we toss it into the garbage bin without a second thought outside of getting rid of some junk. When the enemy attempts to destroy his suffering prey via abuse, rejection, or abandonment, his victim feels like junk from the inside out.

However, God sees us in a different light than we see ourselves or the cracked cup. The Heavenly Father looks down and views a beloved child of His who is so worthy of His unlimited love that He yearns to take up the broken pieces and put His time, love, and efforts into restoring the shattered individual into a vessel that can be far more useful and beautiful than ever before the painful devastation broke it. He patiently waits for us to bring Him all the pieces and cry out to Him for His divine assistance which is our only hope.

The survivor often feels alone, useless, and a complete write-off to God and man, but this is a lie from the enemy with which he seeks to destroy us farther if he can get us to believe it. When the lies of the enemy are renounced and replaced with truth, then we can freely bring the broken shatters of our life to the Master Who is just waiting to put them all together again.

LIE: "I am a worthless write-off to God and man."
TRUTH: "But God commendeth His love toward us in that while we were yet sinners Christ died for us." Jesus wouldn't have died for worthless people.
LIE: "I am too vile and destroyed to ever be of any worth to God."
TRUTH: "What God hath cleansed call not thou unclean. I will restore the years which the locusts have eaten."

PRAYER: Lord, I renounce and break the lie, in the name of Jesus, that _____, and I ask Your forgiveness for believing it. Jesus, please take back all the ground Satan gained in me through this lie, and I yield that ground to Your control and Lordship. Lord, please break and nullify in the name of Jesus all the effects, influence, and bondage that belief in this lie has brought me, my family, and/or my friends, and I ask You take back all that ground also. I ask You, Lord, to teach me Your truth daily. Amen.

Impossible Is Where I Start

My children, come rest in My loving embrace
As I show to you My divine love and grace,
For I have redeemed thee, and called you by name—
To save ruined lives is the reason I came.

Though people and circumstance oft may appear
To be without hope, yet My children draw near:
For I am your God and I still specialize
In things thought impossible—making a prize.

Come, give Me the tatters you don't understand,
The past, bruised and broken—yield all to My hand
The fears of the future and storms of the past
Will transform to joy when on Me they are cast.

From out of the ash heap come nuggets of gold,
Midst heart-shreds of anguish thy heart I now hold,
The dark strands of grief with the gold do I weave—
Creating true beauty, but you must believe!

The rivers of tears turn to wellsprings of life
When I take the shatters of agony's strife,
The lambs, lost and broken, I seek out and find,
Their pained or hard hearts with My healing I bind.

"Impossible" happens to be where I start,
When I create diamonds on pained, wounded heart:
For I will complete all the work I've begun
In each of My daughters and all of My sons!"

KETURAH C. MARTIN

Jesus Is The Answer

Within each human being created there is a vacuum that can be filled only with God. It is not uncommon for the majority of people to attempt to fill this need with other things such as money, prestige, drugs, women/men, alchohol, porn, business, or whatever else the enemy is subtly offering in pretense of satisfying his client.

The survivor may feel even more desperate to fill this need, considering life is in shambles, the pain is unbearable, and the need for some stabilizing force to make life more liveable is imminent. When our inner being is in utter chaos, agony and deficiency, that is a great time to remember that Jesus specializes in things thought impossible—He will never fail you!

I can assure any and all that the world has nothing to offer to fill this need and it in fact detracts from all that God is longing to do for your tattered or unfulfilled life. The devil is busy at every turn, attempting to sell counterfeits to anyone who is vulnerable, searching, angry at God, or completely broken and in desperate need of something. He will stop at nothing to get as many as possible sucked into his heartless deceptions and empty promises so he can keep them from the abundant hope, help, and healing that Jesus Christ offers free of charge. It is a complete waste of time, life, and eternity to bite the enemy's subtle baits and could cost you everything. In addition to trapping you in a life of miserable slavery, he's binding folks in iron fetters with no hope, healing, or relief, but in unending anguish under his control. No matter how hard people try, they can never escape the reality that *nothing and no one can resolve their shattered life except Jesus Christ and all He has to offer.* All these other things serve only to make the agony and confusion greater as the enemy uses you as a game piece to cast aside at his desire when he is tired of the game and has you fully deceived.

Stop, look, and listen! Where do you want the end of the track to be?

PRAYER: Jesus, I choose to seek after You so You can fill my void, and I ask You to bring hope and healing to the mangled mess of my life. Take the tatters in Your hand and take control, Jesus. Thank You Lord for specializing in transforming the things that to us seem impossible! Amen.

Clothed In His Righteousness

My Jesus has love and rich grace so untold,
Which cannot be fathomed—no limit it holds:
It reaches right down to the lowest of low—
To depths of pain's squalor He tenderly goes.

The most broken heart that in deadly shreds lies,
So tattered and downtrod it does naught but cries,
Yet each broken piece doth my Jesus retrieve—
Amid boundless love He doth fully receive.

Though tattered and grimy—just cast out to die,
Yet Jesus, in love will not ever pass by:
For He came to heal all the pained broken hearts,
Despite the shreds caused by rejection's harsh darts.

He brings in His love like a bright, cleansing flood,
Then heals and restores through His powerful blood:
The vile and torn garments of anguish untold,
He casts far away as His child He now holds!

His own robes of righteousness He then brings out—
Enfolds His new child in His robes without doubt;
His love has accepted, restored and made new—
The past is all gone and my Lord is in view!

And now when the world around looks upon me,
The pain, shame, and past they again shall not see,
But only my Savior and His robes of white,
Can they now observe in His transforming light!

KETURAH C. MARTIN

"Child, Give Me Your Mountain"

What towering mountain today do you face?
Which looms with dark anguish surrounding its base?
Its height, insurmountable, brings doubt and fear—
The way seems uncharted and hopelessly drear.
And what's that affliction, encompassing you
With mountainous agony you must go through?
Afflicting your body, emotions, or soul—
Midst fiery trial, which no soul doth know.
That mountain of grief that is looming so high,
Whose peak goes beyond all the blue of the sky,
How do you propose to ascend to its height?
When billows of anguish increase through the night.
And what of those summits, so barren and high?
Rejection's dark glacier, which spreads far and nigh,
Whose cold, frosty breath leaves one lost and alone
To slide on its crust, and to dangers so prone.
Oh, hark, hear the Savior amid life's dark fray—
In love He approaches to show you the way;
He too climbed His mountain at Calvary's hill,
His cross bore to death, as God's plan He fulfilled.
"My Child, I am near, and with you I will walk:
For I'm your Redeemer, your Refuge, and Rock;
No mountain comes nigh thee, except I approve,
And with Me beside thee, that mountain we'll move!
Those treacherous inclines, with drop-offs so sheer,
We'll scale them together—My Child, never fear:
For when I walk with thee, I'm holding thy hand—
Despite pain and danger, with Me you can stand!
Child, give Me thy mountain, its anguish and care:
For I've walked before thee, thy load I will share;
Impossible mountains of pain-crushing weight,
My grace, love and power can now dissipate!"

Insurmountible Mountains?

Do you ever feel hemmed in by mountains that seem insurmountible and looming ever before you? Are there boulders of pain, filth, and shattered pieces lying everywhere, obstructing your path and progress? Sometimes the obstructions in our healing journey are very obviously there, but we may be unaware of what they really are and what to do with them. It is not uncommon for survivors to often feel completely trapped and often incapacitated by the mountains of aftereffects, which they suffer subsequent to the painful horror through which the Lord preserved their life. It is in these trapped moments when despair seems to encircle us that the enemy is craftily attempting to inject his hideous lies to get us to believe that "we are a hopeless case, too hard for God to even care about any more—just a waste of time."

However, we have a God Who specializes in doing the impossible!

"Ah, Lord God! Behold Thou hast created the heaven and earth by Thy great power and stretched out arm and there is nothing too hard for Thee" (Jer. 32:17).

Because of our all-powerful Father, we do not have to stay trapped at the foot of these looming mountains. When we cry out to Him in full faith and confidence, He will hear our cry and will not leave us destitute. He told us to call unto Him and He will answer us and show us great and mighty things which we know not.

FACTS OF HOPE:

- There is not any problem or pain too big for Jesus to take care of.
- There is no mountain too high for Him to climb or tunnel through with us.
- There is no life too mangled for Him to address, fix, and make whole.
- There is no stain, shame, or destruction that His blood cannot cleanse.
- There is no river too wide or turbulent for Jesus to cross with us safely.
- There is no heart too broken, shattered, or defiled but that He can bring complete healing! Praise be to Jesus! Hallelujah! Thank You, Lord!
- There is nothing too hard for God to do!

KETURAH C. MARTIN

One Step At A Time

One step at a time in this darkest of night,
While writhing in anguish, when nothing seems right;
Though life's richest treasures seemed ruined and destroyed—
I must forge ahead and dark pitfalls avoid.

The night is so long and the pain is untold—
If only, midst tears, I some hand could now hold:
A friend to walk with me, one step at a time,
Who understands some of the anguish and grime.

How can I e'en dare to move one step ahead,
When all of my world seems so heavy and dead,
When jeopardy looms and moves in from all sides—
Oh, just for a friend, who with me still abides.

I long to feel safe and all hidden from view
From those who have harmed and emotions have slew—
My heart-broken pieces of life to conceal,
That by Grace Divine, I perhaps may then heal.

Midst pain so intense that it hurts ev'ry breath,
When each step I take, it seems closer to death:
Yet I must move forward one breath at a time:
For God has preserved me midst dark abuse crime!

"Dear soul, take fresh courage and dare to move on:
For 'round the next bend there approaches your dawn;
Your life has been salvaged: for great is your worth—
There's hope, help, and healing beyond this dark dearth!"

PRAYER: Lord, I invite You to walk with me one step at a time in my healing journey so I can know that I am never alone. Please lead me to complete healing and freedom in You Lord, for Your glory. Amen.

A Talk With God

"Oh, Lord, how can I take even one step at a time if there is a sheer wall of rock that is obviously unscaleable, standing right in my face? Why must I be encased with impenetrable obstructions and unfathomed agony while others in life just breeze right on through?"

"My Child, I the Lord am ever near you to walk with you each step of the way. I will not fail or forsake you, but will hold your right hand, saying unto you, 'Fear not, I will help you.' The sheer cliffs of rock are possible to ascend when Christ leads the way: for He walked this road before you, and with thy Lord all things are possible. Though the enemy tried to destroy you, My Child, through these painful circumstances, yet I stepped in on his attempts and have preserved you for a purpose to glorify My name. Look not on those around you who may not have suffered as you, but look rather to My Son Who suffered it all that He might effectively assist you through your anguishing nightmare to perfect healing and restoration. He too suffered abuse on the cross, and in the power of His resurrection, He is fully qualified to bring you a thorough healing when you surrender to Him the pain, the broken pieces, the incidents, and the perpetrators involved. When these things are placed in His hand and under the power of His blood, they will become tools in His hand by which He can perfect and shape you into the vessel I have designed that you should be for My service and the glory of My name. Be always confident that I Who have begun a good work in you will perform it unto the end when I shall gather up all My jewels to My kingdom. I will keep thee as the apple of My eye!"

PRAYER: Lord, I choose to walk each step with You to healing, for without You, I am sunk and drowning in this mangled mess. If You can use Satan's attempts on me as tools to make me a fit vessel, I give all the pain and horrors into Your hand! Thank You for salvaging me from the attempts of the enemy and perserving my life for the glory of Your name! Amen.

God's Eye Is Upon You

The Lord high in heaven looks down from above,
And yearns o'er His children with infinite love;
He sees every soul and He hears your heart-cry—
He draws ever near and will not let you die.

God hears and gives strength for that struggle within,
And stands there beside you amid the dark din;
Christ Jesus will never forsake His dear child,
But leads in full vict'ry, though life's storm is wild.

The Lord sees each tear that may brim from the eye,
And holds in His hand every soul that may cry;
The heart that is breaking in anguish untold—
Within His embrace, He that heart doth enfold.

Come near to His bosom and rest in His love—
Assured that He cares as He sees from above;
He never allows more than what can be borne,
But every dark trial with His strength adorns.

God's eye is upon you as your course He charts,
And tenderly holds you so close to His heart;
He understands fully each trial you face—
Sufficiently showers upon you His grace.

God knoweth the plans that He hath for His child,
And never will fail though the sorrows seem piled;
Despite situations He'll see you right through,
And finish the work He has started on you!

Crying Out To Our Father

Our Father in heaven is yearning over each of His suffering, wounded children, just longing that they would cry out to Him for help, hope, and healing. These things He longs to lavishly pour out upon their painful shatters and dirty tatters if they but come seeking Him and all He has to offer. We are told in Psalm 56:8 that God has all our tears kept in a bottle and recorded in His book. We are so blessed to have a Heavenly Father Who is always there to assist us around the next bend, boulder, or dark night—or just to walk together through the sunshine as we cry to Him and accept the provisions He has made for our journey. In our deepest struggle or darkest night, He tenderly enfolds us in His embrace of love as He offers grace and strength to get through, sometimes just one breath at a time!

There may be many times when you cannot sense that God is anywhere near you, but that is a beautiful opportunity to pour out your heart before Him and cry out to Him with your heart's most inner feelings and longings. In my distress I cried unto the Lord and He heard me.

So often in my experiences, it would feel as if the inner anguish was so intensely excruciating that just to breathe hurt more than words can relay. But so often when I could only cry out, "Lord, please help me," He very noticeably stepped in and/or sent some messenger as doors of hope were opened wide! "He will regard the prayer of the destitute and not despise their prayer" (Psalm 102:17).

He is just waiting for you to cry out to Him: for He will never force Himself on anyone, and is longing to pour out all the riches in glory by which to supply your needs and assist you on the healing journey.

PRAYER: Father God, I come to You with all the empty squalor and rags of pain in my barren soul, and I ask in the name of Jesus that You would do the impossible and bring healing, cleansing, and joy to my life. Lord, it feels as if I am drowning in the filth and agony, and I need Your presence and help to restore my ruined life. I ask You to take charge of my life and help me. Amen.

Don't Quit, My Friend

Don't quit when the tears are falling:
For there's joy around the bend;
Don't quit when the grief engulfs you:
For sufficient grace God sends!
Don't quit when in waves you're sinking:
For the Lord keeps you afloat;
Don't quit when the sails are rending,
For Christ pilots still your boat!
Don't quit when the dark surrounds you:
For God's light of love shines near;
Don't quit midst attack or warfare:
For the Victor, Christ is here!
Don't quit when a soul rejects you:
For your Father cannot fail;
Don't quit when that sting is mounting,
For 'tis Christ Who sets your sail!
Don't quit midst affliction's anguish:
For the Great Physician's near;
Don't quit though the road seems cheerless—
There's a diamond in each tear!
Don't quit in the thick of battle:
For the vict'ry is ahead—
Don't quit in the field of wounded:
For they need you, ere they're dead!
Don't quit at this stage of travel:
For the finish line we see;
Don't quit, my dear friend, forever:
For we're near eternity!

PRAYER: Jesus, I choose to walk with You in Your strength for Your glory, one step at a time. Amen

Don't Ever Quit!

Sometimes while treading the path on the journey to healing, we are engulfed with the magnitude of pain and what looks to us like endless impossibilities of the great distance yet to go. It is more important to focus on all that Jesus has already done, rather than look through our perspective at what He yet wants to do for the perfecting of the work He has begun in us. It is often at this point of being swallowed up in our pain that the enemy will attempt to inject doubt and despair with strong promptings to give up and abandon all hope of complete freedom and healing. If he can get the survivor to doubt the power of what God has done, is doing, and will yet do, then he has gained a crack where he can begin to get a toe-hold in the one he is fighting to destroy. Before he ever gets such a hold, we must cry out to God for the power of the blood of Jesus to banish every attempt of the enemy to defeat us in the healing journey. We must also renounce any lies, doubt, or suggestions Satan has injected into our thought processes, claiming the blood of Jesus over them. Quitting always starts with these poisonous thought-injections, which question our value, hope, salvation, and the healing work Christ is doing. We dare not even give the enemy a second or the thought he injects could take us down a road we would have never dreamed and would always regret!

Satan has already been defeated by the blood and resurrection of Jesus Christ, and we dare not allow him to gain any victories in our experience by just giving up to his wiley suggestions. We are not fighting against the foe for victory, but we fight from the victory that Jesus has already won! Let us therefore rise up, cry out, and claim that victory by the power of Christ's blood through the name of Jesus!

QUITTERS NEVER WIN, AND WINNERS NEVER QUIT

PRAYER: Lord Jesus, I come to You with all the lies, suggestions, and doubts that Satan is trying to ingrain into my mind and heart. I renounce his every attempt, and I claim the power of Your blood over him. Lord, I also claim the victory You have already won for my life and experience. I choose to cling to You, Jesus, no matter what the cost, and I embrace all that You have to offer me in my healing, that You may be glorified. Amen.

A Place For Me

God made the mountains great and tall,
He made the butterfly so small,
But when the Lord created me
He had a special plan, you see:

For in His image I am made—
To Him have worth which cannot fade;
Designed precisely for His will—
God has a place just "Me" can fill!

And so because He has this plan,
I know He'll do whate'er He can
To mend my broken life of pain—
And through it all will bring a gain!

I'll bring to Him each broken piece
So all that's yucky then may cease:
For He will do the best He can
To fix me for His perfect plan!

PRAYER: Jesus, I want to give You all the broken pieces of my heart, mind and past. You alone can bring gain out of this mess and make me useful in Your plan and Your kingdom for Your glory. Amen.

God's Perfect Plan

When we consider the specific care that God put into creating humans in His own image, then through His Son, Jesus, He died in our place to pay our ransom to deliver us from death—it is very clear He has some specific purpose for each one of us created! Praise God! Hallelujah! To wounded survivors, the fact that "God created them for a special purpose" is something they often cannot fathom in their anguished state and filthy tatters. The enemy has blinded them to these facts amid their painful circumstances, which he preys on while attempting to sell them his lies. Because we are created in the image of God, Satan cannot love us and does everything possible to destroy and mar any connection to God we may have. He is the instigator of abuse and seeks to use it to concretize his lies and destruction. However, "If God be for us, who can be against us?" God has made every provision for us to make it possible that His divine plan for our life can be fulfilled, but it is up to us to choose to accept those provisions.

One may be led to believe that "the plan is messed up and destroyed because of the abuses that came to me," but let us reject that concept immediately through the power of the blood of Jesus. Yes, Satan may have waged an all-out attempt to destroy you by using someone (close or a stranger) to destroy you emotionally, spiritually, and/or physically, and God may have allowed it, but it does not have to end there. Praise God! Jesus is just waiting for you to surrender all these broken pieces of life and circumstances of anguish into His hand to deal with in a redemptive way, wherein all the attempts of the enemy against us can be reversed by the power of Jesus' blood and be turned into tools that will defeat further our defeated foe! Christ can change the most devastating pain and degradation that Satan instigated against us into something beautiful that can benefit the kingdom of God and bring greater perfection to God's plan in the end, if we but cry out to Him and invite Him in to do His transforming work!

PRAYER: Jesus, I ask You to please come to me and begin the work in me which will turn the curse of my experience into a tool by which You and Your great power and love will be exalted to the glory of Your name. Amen.

How Can I Hang On?

God promised that He would not let the waters overflow me or the fire burn me, but how can I hang on to hope and His promise when I feel I am sinking and/or the fire is all around me? How can I find Him when the darkness and pain is enshrouded everywhere? If He truly loves me, why does He allow so much pain and darkness? Why can I not see or feel Him near if He is actually with me? If He loves and understands me, why cannot His own people understand?

These typical questions are such that survivors who are just barely "hanging on" need answers for as they yearn for something better.

The first thing we must always bear in mind is that "God is not a man that He should lie, neither the Son of man, that He should repent: hath He said and shall He not do it? or hath He spoken and shall He not make it good?" God can never lie or fail us, and He has a plan despite our pain and/or darkness. As humans we tend to think about God on human terms and fail to remember that His ways, thoughts, and methods of operation are far higher than we can even begin to fathom. When we can see no rhyme or reason, "Wait on the Lord, be of good courage and He shall strengthen your heart; wait, I say on the Lord."

When you are engulfed in pain and darkness and cannot see or feel God near, that is a good time to cry out to Him, choosing to believe by faith that He is beside you regardless of what the tempter says. Often it is Satan who is camouflaging God's presence while attempting to encircle you with darkness, doubt, or anything else to side-track you from the reality of the Lord's nearness: but it is God's sustaining help, love, and presence that are bringing you through it. He will never forsake His own, even when His own children do not understand you and may unknowingly cause pain. Because many of them have not suffered as we have, they have no clue how to understand, counsel, or even be there for the survivor. Jesus can understand us best since He suffered more than tongue can tell, and He will carry you when you can no longer take another step.

PRAYER: Lord, I choose to believe that You are near in my darkest hour, and that the enemy is the instigator of attempting to hide You from me. I renounce Satan, his lies, and attempts, and I claim the blood of Jesus over my life. Amen.

The Secret Door

Within the dark shades of my crushed, broken heart,
A door was there hidden and locked from the start:
For often amid the abuse and despair,
The subsequent horrors I just could not bear.
The trust, oh so splattered, was flung in that room,
Where shadows of hopelessness spelled out my doom;
Unspeakable terrors in there were concealed,
Where horrors of darkness could not be revealed.
So often I secretly vowed in my soul,
That no other being would e'er gain control
Of that old, bent key that I'd buried so deep,
In effort to guard all that this room did keep.
For never again could I ever dare trust,
Considering always it turned to dark rust;
And some things so hidden no soul understood,
Until that new day when came Someone Who could!
'Twas Jesus Who came to the door of my heart—
So crushed, bruised and bleeding and pierced through with darts;
A great transformation of love He had planned—
Where heart-shreds and ashes He took in His hand . . .
But then He took note of that dark, hidden door,
So rusted all closed—to be opened no more;
"My Child, if you seek for a healing complete,
Then all things within must be brought to My feet."
I cried out, "My Lord, I am sure You can't see,
How putrid and vile all the things in there be;
It won't matter much if we just pass it by—
To face those pained fetters will cause me to die!"
"I am Your Creator, My Child, I know all—
My blood is sufficient for all that appalls:
Yet, Child, I'll not enter without your consent,
But I can restore all that's broken and bent.

Cont.

KETURAH C. MARTIN

If we pass it by and leave all there concealed
Then Satan's vile strongholds become more congealed,
But if we shall enter I'll break his dark chains—
Bring light, hope and healing with infinite gains!"
I dug up the key and gave Him full control
Of that barred-off room that had shackled my soul;
He broke every fetter—brought healing profound—
His power and love without limits abounds!

PRAYER: Lord Jesus, even though it feels very scary, I want to choose to surrender the key to this hidden door into Your control. Please go in there with me and clean up this deplorable room of hidden horrors in my life. I choose You Jesus, Your cleansing and the full potential for complete restoration for Your glory. Thank-You Jesus! Amen.

Hidden Closets

We have abundant hope and healing available to our shattered or painful lives because of Jesus and all He suffered on our behalf, after which He rose in triumph over all! Praise God! He also triumphed over Satan, who is the sole instigator of our painful past, and through Jesus we also have victory over him. However, we cannot expect a complete healing or victory if we are unwilling to bring and surrender to Jesus the complete package of pain, rejection, abuse, and all the subsequent effects we may, in terror or anger, be hiding.

Survivors may often hide many things in some back closet without even realizing it, but when Jesus comes looking through the rubble in search of one's ruins, hidden closet doors will usually come to light when His search-light is on. "Thank You, Jesus!" The enemy tries his best to get us to believe all kinds of lies about "what will happen if we tell anyone about the closet or what is behind the door." In my situation he had so many doors completely concealed that I did not even know they existed, but I knew something dreadful was wrong. These closets and doors, which may hide such things as shameful rape, unspeakable horrors, gun-point terror, shattered trust, blood-flowing rituals, tattered heart-shreds, ugly sins, death threats, or you name it, are like the bake-ovens where the devil cooks extensive strongholds and unfathomed bondages in the lives of God's pained child whom the enemy holds captive. Once he has these strongholds, whether known or unknown, he always has a back door entrance to his victim until they are renounced, broken, and reclaimed by the blood of Jesus. The enemy is powerless in the face of Jesus and His blood, and when Christ steps into some such closet, Satan turns into a wimpy coward. We can never be truly free and healed unless everything is brought out of the closet to Jesus, and the best part about it is that He is right beside each one to help bear the pain of looking at these things and helps us deal with them. His grace is sufficient!

PRAYER: Jesus, I ask You to search all the corners of my heart and expose every pain, bondage, sin, and stronghold that has been hidden. I claim Your blood to break and cleanse every hold Satan has on me. Amen.

Be Not Afraid, Only Believe

"Be not afraid, but just believe," for Jesus Christ doth still receive:
Come, burdened heart, to His embrace—experience His freeing grace;
The day of opportunity is still today, friend, don't you see?
The Savior in great love awaits your cumb'ring fears to dissipate.

It matters not how great your load, nor how far down has gone your road,
Despite what shackles bind you tight, there's naught too strong for Jesus' might;
The lies which twine your heart to sin, He'll cast into the garbage bin:
For He can take the blackest heart—complete forgiveness to impart!

And though your heart is bruised and torn because abuse was starkly borne,
Yet God was there and saw you through, now longs to show what He can do:
The broken heart He can repair, cleanse, and restore because He cares:
For Jesus Christ doth specialize from rubbled trash to make a prize!

Arise, my friend, and go straightway to Jesus Christ, Who waits today,
He understands from inside out just how you feel without a doubt;
And there's no bondage in your life, no sin too black or cutting strife,
But that His blood sufficient stands to rescue you from Satan's hands!

When you believe His promise true, assured of what His pow'r can do,
When sought, my Jesus will step in—a transformation then begin;
Then henceforth you'll walk each day through
just as a creature made brand-new—
Take heart therefore and grace receive; the Master waits, only believe!

PRAYER: Lord, I choose to renounce every fear tactic and attempt from the enemy
against me. I choose rather to believe Your promises and all You seek to do when
I yield this heavy load and agony into Your hands. Restore me Lord into what
You have designed and planned me to be, for Your glory. Amen.

What If The Strongholds Are Too Big?

In the Bible, the Lord asks this question: "Is there any thing too hard for Me?" God is all-powerful, all-knowing, merciful, enduring, just, everywhere present, impartial, loving, forgiving, and everlasting!

Jesus told us that "If thou canst believe, all things are possible to him that believeth." There is nothing too big, horrible, or sinful that the power of the blood of Jesus cannot fully address. He is Victor over all!

The following are some lies that the enemy may use in an attempt to strengthen the chains and strongholds he already has in some of his suffering prey:

#1. "I have been made so filthy that only the devil would have anything to do with me."

Truth: "The thief or Satan comes to steal, kill, and destroy, but I am come that you might have life and have it more abundantly."—Jesus

#2. "If I ever told anyone everything, I would be disowned, abhorred, and shunned."

Truth: "He/she that cometh to Me I will in no wise cast out."

#3. "After all I went through, I am just a hunk of worthless trash and deserve to die."

Truth: "I have called thee by thy name, thou art Mine! Ye shall not die, but live, and declare the works of the Lord."

4. God cannot really love me, or He would not have let such terrible things happen to me, but would have rescued me."

Truth: "I the Lord have called thee, and will hold thy hand and will keep thee. When thou passest through the waters I will be with thee and through the rivers, they shall not overflow thee."

PRAYER: Lord, I renounce the lie that _____, and I ask You to forgive me for believing it. I ask, Jesus, that You would take back all the ground Satan gained in me through my belief in this lie, and I yield that ground to Your control and Lordship. Lord, please replace this lie with Your truth and with the power and Presence of Your Spirit in my life. I choose to renounce Satan and all his schemes and I embrace Jesus Christ. Amen.

KETURAH C. MARTIN

These Tatters And Tangles

"Lord, what shall I do with the tatters of pain?
How can I be free from abused rags and stains?
Can I escape ever the tangles of shame?
So tightly all knotted with harsh, ragged blame.
Rejection's dark splinters like glass at my feet,
Create a deep agony none could yet meet;
What value can come from the heart-shreds untold?
Abandoned, forsaken, and left in the cold.
From misunderstandings thrown out like a noose,
Can I be exonerated and let loose?
In all of these tangles and tatters that be,
My Lord, I know not what is truly just 'me.'"

"My Child, come and rest in your Father's embrace,
While I show to you all the hope through My grace—
You're not 'a lost cause' though so ragged and torn,
But midst anguished tatters new life can be born!
Bring Me every rag with abuse so defiled—
Each rope of untruth that around thee is piled,
Surrender the tatters of pain none can know,
And yield all the splinters rejection doth blow.
Commit to My hand all the tangles of shame,
Along with the 'blame' that knots into thy name;
The noose which doth tear at thy ripped, bleeding heart,
Put into My hand, with each pain-throbbing dart.
These dark, bleeding tatters which so worthless seem,
With big wounded tangles—My blood can redeem;
There's nothing too hard for My grace to restore,
Which you bring to Me and then walk through hope's door.
The dark, throbbing shatters I mix with pure gold,
Creating new beauty with value untold;
The rags made so dirty that you would cast out
I change to bright strands which My glory will shout!
Cont.

The ropes which have bound you with lies from the pit,
I cut them right off and with truth ye shall sit;
All dark devastations the enemy wrought
Are changed to bright sunshine and then brought to naught."
In place of pained tatters, true beauty I give;
With death-chains all broken, My Child, ye shall live:
For I have redeemed thee from all that was loss,
To spread hope and healing while bearing My cross!"

Jesus Is Bigger!

Even though the world is filled with bruised, broken, and destroyed people who suffer daily, yet Jesus is a bigger solution than all pain heaped together in one place. To say that the abuse, pain and destructions we survived is too massive or devastating for Jesus to heal, is putting a limit on the power of God and all He wants to do for us.

I too know the inexpressible agony within where one's heart feels as if it is literally torn into bleeding shreds. The ragged tatters are so obvious to us, but the outside world sees nothing and understanding is often nil. But dear friend, take heart: there is Someone Who understands and has suffered abuse far worse than any of us! Jesus is the only One Who understands everything all the time. He is waiting to take you into His arms—tatters and all—and to love you just as you are. Jesus specializes in taking all those agonizing heart-shreds—those writhing splinters—and make something valuable out of them. Yes, I know that feels so far-fetched when everything inside is so anguishing and misunderstood. At one point I too was enduring unspeakable pain to such extreme that it was impossible to see even a spark of hope beyond it. The bleeding tatters of my shredded heart were undefinably destroyed. But one day I dared to talk to Jesus about these heart-shreds. I just dared to begin placing all those painful items in the hand of Jesus for Him to deal with. He really can fix impossible heart-shreds and turn hopeless shatters into strands of pure gold if we but ask for His help!

PRAYER: Jesus, please help me! Everything hurts so badly inside and I'm scared to trust anyone. Is it safe to bring my broken heart to You? If You can fix these tatters of destruction, I choose to bring each one to You and yield it to Your control. I choose to believe You, Jesus, even when it hurts. I choose to entrust my healing into Your Hands, Jesus. Amen.

Success

Success begins by pressing on
Through dreary storms, toward the dawn;
Success that's true will set a goal,
Then do the best in its control.

Success, midst heartache won't give up,
Despite the sorrow in its cup,
But looks to God for courage, true:
For strength each day, that He'll renew.

Success will look out for the best,
And tackle life with fervent zest:
Life's problems work out one by one
Until the victory is won.

Success is failure turned about:
The wings of hope, instead of doubt,
The battle's vict'ry—not defeat,
Life's pressing forward—not retreat!

Success will be most ultimate
When we succeed to heaven's gate:
Success we'll know when Christ we see—
Know heaven's ours eternally.

PRAYER: Lord Jesus, I ask You to walk with me every step of the way. Whether through rivers of sorrow or over mountains of pain – I entrust my life, healing and future into Your control. Be glorified, Jesus, in and through me, and please don't waste my pain but transform it into something good for Your praise. Amen

Success For Survivors

True success and ultimate healing is possible in the most complete sense when Jesus is the Great Physician overseeing the entire healing process. When He is allowed and invited to be present—and it is He to whom one can bring all the filth, anguish, and destruction—then begins the truest journey of success and freedom. When He is done helping people to work through their heart-shreds and shatters, there is nothing left of buried pain or deadly hopelessness to haunt, but rather all the adverse experiences have been turned into tools of joy. Consequently, the enemy of our soul slinks away in defeat: for it was his scheme to use the horrific abuse to totally destroy. Because of Jesus being involved in the healing, every plot of the devil has gone in completely the opposite direction of what he had intended.

One may often hear that to *forgive and forget* is the way to gain successful healing. This concept, however, is spoken in ignorance and is intertwined with a deadly myth that can ultimately devastate the unsuspecting survivors of trauma or abuse.

It is quite true that we must always choose to forgive and release to God anyone who has rejected, abused, or hurt us in any way. To avoid or downplay this step will in the end result in being eaten alive by bitterness, hatred, and/or revenge. To take the bitter route is to ultimately choose destruction and death. To propagate the idealistic concept that one must forget the abuse in order to be free or healed is not of God regardless of who says or believes it and can result in a lot of counter-productivity and painful confusion in the healing journey.

Just as God does not intend that we throw out the baby with the bath water, so He has made it possible for the healed survivor of abuse to remember without the pain. Because through Christ, this is possible; it enables that we can take all the tools God has used in our healing and pass them on to benefit in the healing journey of others. Just as you cannot forget the scar that resulted from your finger being chopped off, so you cannot humanly expect a survivor to completely forget what degree of healing God has performed in a ruined life, or from what ruins the Lord restored from.

PRAYER: Lord, I want to choose the successful healing that only You can bring me through the finished work of Jesus. I ask You would give me beauty for ashes as You completely heal the pain of the past and turn it all into tools that will benefit others for Your glory. Amen.

Lord, Why Did I Suffer?

For years I asked, "Why, Lord, did I suffer so?
Through anguish untold, Lord, just why did I go?
Why did You not spare me from agonized pain?
How in pain's dark horror could there be some gain?"
"My Child, come and rest in My loving embrace
As I show to you My great will, love, and grace:
For on you since birth, Child, My eye hath been cast,
And under you daily My hand held you fast.
Midst grievous affliction I had a great plan,
To purge and prepare you for work I began;
Though Satan's tried hard to destroy you, dear soul,
I've sheltered you safe 'neath My love and control.
I could have erased all your pain with one touch,
Delighting to do so—I love you so much,
But I want to teach you to cling to My hand,
And fully to trust, though you don't understand.
The bigger your anguish, the damage or pain,
So grows My rich grace that has fully sustained;
The enemy tried every way to destroy,
But I have preserved you for My praise and joy!
You've suffered, My Child, for you're chosen to be
A light for the hurting—a witness for Me.
While trav'ling life's path that I've laid out for you,
You'll meet many hearts that are suffering too.
Because of deep waters that you have come through—
While looking to Me for the healing so true—
You'll know the stark anguish and suffering they feel:
My love you can show them and help them to heal!
I've chosen you, Child, to be My hands and feet,
To minister love to the hurting you meet,
Uplifting the downtrod, assisting the blind—
That hope, help and healing in Christ they can find!"
"Lord, now I can thank You for Your plan divine,
And ask that Your will may be done, Lord, not mine;
The deepest of pain You have shown can be healed—
My Jesus Physician must now be revealed!"

KETURAH C. MARTIN

"Why, Lord?"

For years, in writhing agony, I repeatedly asked God, "Why did You allow all these painful abuses to happen to me? Why did You not stop all the bad people that hurt and rejected me?" I could never understand how a loving God could just stand by with folded arms and watch innocent victims of atrocities suffer helplessly.

Years later (after suffering at the hands of many different perpetrators), the previous poem was born on a night wherein I cried out to God with my heartrending questions. Amazingly it was almost as though I heard the answers audibly, which were so clear and comforting! Suddenly all of the whys did not matter so much anymore because of the wonderful messages I had just received!

- ➤ "God has been involved and watching out for me since birth and even before that!"
- ➤ "He has a plan for my life despite the pain, abuse, and rejection."
- ➤ "The Lord has been fighting unseen battles on my behalf against Satan, who has attempted my destruction!" Wow!
- ➤ "God loves me despite the shatters and circumstances, enough to invest in my long-term well-being."
- ➤ "The grace of God is so rich and unlimited that it freely expands to meet the biggest and most desperate need or agonizing devastation!"
- ➤ "It was God Who preserved me in the face of death for some purpose."
- ➤ "I am chosen by God to be an instrument in His hand through whom He can touch other broken lives!"

Equipped with the knowledge of all God had shown me, I was beginning to experience some gratitude to Him for the way He was planning to use what the enemy meant for destruction to further His plan and purpose!

PRAYER: Lord, thank You for fighting for me, preserving me, and purposing to use the enemy's plots for the praise and glory of Your name! Thank You for walking with me through the pain and giving the grace to bear it all. Thanks Jesus for transforming me and my past into a redeemed instrument to touch others with Your love, for Your glory! Amen.

My Lord Can Restore

Though one is abandoned, or just cast aside,
Controlled as a robot, and harshly denied,
Though you've been sore torn by deliberate abuse,
The Lord Jesus calls you despite the misuse.

"Come, Child, unto Me, though you're tattered and torn—
I see how your load is too great to be borne;
Do not labor on with this luggage immense,
But bring Me your burdens, and I'll help you hence!"

My Jesus too faced great abuse on the cross:
The sting of betrayal, its anguish and loss,
The shame of exposure, the beatings so wild—
Degraded and spat on as nails pierced God's Child.

"Dear Father, forgive them," He cried out aloud,
And loved each one fully, amid abuse cloud;
He too knows the anguish of things we've gone through—
Impossible pain He will carry for you!

Although you've been trampled, dear soul, you have worth:
For you, Jesus died on this sin-cursed old earth;
And now He stands waiting to mend broken hearts—
To lift you above all the enemy's darts.

For Christ is a Specialist—He'll beautify
The most ragged heart that abuse left to die;
The shards of deep pain He removes, and will heal
The pangs of dark shame, which you always now feel.

So tell Him each detail of what you've been through—
Release to Him damage, and those who hurt you;
Just yield Him your tatters and crushed heart so sore—
Impossible ruins, my Lord can restore!

KETURAH C. MARTIN

MARCH 12
READING: ROMANS 8:34 AND 1 JOHN 2:1, 2

Jesus, Advocate For The Abused

Jesus is the only Advocate we will ever need who can understand 100 percent of everything we have experienced, suffered, and survived. He understands all the endless anguish and filthy shame that comes after abuse. Jesus faced a multitude of abuses while He walked this earth among men. He was repeatedly shot down verbally while He endured emotionally the contempt and degradations of the religious leaders of that day. On the day that Jesus was crucified and died in our place to save us, He was physically and sexually abused, in addition to all the other abuses. Just before He died He called out to God and said, "Father, forgive them for they know not what they do."

Three days later Jesus conquered death (Matthew 28:5, 6) and arose from the grave in triumph! Now He is forever at the right hand of God where He makes intercession for us. Not only does He intercede, work, and oversee everything on our behalf, but He is also the only One Who is completely qualified to bring us healing and freedom from horrors past. Because Jesus died for us, He has a vested interest in our painful past, our current demolitions, and our future, which He longs to make bright again.

It doesn't matter how destroyed one feels or even how shattered one actually is when it comes to meeting with Jesus, our Advocate. There is nothing too hard for Jesus to fix, though to the survivor it may often seem to be all hopelessly irreparable. He specializes in the most impossible situations of abuse, trauma, grief, and shatters of destruction. When nobody understands or validates you and where you are, that is when Jesus our Advocate picks you up and carries you close to His bosom! He can never fail you! When He begins to work on you, nobody can stop Him!

PRAYER: Jesus, I am so glad You are Someone Who can understand how it feels to be hurt and destroyed. Take all these shatters and agony within. Please make them into something of value. Please help me to get through all this mess, Jesus. Amen.

"By My Hand Ye Are Led"

"My Child, despite storm clouds which darken the sky,
I see thy life picture and hear ev'ry cry,
So do not despair, though the path may grow dark:
For I AM thy Captain Who holds thy frail bark.

Though circumstance darkens and few understand,
My Child, be assured I have all in My hand:
For just before dawn comes the darkest of night—
So, Child, midst thy anguish I bring truth and light!

I see the full picture which none else can see,
And through darkest hours thy comfort shall be:
For I know My thoughts toward thee and My plans—
My Child, know My grace still sufficiently stands.

Each day and each step I My great plans progress,
Which I work in thee, though in joy or distress:
For when you commit thy dark trials to Me
I take full control and thy Refuge shall be.

No wave shall o'erflow thee—no depth cause thee harm:
For I AM thy God and uphold with My arm;
My most perfect peace shall reside in thee, Child—
Though storms and dark tempest surround thee so wild.

My Child, keep thy focus on Jesus thy Lord:
For guidance and grace He in full doth afford—
Look past all the boulders, affliction, and pain:
For My plans do work for your infinite gain!"

—Your Heavenly Father,
the Great I AM

God's Plans For Me

For everyone whom He created, God has a perfect plan and divine purpose. His thoughts, ways, and plans are so much above and beyond what we can fathom that we may often lose sight that He even has a plan for us. Our own choices can often mess up God's plans for us. Likewise, the decisions of others taken against us in such matters as abuse, rejection, and trafficking are also against God's perfect will and foul up what He had planned. During such incidents, if He wouldn't have stepped in with His presence to preserve us, in some cases, we could very well have died. But He cared enough to preserve both us and His plan despite outward circumstances.

Our God has such limitless love and infinite plans for us that regardless of our past or what we have endured, He can turn it all around for our best and His glory. He does, however, respect our choices; so it is up to us to give Him the green light to go ahead and transform painful pasts into channels of living hope. He can turn heart-shreds of agony into strands of gold, barren desert sands into lush and blooming meadows, and He can transform heaps of trashed rubble into value untold! The possibilities of what Jesus can do with the impossible situations some of us face bring about a great hope for our future despite the past! Although pain, abuse, and destruction are not God's will or plan, yet they can become tools in His hand if we surrender the contents of our heart into His control and invite Him to work in us. He can turn all the attempts of the enemy into something of great worth, while at the same time defeating Satan's schemes against us. The enemy's intent is to steal, kill, and destroy, but he cannot touch us when we are in the hand and control of God.

PRAYER: Jesus, when the storm around me is so dark that I cannot see You, please hold my hand. When the pain within my being obliterates Your face, will You please help me and hold me? When those around me do not understand and speak or act in detrimental ways, please walk with me and be my support: for I know You alone can fully understand. I renounce every attempt of Satan on my life and I claim Your protection. Take all the pain, heartache, and ashes, Lord, and please turn them into something beautiful by which You can be glorified. Thank You, Jesus for loving, caring, and understanding me! Amen.

I Carried You Through For My Praise And Joy

There wandered alone, in the darkness of night,
A little girl labelled with Leprosy's plight;
Cast out and forsaken by standards of men—
Rejected as "worthless" again and again.
God's people had branded her "bad, without use"
Because she survived dark, horrific abuse;
Their sad lack of knowledge erected thick walls,
Which banned her as "leper" with all that appalls.
Shut out in the cold with a pained, bleeding heart,
Condemned for destruction abuse did impart;
She crouched in dark shame midst an anguish untold
While scorned for surviving abuse stark and cold.
Why did she not die midst those years of abuse?
How can one so leprous become of some use?
Why is it a sin to survive horrors past?
Why, outside the camp must she always be cast?

Outside of the camp so alone she remains—
'Twas solely the Lord Who's preserved and sustained:
For midst deepest pain of rejection's dark night,
His Presence surrounds her lone form as a Light.

"My Child, you are Mine, despite men's verdict grim,
And My understanding makes theirs grow so dim;
I've planned and preserved you midst pain so untold,
And I provide healing as your hand I hold.
So yield Me the scorner, the skeptic, and judge,
And don't let dark bitterness drown you in sludge;
Though man understands not—support may not show,
Yet I am the Lord, and My plans for you know.
I saved you from death—your salvation have paid,
Cont.

And countless times over at your side I've stayed;
Though Satan, through man, all your life would destroy,
I've carried you through, Child, for My praise and joy!
Though waves of rejection may dash in your face,
Yet I am the Lord and supply you with grace;
I hold your full healing and carry you through—
My arms everlasting remain under you!"

Jesus Loved The Lepers

When Jesus was here on earth and walked among men, He went about doing good to all men, women, and children. There was no respect of persons with Him, regardless of station. He loved and accepted the people infected with the disease of leprosy just as much as anyone else He was in contact with. He was not afraid of public opinion and judgment, even to the point of exemplifying His love by touching a leprous man to heal him of his sickness. The mobs went wild with this act of love because they were living in the law rather than in love. Jesus came to show a new way of living, loving, and relating, which puts love in action toward the sick, abused, fatherless, homeless, and rejected.

The little girl in the poem was threatened and abused while being told that "If you ever tell anything that happened to you in here, the churches will reject you and cast you away forever!" Twenty-five years later, she could look back on a history of rejection, just as the perpetrator predicted in harsh tones. Repeatedly she was kept outside the gate where she looked in with longing, but was told by many that her history was too horrible to be looked at.

However, Jesus has a different viewpoint of the little girl sitting outside the gate, and anyone else who may be in similar situation. It is for the bruised, rejected, broken, and the ones dying alone that Jesus came to help, heal, and offer hope (see Mark 2:17). Tenderly He went to the lonely and cast-out little girl, where He took her in His arms and gently held her to His bosom. His words and touch whispered love, acceptance, and peace into her heart as He assured her that He had come to her side to help regardless of what man, churches, or anyone else may think or how they may act. He explained to her that it is actually Satan working through man when people reject, condemn, and cast out His hurting children. Then He urged her to always choose to put this type of people with their rejections into His hand so she would not be swallowed up in bitterness. What a comfort to rest in His arms and assurances, which are so much more valuable than anything that man can offer!

PRAYER: Lord Jesus, I bring You all the rejection, worthlessness, and loneliness of being cast out or kept out from a group of people. Bless each one responsible and help me to love them as You do. Thank You for Your love, assurances, and acceptance, regardless of popular opinion. Amen.

Under The Wings Of God

What better place could one be than under the protection and safety of the wings of God Himself? He Who created us and knows our life from start to finish also has a vested interest in every human being because of coming to earth in the form of His Son, Jesus, Who gave His life for all.

To be sheltered under His wings is the safest place one could ever be, but especially so for the wounded ones who may be more vulnerable, or not be understood anywhere else. Often others (who because they have never been there) cannot even begin to comprehend what we are experiencing. Due to their lack of knowledge and how to relate, they may say or do things that are hurtful without meaning to do so. Whether someone deliberately hurts another with his words and scant understanding or whether it is unintentional, either way we must immediately run to the Source of our grace and strength, which is Jesus. He fully understands the misunderstood, and He is right there to walk with them each step. He is willing and ready to be a shield for us, taking whatever darts and arrows may come.

Though human nature tends to judge others by appearance and then believe they are on track with what they assume, yet it is only the Lord Who knows the absolute truth about everything unseen. Jesus said, "Judge not according to appearance, but judge righteous judgment" (John 7:24). It is very comforting to know that Jesus knows the truth even when nobody else seems to. In fact, He experienced the very same thing when He was on earth—always facing judgment, scorn, unbelief, and ridicule. Jesus not only understands us completely without judgment, but He also travelled the road before us. The example He left for us is a helpful tool which can lead us through the anguish of not being understood or accepted.

PRAYER: Lord, I choose to forgive and release into Your hand every person who does not see and understand the full picture. Their every word, thought, attitude, and action I release into Your control. Take back any ground the enemy may have taken through all this, and please fill me with Your love. Thank You, Jesus, for understanding, caring, and loving me. Amen.

A Walk Through The Lord's Garden

At sunrise I come to Your garden each morn,
Where daily, new sunbeams the flowers adorn;
I walk with You, Jesus, midst lilies so white,
Which tell of Your wonders just after dark night.
The bowers of roses which climb up so high,
Shout forth the thorn story of One Who would die:
For me, Lord, You wore piercing thorns on Your head
Before You were nailed to the cross in my stead.

The violets so tender, in dark purple hues,
Bring out a sweet message midst new morning dews:
They whisper in awe of the most gentle touch—
The Master restoring when needed so much.
The bleeding heart flowers in brightness hang low,
Midst heart-pains rejuvenate hope none can know,
Ecstatically shouting of Jesus, my King,
Who mends broken heart-shreds and makes ruins sing!

The lily of valley determinedly grows,
And out from a crevice in rock it now shows:
For it sought the sunshine and light from above—
No obstacle, hard, could deter it from love!
The sunflowers loom near the garden's far wall,
In brightness so cheering, still loudly they call;
They laud the bright sunshine so full in the face—
Remind me of Jesus—His love, light, and grace.

And then come the grape vines all climbing about,
With never a shadow of worry or doubt:
For if they abide in the true vine alway,
The life is sustained in them, come then what may.
And Lord, the rock walls that surrounding I see,
Reminds of protection You put around me:
For You are the Gardener of this my heart—
Completing in full ev'ry work You do start!

KETURAH C. MARTIN

The Lord's Garden

Walking through the Lord's garden is an experience of awe, as one takes time to consider the intricate grandeur of the Master Gardener's work. He spoke the world and each minute detail into place by His great power and stretched-out arm. The same hand that holds the universe in its place can reach right into an agonized or devastated heart with a touch of love and begin His work of restoration. Just as He fashioned the delicate violet, so He can create exquisite beauty out of ashes in a destroyed heart.

As we advance under the arbor of climbing roses, I cannot help but think of the piercing thorns my Savior wore. But to look at the roses from another perspective tells yet another story. Just as the roses pushed beyond the thorns into fragrant blooms, so we with the Gardener's help can also push beyond the briars of adversity, inner agony, or any other circumstance we face. We need not concentrate on the thorns of the rose bush, but praise God for the rose. Even so, the thorns and aftermath of abuse can also lose their sting and sharpness of pain, grime, and memory as Jesus, the Rose of Sharon, blooms in the heart which He has restored. However, we must never presume that one's painful past can be buried, ignored, or untouched, or Satan will retain unseen footholds spelling ultimate defeat. These footholds can easily produce blight, bug invasions, and ultimate death. Rather, we must allow and invite Jesus, the Gardener of our heart, to dig and work the soil therein, and to remove whatever He finds there that can hinder growth. He can find all the shards of broken glass, life-choking weeds of doubt and deceptions, and everything else that needs to be taken care of.

May we seek to persevere through hardship like the lily of the valley; shine as the sunflower; connect to the Vine as the grape branches; and reflect the touch of God like the violets. May our mended hearts shout the hope and praise that the beauty of the bleeding hearts promote in their undeniable uniqueness and gorgeous grandeur.

PRAYER: Lord, please take control of the garden of my heart. I ask You to work the soil and remove all the thorns of pain and shards of rejection. Cause my heart to bloom with the presence of Your love and healing. Amen.

Blessings In Disguise

Lord, I thank You for each hardship,
Which in faithfulness You send—
Though the agony has harsh grip,
Yet sufficient grace You lend!
For dark trials can be blessings,
Which disguised, are in Your hand,
That You seek to use as lessons
And enhance my growth as planned.
I rejoice, Lord, for Thy insight,
Which discerns my deepest needs—
For the blessings of the dark night,
And sufficient light indeed!
Midst the ash heap of dark trouble
Where the ruins writhe in grief—
Though pained circumstance may double,
Yet my Lord can bring relief!
Ev'ry trial, tear and heartache,
Are rich blessings in disguise—
Which endured by grace for Your sake,
You in turn can make a prize!
So for circumstance of anguish,
I do praise Thee, Lord of mine—
Though o'erflowing seems my life dish—
Yet Your plan remains divine.
For these blessings Lord, I thank Thee,
Though disguised amid much pain—
For Your strength, so perfect I see,
And in weakness You bring gain!
Lord, when trials come from all sides—
Then Your blessings freely flow;
Though midst fire I am oft tried
You, Your purpose fully know!
For the fullest picture You see
From beginning to the end;
The disguised blessings I give Thee,
With Thy perfect will to blend.

KETURAH C. MARTIN

Disguised Blessings

When one is experiencing depths of pain, sorrow, or the tempestuous aftereffects of some sort of abuse, it feels literally impossible to see anything good in it. Only with the help of Jesus can one be given divine insight to see beyond the agony, shame, grief, and/or tears. But Jesus—as the Master Designer of our life, purpose, and future—has the utmost capability of turning shambled ruins into gems of value. He specializes in taking the pain and rubble of shattered lives, and turning them into tools with infinite worth which can transform us completely. The subtle scheming and repeated attempts of Satan to destroy through another human can be totally reversed when Jesus Christ steps in.

It is important for us to surrender into His hand all the anguishing heart-shreds we may be engulfed in. When He has all the pieces, that is when He can truly foil the attempts of the enemy against us. He then re-creates the trampled pieces and tangled heart-shreds into disguised blessings, which benefit us eternally, if we but let Him do the work in us.

The enemy seethes in rage as he observes the pain and havoc he wreaked in us turn into tools which work for our santification. His anger grows as the absolute destruction he instigated in some individuals transforms into jewels of infinite value by the power and love of Jesus. The enemy does not want the survivor of his destructions to know and embrace these truths: "The power, grace, and love of Jesus can transform the deepest form of abuse and destruction into clear, tranquil streams of living water and peaceful pastures. There is nothing too hard or destroyed for Him to bring healing to."

What we may have termed as hopeless rubble Jesus can turn into sparkling diamonds. The agonized and bloody heart-shreds He transforms into strands of pure gold, which He weaves into our life picture beside the dark ones. What we thought was a heap of ashes and grimy charcoal, He perfects into pure, white linen of priceless value. The unbearable agony He fashions into unique tools of great worth and thus foils the schemes of the enemy to derail us.

PRAYER: Jesus, I choose to bring You the pain, destruction, and aftermath of all I have been subjected to in the past. I choose to believe beyond the darkness and anguish that You can do the impossible and restore my life into something of value. I entrust my life and future to Your divine plan and work of love. Amen.

My Refuge Is My God

Though I must pass through the fire in the darkest of my night
Should the flames arise still higher, yet the Lord remains my Light;
He provides for me to dwell in a safe secret place near Him,
Where in spite of heat and dark din, there is peace though life looks grim.

For my Refuge and my Fortress is my God in Whom I trust,
Who, despite what trials oft press, He doth shield from ev'ry gust;
From dark snares He doth deliver, midst the trouble on all sides:
For of life He is my Giver and so constantly abides.

With His feathers He doth cover when the storm is raging sore,
Of my soul He is the Lover and has great things yet in store:
For beneath His wings abiding, I in trust am not afraid,
But behind His shield I'm hiding till the outward storm is stayed.

There's no terror can affright me with His shield of truth before,
Though dark arrows daily I see, He my Buckler helps the more;
When destruction round me rages, He's my Refuge day and night:
For my Lord, the God of ages, is my constant Guide and Light!

Ev'ry circumstance encountered doth the Lord hold in His hand:
For my call to heav'n is answered by a God Who understands;
Though dark peril lurks around me and the trouble piles up high,
Yet my Refuge shall the Lord be, with His love and grace so nigh.

From beginning to the ending, my life picture doth God see,
So life's joys and trials blending, He works patiently with me;
Each experience He uses to enhance His plan divine,
And no soul with Him e'er loses as He works in perfect time.

Ev'ry trying situation God works out for my own good,
Which is used in preparation, to mold me just as He would;
So within His hand of power I commit my life anew,
Who sustains me ev'ry hour and doth see me safely through!

KETURAH C. MARTIN

A Safe Refuge And Fortress

While travelling the road to healing, it is imperative to have a safe place where one can go if healing is to advance. A safe place to a survivor means that there is no threat of harm or abuse, understanding and validation are prominent, confidentiality is 100 percent present, protection is paramount, judgment is totally absent, and living out true love is unconditional. To someone fleeing abuse, trafficking, death, and terror, this description in action would be a haven indeed!

Sometimes it may feel as if your whole world is crashing on you and all the unresolved anguish you may carry. There is no place to turn, and no one who cares enough to understand the crushing pain or to take the time to be involved. At such a time is when a safe refuge wherein to retreat would be most welcome.

After years of rejection and various repeated abuses across the continent, God began to teach me about a safe place where people can always go, no matter where they are geographically. It is Jesus Who provides this safe refuge and fortress while travelling the anguishing road to healing.

Sometimes before survivors come to complete healing, they may inwardly experience explosive interruptions while outwardly relationships and circumstances are spiraling destructively downward amid unlimited inner agony. When we are trapped, misunderstood, and crying out for hope, help, and mercy, this is when Jesus steps in and carries us near to His bosom. Often we may not even be aware at the onset that He has gently picked us up with the loving intent of walking us through what would be unbearable alone. It is important to specifically request Him to be our Guide: for He never forces His way in on anyone. Without Him as Guide, we are more apt to take shortcuts in our healing and become vulnerable to quick fixes, band-aid solutions, and the detrimental input of those who do not understand, resulting in additional injury and setbacks. Doing it our way can also give Satan more opportunity to attempt some foothold in areas we sought to bypass. With Jesus as Guide, we have a safe Refuge right beside us, and He will never fail, forsake, or betray us. He understands and validates us and offers supernatural protection in every circumstance or painful encounter. He also knows the truth, even when most others seem blinded, and His love is unconditional.

PRAYER: Jesus, I ask You to be my Guide and walk with me throughout this entire healing journey. When the way is dark and the pain unbearable, please hold me close to Your bosom and carry me through to peace and safety. I choose to give You my past, present, and future. I ask that You bring me to complete healing for Your glory. Amen.

Pain Signals Your Dawn

"Dear God, take my hand in this darkest of night:
For I cannot stand, save, dear Lord, by Thy might;
The path I can't see midst stark anguish untold—
Come, Lord, near to me and my hand firmly hold.
I can't understand this deep pain made alive,
So, Lord, with me band that for Thee I may strive;
Help me to be true as I give Thee my life—
Surrend'ring to You, pain which cuts like a knife.
Dear Jesus, tell me—what in this You have planned?
Lord, how could it be all allowed by Thy hand?
This agony, deep, I alone cannot bear—
Awake or asleep, it doth surge in despair."
—Survivor, come alive emotionally

"My Child, don't despair, midst the anguish so grim:
For I, your load share, which o'erflows from the brim;
The feelings once dead that abuse did destroy,
I've touched now instead: for I seek to bring joy.
I've chosen you, Child, for your value is high,
Though pain mounts so wild that your heart always cries;
My grace on you pours—I thy needs understand—
Your heart bleeding sore, I now hold in My hand.
Because you can feel this stark pain, grim and cold,
You also can heal to degrees manifold:
For when all is dead, healing cannot move on,
So take heart instead: for pain signals thy dawn!
Child, yield Me each thorn which now pierces thy heart,
Each flashback so torn where the anguish all starts,
Surrender each piece of the pain to My hand,
Then healing's release can take place as I've planned.

Cont.

When healing complete I've restored unto thee,
Your joy will be sweet and thy heart be pain-free;
You'll then be equipped to go work in My name
And touch souls all ripped by abuse and dark shame;
Then joy, life and love will burst forth from thy soul
When healed from above—which is My highest goal!"

—Jesus, in reply

MARCH 25
READING: ROMANS 8:15-19

A Painful Dawn

The journey to healing is sometimes dark and agonizing with only short breaks of light or strands of hope. Other times there may be a bright rainbow after a wild, stormy night. Whatever the case, it is a long arduous and painful journey, despite the fact that those around us may often urge for short-cuts, cover-ups, or quick fixes.

One particular dark time in the journey is when one's emotional system comes alive after a long period of having been unknowingly shut down just to survive the previous destructions faced. The excruciation one may experience when the dormant emotions throb to life may be far beyond what words can even begin to express. During this time in my experience, the tears flowed 24/7 for three weeks nonstop, and to a lesser degree for several weeks beyond, as my heart felt literally as though it were ripping into bloody shreds. The vivid writhing of internal agony, added to the external physical distress of PTSD, can easily obliterate hope, but for the unseen presence of Jesus.

Though humanly speaking it seems impossible, yet we need to thank God for allowing and ensuring that our emotions come alive. It is not possible for us to heal from something which we cannot feel. God, Who created us, knows this well and, in His love, does not allow anything to remain forever dormant or secretly rotting away. When His timing is right, He will gently walk through the tangled mess of the heart's garden to waken the emotions out of dormacy. However, He faithfully remains at one's side with the most tender yearning to assist in the healing of all that surrounds the unspeakable pain. It then becomes our choice to either implore His aid, healing, and sustenance or plunge forward on our own strength to try to resolve what is humanly impossible to do on our own. Without His involvement we are setting ourselves up for defeat, frustration, additional pain and chaos, and ultimately a possible case of emotional, physical, and spiritual burn-out while being no further ahead.

PRAYER: Lord Jesus, I ask You to be my constant companion and sustenance throughout this journey to healing. I cannot carry this throbbing pain all alone and I ask You to be present and take it all into Your hand to bring healing. Defeat the enemy's intentions against me and use this pain to build me for You. Amen.

KETURAH C. MARTIN

What Would Jesus Do?

Would Jesus Christ refuse to hear another's pain, discount their tears?
Would He reject their pleas for aid, of tortures complex be afraid?
Would Jesus judge one in advance before He knows their circumstance?
Does He withhold His love and care—pretend that heartache is not there?
Would He refuse to understand and show no love, nor lend a hand?
Because a person's been abused—subject to horrors, beat and used.
Would Jesus wound the broken heart, refuse to help and speak "Depart,"
For fear of what men think or say—a soul at stake thus turn away?
Would Jesus lift the carpet high, shove pain beneath—perchance to die?
Would He deny the aching heart of love and caring from the start?
On shredded hearts would Jesus walk, and of assumptions only talk?
Or would He seek out truth alone, despite away from comfort zones?
Would Jesus shoot out judging darts—aim them directly at the heart?
And would He trash the wounded soul for dark abuse beyond control?
Would He attempt a bypass route because the truth's concealed with doubt?
Does He condone "to cover sin" just to avoid a raucous din?
Does He condemn a victim's mind for pain and anguish undefined?
Would He reject the longing heart, and heap more injury from the start?
Sometimes we're tempted to surmise, another's anguish criticize:
"Pull up your bootstraps, move along, forget the past, and sing a song."
But Jesus came, a Shepherd kind—the brokenhearted souls to bind,
He came to set the captives free, the bruised to set at liberty;
Christ did not judge the shattered heart—He loved each leper from the start,
He poured His love out to the lame and touched each soul who to Him came.
Our human nature often tends to push and judge, one's heart to rend:
Care not that they are hurting sore, but oft will wound them even more.
May Jesus guide our words and thoughts, all fears, opinions bring to naught:
Let's live God's love each step, each mile: without condition, love compile.
Then when our journey is complete and we will rest at Jesus' feet
To you, will God say "Child, well done—enter My joy with Christ My Son?"

WILL YOU DO WHAT JESUS WOULD DO?

How Does Jesus Relate To The Abused?

When Jesus walked this earth, how did He respond to the ones who came to Him in anguish of soul and body, looking for help and hope?

> ➤ He stopped and took time to help them, addressing the core need of their heart and life. He accepted them where they were and loved them without judgment.

How did Jesus treat those who lived daily in emotional pain and/or physical debilitations?

> ➤ Even though Jesus knew each detail about all who came to Him, He always took an interest in them and inquired about what was happening in their life and how He could help. A touch or a word would often heal them, accompanied with their faith and His divine love in action.

What kind of time and effort did He put into the little children, some of whom were very likely survivors of abuse?

> ➤ He took time for them as He held them in His arms, blessed them, and likened them to those who would inherit the kingdom of heaven.

Did Jesus reject and condemn individuals because they were oppressed within or without with demonic powers?

> ➤ Jesus always separated the person from the evil power. He accepted and loved the individual, but the demonic entity He cast away, bringing freedom. He never judged by appearance, but looked on the heart.

Did Jesus care what others observed, said, or thought about Him as He went about helping, loving, and healing those in need?

> ➤ He did not care that the religious leaders were always in a state of jealous contempt against Him for extending Himself to the broken, dying, sick, and outcasts. Jesus clearly portrayed that all are equal and deserve love.

When Jesus met abuse survivors, did He condemn and ostracize them while ordering them to forget the pain of the past and get on with their lives?

> ➤ Jesus specifically said, "I came to heal the brokenhearted, to deliver the captive, give sight to the blind, and to set the bruised at liberty."

PRAYER: Jesus please help me to live Your love in every circumstance. Amen.

On Eagle Wings Thou Shalt Mount

When life seems so dreary and burdened with care,
As clouds of dread darkness breathe out black despair,
Dear soul, take fresh courage, look up, and behold:
For Jesus has planned you a future untold.

Wait now on the Lord and your strength He'll renew,
As on eagle wings you shall mount and take view
Of ev'ry bright promise, which through the clouds beam,
As sunbeams of hope on your sordid life gleam.

He hears you above all your pain and dark past,
As each painful heartache on Him you now cast:
For He is the Healer of sad, broken hearts—
It's here that His infinite plan for you starts!

So as with the eagles you mount up so high,
Give Christ ev'ry anguish that makes your heart cry:
For as you are borne near the Savior's own breast,
He works within you to bring healing and rest.

He brings you a freedom and healing complete,
As all you surrender and lay at His feet;
The shatters of heart-break and strands of dark pain
He blends with bright gold of most infinite gain.

And then He equips you by His grace divine,
To soar still with eagles and says "Child, you're Mine;
You shall not grow faint when I walk by your side:
For I'll light your path and so near will abide!"

On Eagle Wings

Waiting is often a very difficult process, especially when one is in the midst of suffering, abuse, pain, and/or rejection. Why must we wait on an all-powerful God Who could stop all the outside circumstances of agony with a word? For thirty-five agonizing years I waited, longed for, and cried out for hope, help, understanding, and deliverance from continuous abuses of every nature. Why did it seem that my desperate cry was ignored or cast aside? Where was the God of love I had heard so much about?

Years later, after God had sent messengers to rescue us from deadly abuse, the voice of Jesus was heard very distinctly. He brought an answer to my cry, which set so much of it straight despite the need to look at some deeper things further. "I planned you before the world began and have loved you with an everlasting love. I have understood you since the time I was forming you in the womb; and it is because of My presence, sustenance, and divine aid that you survived everything adversely painful throughout your life. Though humans have not always understood, or known how to love and help you, yet I the Lord can never fail you!"

This message straight from my heavenly Father brought about a great renewing of my emotional strength and courage, as light from heaven burst upon my darkness. The joyous assurance of God sustaining and preserving me all the years to the present made the waiting, and even the agony, worth it all. Now there is no question about where He was, because I know He was right there, standing between me and the many abusers. Had He removed Himself from scenes of terror, agony, and horror, He would have removed life itself, as men were being used as a pawn of Satan to destroy me.

To receive the words from my Father that He gave that day was a blessed experience of mounting up with the eagles as the Lord renewed my strength. The courage and hope that before was continually dwindling now became vibrantly alive in the face of my Father and the knowledge of His preserving hand.

PRAYER: My heavenly Father, I choose to embrace You as the Source and preservation of my life. Thank You for being there to keep me alive when all around was just excruciating darkness and filthy pain. Thank You for lifting me out of the rubble pile so You could bring healing and transform me into a vessel through whom You can pour Your love. I give You my past, present, and future: for it is You alone Who can restore and make me soar with the eagles. Amen.

The Destroyed Rose Made New

My life, like a rose had burst forth in full bloom,
Each soft, fragrant petal dispelled shades of gloom,
But then in the twilight somebody drew near
And stomped the plush rose into dirt's mucky smear.

The stem had been broken, the leaves rent and torn—
The delicate petals, the worst part had borne:
For they lay in ruins, all scattered about,
In pain's dirty mire were now tramped beyond doubt.

The core of the flower drooped hopeless and grim,
Now stripped of all beauty—a silhouette dim;
The future was gone—in a moment destroyed—
So barren and useless, of beauty devoid.

The Master of Gardeners, one day did appear,
Approaching the rose that was tattered and drear;
He quickly observed the destruction it bore,
But didn't pass by, as all others before.

Christ picked up each petal, though dirty and torn,
So tenderly gathering each one, forlorn;
He washed and restored them by power divine,
And put them together—a flower refined.

The rose, without petals, had been incomplete,
And gone was its wholeness and beauty so sweet,
But Jesus has done the impossible thing—
His hope, life, and healing midst ruins did bring!

Despite the destruction one's life may have faced,
God's love, grace and power can fully erase
The damage and anguish, the grief, shame and night—
In full restorations, my Jesus delights!

Trampled And Made New

Each soul that God creates, He does so with a specific purpose in mind for that individual to fill. He creates each individual person with a unique beauty and in His own image. Just as a rose bud that is bursting into bloom has an amazing beauty, so is each girl and boy He brings into this world as a baby.

God does not condone abuse and all the ugly aftereffects that may project far into the future of the survivor. However, because He has given man the power of choice, and many choices are against His perfect will, therefore many innocent victims suffer through unmentionable crime, horror, and abuse.

But despite what any perpetrator has done against another human being, when Jesus comes walking through the garden of life and finds one of His blooms crushed, He stops to investigate and bring about restoration. Sometimes individuals are so destroyed that they are merely lying in pieces and strewn about in devastastion when Jesus, the Master Gardener finds them. Gently He picks up all the fragmented pieces of the precious lives and begins the work of restoration that He alone is capable of doing.

When we observe a broken rose with the petals all shredded on the ground and the flower itself a skeletical remains, we would say that it is beyond hope of ever being a beautiful flower again. Even so, abuse and rejection too can result in shattered lives lying in broken pieces, which may be repeatedly trampled and disregarded. But all is not hopeless when God is involved and when Jesus the Master Gardener is invited to be the one in charge of restoration and healing. His touch of love manifested toward each broken piece of the life involved can produce a healing and restoration that with man is impossible. There is nothing too hard for God, but rather He delights in specializing in those things which to the human mind seem utterly impossible! The most destroyed life which may have been shattered to hundreds of pieces or ground to powder He can definitely restore!

PRAYER: Lord Jesus, I bring You all the shattered and trampled pieces of my life and ask that You do a work of restoration which only You can do. Thank You for loving and caring enough for me that You would be willing to stoop down and retrieve me from the dust. I invite You to do the work at hand. Amen.

Dissociative Identity Disorder

The Lord, Creator of mankind, has fully planned, designed the mind:
Techniques He gave—life to advance—dissociation gives a chance.
So often it's misunderstood, thought of as "evil," never "good";
When misdiagnosed and treated wrong, then shattered lives
can't sing hope's song.

When trauma's vice becomes one's fate, or when abuse will dominate,
A victim's mind may helpless rend and split, as life it will defend.
As lightning rends the blackened sky, which helpless hangs midst storms so nigh:
Just so, the mind in anguished plight may split, as death it seeks to fight!

When perpetrators hurl with force abusive anguish vile and coarse,
Upon their victims, trapped and bound, without a friend or soul around:
There's just so much the mind can take when life and sanity's at stake—
The mind then sets survival stance before pained death is full advanced.

The mind then tears, beyond control, midst agony, emotional—
A new identity sets up, who stores that pain in memory's cup.
The host may oft be unaware of what each part in anguish shares;
Each day is filled with loss so grim and all the future's hope is dim:

Because days, hours, months and weeks are oft unknown, so dark and bleak,
As vivid time loss overrules these pained survivors in shame's pool:
Past, present, future's just a haze of dim reality and maze,
Black hopelessness looms ever near: for few do know the anguish here.

Dissociation's a device God gave the mind, though high its price,
But it allows one to survive—though great its pain, keeps them alive;
Dissociation is a route God gave the mind, there is no doubt,
To use midst trauma's tragedy, escaping death—now life's for me!

PRAYER: Jesus I invite You into this mess of broken and dissociated pieces which
writhe in unspeakable anguish and endless clamoring confusion. I ask You Lord
to find every disconnected piece of me and bring us all into complete healing
and freedom. Amen.

Dissociative Identity Preservation

There are many things about God that are far deeper than our human minds can comprehend. He made and understands the intricate recesses of our mind and brain, and just how it all works together with the body and soul. One thing very difficult for the majority of the population to fathom (unless they've been there) is how God designed the mind to sanely survive unbearable and repetitious trauma or abuse.

When enduring and surviving the blows of repeated or continuous abuse and violence, the mind is as a chunk of wood on the chopping block. The swinging axe is the deadly abuse, and the hand swinging it is the perpetrator. Every time the axe strikes there is damage done to the whole piece of wood. At a certain point of impact after repeated blows, the wood will split into an entirely separate piece of wood with its own shape and identity. This is a picture of what can happen with the mind of an abuse victim under the impacting blows of abuse. When it reaches a certain point of its endurance it can split into a separate identity of memory and consciousness. This piece holds certain aspects of the abuse, such as the memory, pain, and/or other details of threats, filth, or shame.

Because God created the mind with the capability of splitting while in a survival stance, we know He is also capable of bringing healing to individuals who are split up like a piece of wood. He cares for each broken-off piece, for each one helps make up the whole of His wounded child. Each separate piece must be accepted and validated in order for complete healing to take place in the suvivor as a whole.

I praise and thank God for preserving my life, being, and sanity by allowing me to split in the face of death and abuse, for He ensured my survival and has a plan for me! Living in this split condition is one of the most difficult and unwanted things that there could possibly be and is one of the most misunderstood. But when Jesus is part of the healing and begins touching each piece personally, that is when true freedom, hope, and healing begin!

PRAYER: Thank You, Lord, for preserving my life and planning my future. Even though many cannot understand my survival and healing, yet I praise You for Your infinite understanding and Your touch of love to every part of me! Amen.

My Jesus Was Always There!

Sometimes it is hard to at all understand,
Just what in dark trial my Lord may have planned:
How could He allow all the suff'ring and pain?
Why did He not stop all the anguish that rained?
So often I've stared within death's darkest face,
Not knowing if morning my breath would still trace;
And one could well wonder, "Was God really there?
Did He even help in the midst of despair?"

My friend, let me tell you in tones full of trust,
That "Jesus was there despite rubble and dust—
When dark death was lurking midst pain none can rate,
The power of God I cannot estimate!"
For it was my Jesus Who always was there—
He salvaged my life from the depth of despair;
For had He not been there, all hope would have fled:
And I would have perished—been found only dead!

He tenderly held me within His embrace—
Though crushed, bruised, and bleeding, He offered His grace;
Although when in anguish one can't understand—
Assured we can be that God has each life planned.
Christ picked up the ruins of agony, dark—
In love's tender care He preserved my torn bark;
The tatters of agony, mixed He with gold,
Producing a treasure with value untold.

I praise my dear Savior that He understands—
For using torn pieces in His divine plans—
For salvaging life midst the ruins of pain—
For using the anguish for infinite gain!
For pain I do thank Him, and praise Him anew
For each darkened trial that He's called me through;
I thank Him for using abuse so untold
To teach me His love as His purpose unfolds!

READING: DEUTERONOMY 32:10, 11 AND ZECHARIAH 2:8

The Saving Presence Of Jesus

When I was writhing in terror and pain while lying in shards upon the dust of a rubble pile, where was Jesus? When it felt as if peril and death were staring me in the face with relentless agony, did Jesus see or even care? Did He actually know the countless times when my heart was brutally ripped out, torn into tidbits, and trampled underfoot? Where was He when I laid down my life and body into the paws of death and violence just to help save someone else from being hurt? When children and victims are suffering intense abuse, pain, and rejection, does God just fold His arms and passively watch the destruction of His child? Where is God when every day babies and children are being sold into sex trafficking and slavery? Does He really care?

These are all questions that have been often voiced by countless survivors of all manner of abuse. Very often it may feel as if "there are no answers, and that the evidence and aftereffects of abuse prove that He just passively stood by—not really caring."

Some perpetrators use the power of Satan to verbally and mentally portray graphic pictures of Jesus assisting them in hurting the helpless victim or of Him just walking away. Because of experiencing this devastating phenomenon, I had no peace of mind about the foremost question until I had brought it specifically for an answer. "Lord, where were You while I was being violently destroyed, or looking down the barrel of the gun?" His loving, gentle response brought me to tears of ceaseless gratitude, and answered my question once for all.

"My Child, I cannot stop the wrong choices of evil men, but when Satan used them in attempt to destroy you, that is when I stood between them and you. I held you close to My breast, and when the pain, filth, and shame were more than could be borne, I carried you through it all. I was actively present and stayed right beside you through all that you encountered so I could preserve you by My power and for My glory."

PRAYER: Thank You, Jesus, for preserving me, carrying me, and delivering me from the entirety of what the enemy intended to do. Thank You for standing between, and I surrender all the broken pieces to You so that You can bring beauty out of the ashes for Your glory. Amen.

Even Greater My Grace

"When burdens and trials, My Child, do come near,
When heartache and grief seem to drive away cheer,
Come closer to Me, Child, and bring all thy care:
For I, as your Savior, each heartache will share.

My grace, all-sufficient, is given anew
For each darkened hardship that you may go through;
And, Child, e'er remember, My love shall enfold
You close to My breast as thy right hand I hold.

The greater the heartache or trial you face,
My Child, even greater is My strength and grace:
For I walk beside thee to guide and to save—
Affliction's dark waters together we'll brave.

The floods of great waters are held by My hand
And cannot surpass all My will and command—
Midst turbulent trials with you I do walk,
And in sweet communion together we talk.

Though mountains immense may forebodingly rise,
My Child, I'm thy God, and I still specialize
In things that to you may impossible seem—
Midst mountainous troubles I fully redeem!

I've called thee by name, and I know thou art Mine;
No dross shall remain when thy soul I refine:
So yield Me your trials—thy heart I now hold,
And you shall come forth as the purest of gold!"

READING: 2 CORINTHIANS 9:8 AND HEBREWS 4:16

My Grace Is Sufficient

Jesus told Apostle Paul, "My grace is sufficient for thee: for my strength is made perfect in weakness," when he was asking God to remove some thorn in the flesh that he was suffering from.

Very often in the healing journey, it is only by the grace and help of God that one can endure and go on amid insufferable aftereffects. God will never allow anything to happen to us but that He Himself will walk through it with us. Sometimes when an experience yields so much turmoil, pain, or shame that it feels impossible to even take one step more, that is when the grace of God grows to immense proportions to meet the need at hand. He will never just let us sit without sufficient grace and His divine presence to draw from. When the pain is so intense and the night so dark that you cannot feel Him near, that is when He is in the process of carrying you through it all, even as the enemy attempts to camouflage His presence.

We don't ever need to be afraid of coming too much to the throne of grace to obtain help in a time of need. The storehouse of God's grace is exhaustless, and He supplies our needs according to His riches in glory from His unlimited supply. This fact alone should give us great confidence even in the thick of our darkest night or most unbearable inner excruciation. For if God's grace supply is unlimited, that means we do not have to fear the pain, trial, or hardship, but rather commit it into the hand of our divine God Who expands His grace to fit the specific need at hand.

In our weakness and anguish, the strength of Jesus Christ is perfected in us and our entire situation as He literally becomes our sole strength, help, and preservation. At the same time He is receiving praise and glory as we and all those around us can see without any doubt that Jesus alone is the Strength in the particular turbulence at hand.

PRAYER: Lord Jesus, I want to thank You for the riches of Your grace that You have shown in the past and continue to shower on me. Thank You for whatever adverse experiences in my life that can manifest Your strength, power, and grace in and through me for Your glory. I ask You to continue to walk with me throughout this journey. Amen.

KETURAH C. MARTIN

The Carpet Of Denial

The mat of *No Knowledge* is humped up and drear,
Where skeptics and scorners oft gather so near;
Here some folks will walk in denial's dread shoes—
Avoiding the truth, even though they will lose.
The truth remains true, despite race, wish or creed,
And so, unfulfilled, is a need still a need;
There's not a survivor alive in this land,
But that they need hope and a true, loving hand.

Denying the need won't diminish its throb,
But rather denial is out to just rob . . .
It robs people blind, who deserve living love,
And misrepresents the dear Father above.
Our soul's fiercest enemy roams in the dark,
And seeks the destruction of anyone's bark;
He loves to gain footholds when truth he conceals—
With lies and deception so subtle he deals.

He seeks to enforce that the truth be denied,
Though scores are so battered, and many have died;
But do not despair, Child, though wounded and bruised:
For Jesus Christ cares for the lame and abused.
Our Lord knows the truth which so many deny,
He's seen every tear and He hears every cry;
His heart too was weeping when dark death you faced,
And then by His love you were fully embraced.

He carried you tenderly close to His heart
Away from dark secrecy death did impart;
He held you so close when no one understood—
Assuring in love, "I'll work this out for good."
Surrender the tatters and pain to His hand,
And items which some would conceal or make banned;
Give Him full control to heal freely in love,
Then He will reward you in heaven above!

Dismiss Denial

This world is full of hurting, broken people, who most often have fallen prey to instruments of evil. There are many cultures, groups, and traditions that may have a tendency to take these episodes of abuse, trauma, and destruction, and just bury it all away from the eye of the public. This pains my heart to know that there are suffering children and survivors who are repetitiously destroyed and disregarded. Very often in such cases, the unspeakable aftermath and agony of abuse is silently swept under the carpet where observers will not notice and those who should be helping and supportive can try to forget about the intense need to become involved.

In some cases, it often goes a few steps farther, to a point where the survivor is invalidated 75-100 percent, but the perpetrator is believed, accepted, and given a wide open door to plant deceptions. "Woe unto them that call evil good, and good evil; that put darkness for light, and light for darkness; that put bitter for sweet, and sweet for bitter!" Isaiah 5:20

To be supportive or involved with a broken, needy person and/or abuse survivor does not take a college degree or something out of reach. In all reality it involves only a servant heart that is full and overflowing with the unconditional love of Jesus. It requires the same non-judging compassion which Jesus displayed in action to everyone He met, especially those in need. He put special effort and love into the outcasts of the day, the sick and lame, the individuals oppressed by demons, the lepers, and those who were not high on the popular list or social ladder. He made specific effort to not avoid those who were deliberately avoided or disdained by others. This put Him in a bracket of disdain where He was despised and scorned by the religious leaders for choosing to associate and help the very ones whom they rejected. Jesus didn't care what these leaders thought of Him, because it was more important to Him to touch the needy with the love of His Father than to be bound by the opinion of those bound in chains of the untruth.

PRAYER: Lord Jesus, will You please search my heart to see if there is anything hidden there that needs Your cleansing touch and healing? I ask that Your Spirit would bring everything to light and make the truth manifest in every area. If there are those who do not understand the work You are doing in me, I commit them into Your hand and ask You to bless them. Amen.

Victory In The Battle!

Fellow soldiers marching forward in the battle thick and sore,
We as foreigners and pilgrims, headed to the heav'nly shore:
For our Savior's blood has bought us from the devil's grip of death—
By His grace and endless mercy He forgives and gave life's breath.

But our enemy is raging—seeks to capture us again,
This, our foe is whom we battle—it is not women or men:
For he knows his time is short now to ensnare more souls to hell,
Thus he wages war against those who redemption's song can tell.

I would warn you most sincerely, "Never give him e'en an inch,
Or he'll steal from you a hectare as in darkness you will flinch;
Slam and lock the door before you—do not open it a crack,
Or he'll burst right on in through it and will stab you in the back!

Do not trifle with allurements he has baited on your way:
For his traps of death await you when with canons, hot, you play;
Snaring lies he will have hanging from the limb of ev'ry tree—
Do not stop to view their makings lest the noose will tighten thee!

Run, my Comrade, to the Savior, our Commanding Conqueror:
For when covered by His blood-flow, we have vict'ry in this war;
Jesus Christ arose triumphant over Satan, sin, and hell,
And in Him we claim the power as He all our foes doth quell!

Fellow soldiers, gird your armor, never putting down your Sword,
With the righteous breastplate o'er you, and your shield—faith in the Lord;
Take the helmet of salvation—keep it always in its place,
With the Truth all girt about you—fiery darts then find no space.

Pressing forward, on and upward, our Commander, Christ, in lead,
For we know our foe's defeated and all hell one day will feed.
Never swerve from off the pathway, but let snipers wait in vain:
For we have the cross before us, and the crown we shall obtain!

READING: ISAIAH 25:8 AND LUKE 10:19

Victory Through Jesus

One thing we must always remember is that if Jesus had withdrawn His presence during our abuse, we could well have died. We often wonder where He was, but I am 100 percent positive that He was right there holding you in His arms so Satan could not destroy you as much as he wanted to.

When one is enduring and surviving abuse, the soul, mind, and body are made extremely vulnerable and completely helpless. Satan, who is out to steal, kill, and destroy, takes advantage of this extreme vulnerability. It is he and his demons that are responsible for working destruction through the perpetrator. At the same time, they attempt every possible means to latch on to some aspect of the victim during those vulnerable moments of surviving deadly abuse and terrifying horror. When this happens, it is not the fault of the victims, nor does it put them under God's condemnation. Rather it means that the enemy of their soul has attempted to plant a secret foothold in their lives, through which he intends to wreak havoc at a later unsuspecting time. Just as he is cruel and heartless, so Jesus sees his every attempt and draws near. As He gathers you in His arms, He gently whispers, "I love and accept you just as you are and have won the victory over Satan. Because he is a defeated foe, My blood, power, and love can make you completely free, safe, and whole!"

Jesus has died for us, shed His blood, and then arose triumphant over death, sin, and Satan in abundant life. Because of His triumphant victory over Satan, we as God's children are entitled to freedom and victory over every attempt of the enemy to conceal hidden footholds within us. Through Jesus and the power of His blood and resurrection, every demon of hell is defeated! Any enemy that has taken advantage of the Master's vulnerable lambs in the midst of abuse must be vanquished by the blood of Jesus: for He is Lord and Shepherd of His sheep. Jesus yearns over every broken lamb and holds you lovingly in His arms as He brings healing and freedom to every area of your life. He will never give up on you no matter who else may.

PRAYER: Jesus, I renounce every demon of hell and all attempts of Satan to destroy me or gain some type of hold on me. I claim Your blood over my body, heart, mind, and soul and yield them to Your control. Amen.

God Has An Infinite Purpose

My Jesus, I thank You for Your purpose true:
For reasons unseen in the things that You do,
For sending Your angels to touch broken hearts,
For dew-drops of prayer when the teardrops do start.
It may be that we can't in full understand
How hardship and suff'ring fit into God's plan,
But God has an infinite purpose for pain,
And it is the Lord Who can see the full gain.

For His ways are higher than we comprehend—
He views the eternal in all that He sends;
He only desires that we yield complete,
Each trial and pain to His own pierced feet.
For through pain and suff'ring the Lord can maintain
Our life and His purpose to bring forth great gain:
For He is the Master of suffering's school—
When yielded to Him, it becomes a blest tool!

Though in the dark agony, darkness surrounds,
Yet it is assured that the Lord's grace abounds;
The Angel of God's blessed Presence is near,
To carry us through the dark night and pained tears.
So gently He holds us within His embrace,
While giving assurance of unending grace;
His heart throbs with ours midst the pain of the hour,
As His divine Presence around us doth show'r.

In love's tender tones He so kindly makes clear,
That with Him beside us, the pain we'll not fear:
For each shred of agony placed in His hand,
Is transformed by Him into bright golden strands!
He weaves it so tenderly midst love and grace,
As He beholds kindly each tear on our face;
With Christ there's no pain or destruction too great,
But His work of love can in full, dissipate!

Transforming Pain To Gold

God's ways, thoughts, and plans are so much higher than what mortal man or woman can comprehend that we often find ourselves even questioning His wisdom about allowing the adverse circumstances we have faced. We have only limited vision and knowledge, but the Lord knows and sees all—right down to every buried, secret, or hidden thought. He knows every heart-shred of anguish that pierces the soul with unceasing excrucation and feels that pain with us. But one of the most beautiful items of knowledge that our Lord holds is that of knowing and having the power to take broken life tatters of pain and turn them into something of value and beauty!

Jesus has won complete victory over Satan, our enemy who is the instigator of every evil perpetrated against us. Jesus Christ, as both God and human, experienced tremendous abuse on behalf of all mankind. Before Calvary and also while dying on the cross, He suffered verbal, emotional, sexual, and physical abuse in proportions far greater than any other human has or will suffer. This degree of suffering and abuse He chose to go through because of His great love with which He paid for our ransom from everlasting death by the power of His shed blood. Jesus not only knows every detail of what you or your loved one may have suffered at the hand of evil men but also understands to the fullest extent. Because Jesus has completely defeated Satan and every plot of destruction he launches against God and His people, Christ can turn all the pain and devastation into something beautiful, if we but let Him do so. In order for Jesus to do this astounding work of transformation amid the rubble of a ruined life, we must be willing to yield Him every morsel of pain, strand of filth, and chain of fear. When He has unrestricted access to a life of anguishing tatters, He can turn every attempt of the enemy to destroy us into tools and vessels through which the Lord of heaven and earth can be exalted. Praise be to His name!

PRAYER: Dear Jesus, will You please search my life and see if there is anything hidden that would hinder Your healing work in my life? I choose to yield to Your hand all the pain and destruction so that Satan will be defeated and the glory of Your power and love can be exalted in my life and future. I choose to believe that there is nothing too hard for You. Amen.

KETURAH C. MARTIN

Peace In The Eye Of The Storm

The dark devastation of storm had begun—
The day grew so dark—one could not see the sun,
Then pending destruction appeared stark and grim
As tornado fury spilled out on earth's brim.

Yet right in the eye of the storm could be seen
A place of sweet peace, bathed in sunshine, serene—
Destruction so grim, ravaged havoc around,
As buildings and fields were destroyed to the ground!

Just so is the peace which to us can belong,
As children of God, though it seems all goes wrong:
For when in the center of God's divine will,
We find a sweet haven so peaceful and still.

Though trials and burdens upon us may pour,
And we are afraid to take just one step more:
The tempest of life in its fury may blast,
But there "in the center" His hand holds us fast!

This haven so sweet is in God's loving hand,
Where peace He gives fully and helps us to stand;
As we yield our problems, our will, life, and all,
He shelters us safely despite what befall!

Let's yield up our will to the Father, Divine,
And whisper each breath, "Lord, not my will, but Thine:"
For peace will not come through a life of sweet ease,
But in full surrender, through Christ, on our knees!

There's peace in the center of God's will, divine,
There's peace when we know that He holds our lifeline;
Midst tempest and pain there is peace in our soul
When Jesus is Pilot and has full control!

In The Eye Of The Storm

Little Mandie clutched her teddy bear fearfully as the violent storm howled around the corner of the barn. Her five-year-old heart quaked as a tin pail clattered ahead of the wind, and over in the barnyard a giant oak tree was suddenly uprooted as the darkness of the storm approached her. Bits of debris flew over her head as she cried out in terror. As she looked in the other direction, she saw with horror that the front door of her home was violently ripped from its hinges and tossed like paper into the air.

"Jesus, please help me find my mommy!" she cried out in terror as she glanced fearfully around at the progressive damage.

Suddenly, a bright beam of sunlight filtered down over the terrified child and a very still peace was all about her form. Looking up, the brilliance of sunshine illuminated her face, even though all around her she viewed massive destruction and darkness.

"Jesus heard me! He keeps me safe in His sunshine!" Mandie exclaimed with a happy heart as she looked up into the bright porthole of the sky.

Just so, we have the privilege and opportunity amid the storms of unspeakable agony and inner tempest, to cry out to the only One Who can actually walk through it with us. It is only with Jesus at our side that we can experience peace and calm in the eye of the storm. So often we focus mostly on the storm and its effects all around and may not even think to call out to God for help, protection, and healing. When He is in control of us and our surroundings, there is nothing that can touch or harm us, regardless of the storm's severity. If He allows us to go through something painful or difficult, that is a sure indication that He intends to take the time to walk through it with us. He will also give an abundance of grace from His limitless storehouse to meet every piercing need, thunderbolt of pain, and the aftermath of abuse.

PRAYER: Dear Jesus, please put Your hand around me and protect me from all the storm. Give me Your peace and let me feel Your presence, for when I am with You, there is nothing to fear. Bring me calm both within and without, as You continue to perform the work of healing in my life that You have started and will complete. Amen.

God Holds The Future

The future is a mystery, of hidden things that we can't see:
At times we long to see ahead—plan how to walk the path we'll tread;
We'd like to see the rocks and curves, the muddy slopes, the upward swerves,
The trials that may be in store, the stormy days that rain and pour.

So often we would like to know, just how our circumstance will go:
Will there be light to cheer our day? Will pain and heartache go away?
God holds the future in His hand—our life each day by Him is planned:
He sees our life from start to end—gives strength, as bit by bit He'll send.

He knows that we could not withstand to see the future—all that's planned:
He only asks that we trust Him each moment, whether bright or dim.
The Lord allows our grief and pain, and monitors dark days of rain;
He seeks to build our heart and soul, as we allow His full control!

When painful billows lash and roar, and rip one's heart right to the core,
In anger one may often feel that "God allowed this rotten deal,"
But fail to know the truth concealed, midst lies of Satan all congealed:
The truth remains: God's always there to help you ev'ry load to bear.

The devil is the one who brings the dark destruction of all things,
Initiating vile abuse and every method of misuse;
He seeks to steal, kill, and destroy, and squelch completely ev'ry joy,
And then to truth he blinds our eyes—blames God for his vile enterprise.

It is the Lord Who is your Rock, and Satan's worst from you doth block,
Hold hard and fast to His big hand e'en though you do not understand:
For He's the Source of all your hope and helps you up each slippery slope:
Against the foe for you He fights and banishes the lies of night.

Yield all your pain to God's control, defeating Satan's wily goal,
Our circumstance of grief or pain the Lord can use creating gain;
Then when our journey is complete, and we will rest at Jesus' feet,
We'll clearly know the purpose true, of everything He's brought you through!

The Untraveled Path

Often our human nature yearns to see down the road ahead so we can figure out what's coming and prepare for it. We don't like to feel as if we are hanging in limbo or cannot see what is coming just around the corner.

God is very gracious to us as His children, by not allowing us to see into the future as He does. He, Who created us, knows that if we in our finite mind and body could see all the future holds for us, we would not be capable of enduring, and trusting our Heavenly Father may become even more difficult.

Lovingly, He gives us one day at a time and asks us to walk just a step at time. There are sometimes situations where we can only take a breath at a time, but even that bit of progress is enough in the eyes of God. He understands the pain that is often evident with each breath taken while walking the journey to healing. He also understands how the frailty of our human make-up could not handle the entire picture of what our future path holds or where it may lead. It is in His love and caring for us that He has made it possible for us to live a day at a time, a step at a time, and alone in His grace divine!

We need not know what the future holds, but we must know only Who holds our future! When we are assured in our heart that the Lord God holds, plans, and controls our life circumstances and future, then we can rest in His care without any concern or worry. He does not plan that evil men may choose to inflict harm on His child, but if such choices are made, it is the Lord Himself Who sustains and upholds us while expanding His grace to meet the need of the moment.

It is of utmost importance to our eternal well-being and healing that we commit our will into the hand of God. When this is done, He can help us make His will our own as we die to self, accept the cross, and embrace whatever He has planned for our earthly future and eternal well-being. When He holds the future, there is nothing too painful or fearful to face: for His sustaining grace and presence is all we need to carry us through.

PRAYER: Father in heaven, I choose to surrender my will, life, tatters, and future into Your all-knowing and sustaining hand. Please help me walk one step at a time to complete healing, that You may be glorified through the work of transformation. I renounce every fear and embrace Your grace, love, and truth. Amen.

Borne Up As The Eagle

Midst storm clouds low hanging, as thunder rolls by,
And e'en though the lightning may pierce through the sky:
Be still now, my soul, on the Lord God to wait,
Your strength He'll renew and the storm dissipate.

When torrents of rain may start pelting in haste,
Life's burdens and anguish may seem all a waste
Fly upward to God by His power divine,
Midst storms He then whispers, "You, Child, are all Mine!"

On wings as an eagle He bears us on high,
Thus unto Himself He then brings us so nigh;
In love, grace, and power He helps us attain
An altitude, calm, far above stormy rain.

Borne up as the eagle beyond stormy night,
We soar in God's Presence of love's sun so bright;
We tell Him our sorrows, the pain He well knows,
Then waiting we listen, His will He thus shows.

"My Child, your great value can never compare
With all of earth's wealth or a life free from care;
Your burdens and anguish, the storm and the pain,
To Me, when surrendered, bring infinite gain.

I have for your future and life a great plan,
Which you must submit to My all-knowing hand:
For I know the things which My child must endure—
Enhancing soul beauty, My plan to secure.

Sweep down with the eagle: for gone is the storm,
Allowing My grace to sufficiently warm;
My grace expands freely to meet pain untold,
Which yielded to Me shall come forth as pure gold!"

Out Of The Comfort Zone

When a mother eagle decides it is time for her eaglets to learn to fly, she takes deliberate action to make it happen. Stirring up her nest (which can be up to twenty feet across), she intentionally makes uncomfortable what previously was comfortable and causes the sticks to poke upward. This creates evident cause for discomfort to her young who can now find no comfortable resting spot. As she flutters over her young, they are gently but purposely nudged toward the edge of the nest and out of their comfort zone. It doesn't take long until they flutter helplessly over the edge where they plummet toward the earth's floor, flapping and screaming out. High above on a crag of rock, the father eagle watches the whole procedure with keen eye. As his offspring scream and flap in terror while dropping toward obvious doom, father eagle observes with piercing eye and obvious intent. Suddenly, as the little ones advance closer to a perilous end, he dives downward at a speed of 150-200 miles per hour. Swooping beneath them, they land on his back, and he bears them up high beyond the clouds and out of the danger zone. Then without notice, he dives downward from under them, giving them opportunity to again attempt their flight outside their comfort zone. Once again father eagle will dive under them and bear the little ones up when nearing a perilous landing.

The father eagle relates to his young in like manner as our Heavenly Father does to His children. God will deliberately take us out of our comfort zone to help teach us how to fly, trust, and survive. He may take individuals out of their comfort zones when He is preparing them to become ready to minister to the brokenhearted or needy around them. Those eaglets that would refuse to learn to fly will ultimately die as a result.

Even so, those who may have been broken, bruised, and rejected must persevere far beyond their comfort zone in order to gain complete healing. To give up in the face of fear, flying, or falling is to relinquish hope and abandon survival.

PRAYER: My Father in heaven, please make me to be open to learning how to persevere and keep trying. Thank You for bearing me up and teaching me to move forward under Your watchful eye and loving care. Please bring me Your complete healing and teach me to soar with the eagles in the sunlight of Your love, above the painful past. Amen.

KETURAH C. MARTIN

Flying With The Eagles

When eaglets are falling, attempting to fly,
And plummet with speed from the heights of the sky,
With squawking and flapping they cry out in fear—
Alone and so helpless with no help that's near.

With breath all abated and desperate eyes keen,
Now swooping beneath them a figure is seen:
The plumage of father they feel at their breast—
Their fall is now broken and comes to sweet rest.

With power and grace does the father bird soar,
Above all the obstacles on the earth's floor;
On strong eagle wings he then bears them on high,
While calming their spirit and hushing their cry.

He knows the small eagles must learn how to fly:
For that is imperative, else they will die—
He then makes a dive giving them a new chance
To strengthen their wings, that their growth may advance.

Surrender and trust are the wings they must use
To persevere on, and to live they must choose:
Beneath the keen eye of their father in flight,
They exercise trust and press on to new heights.

Just so, does our Heavenly Father lead on,
While guiding our flight toward hope's healing dawn;
Each obstacle flees before His loving pow'r,
And He stays beside us each day and each hour!

We must trust our Father to bear us on high,
Surrendering all that restricts from the sky;
His power and love can transform all the pain,
Creating a vessel of infinite gain!

Choosing Ownership

*For you are brought with a price, therefore glorify God
in your <u>body and your spirit which are God's.</u>*

******

*No human can serve two masters for either he will hate the one and love the other
or else he will hold to the one and despise the other.
You cannot serve God and mammon.
Matthew 6:24*

******

Make a list of all the people and/or spirits whom you believe own you in body, mind or soul and hold control over you — those who controlled you via abuse/torture. D.I.D survivors may have many confused & controlled inner members who need strongholds broken in order to see Jesus more clearly.

*
*
*
*
*
*
*
*
*
*

"Lord, I choose to completely renounce all ownership ties, blood pacts and assignments that bind me to _____ and reject every attempt of satan to own me. I reject through the blood of Jesus, every chain of bandage, blood-sealed commission and soul tie that has ever held me captive through the abuse, bondage and torture perpetrated against me by _____, and I acknowledge and claim Jesus Christ as my Lord and Savior through the power of His blood and resurrection."

KETURAH C. MARTIN

The Lord's Touch Can Be Seen

The sunrise is casting its radiant light—
Has conquered in full the dark shadows of night;
With quivering breath see it racing along,
Awakening life and creating new song!

The animals stir from their dens, nest, and lair,
Or for a day's sleep may so hasty prepare;
Wherever I look the Lord's touch can be seen,
And I see the places His Presence has been.

The dew on the roses, like balm from above,
So sweetly reflects the Creator of love—
Refreshed, despite thorns, the rose faces new day,
Revived to keep blooming along this life's way.

The birds begin warbling and trilling their song,
While praising their Maker through all the day long;
He cares for the sparrow, the robin and wren,
And God cares for you, Child, again and again!

He keeps His watch over you all through the night,
And bathes your brow gently with new morning light;
Although your path often may yield rocks and thorns,
Yet He guides you upward midst love that adorns.

God's Presence around you, like dew on the rose,
Refreshes you daily and tenderly blows;
No evil can touch you and naught cause you harm,
When you are sustained by His powerful arm!

So bask in His presence each hour of the day,
Assured He walks with you each step of the way;
He never will fail you though storms may blow wild:
For you are His chosen, His prize, and His child!

The Greatness Of Our God

We have a great big God Who is fully capable of taking care of everything and everyone in His creation! He never grows weary or falls behind on the job! "Hast thou not known? Hast thou not heard that the everlasting God, the LORD, the Creator of the ends of the earth, fainteth not, neither is weary? There is no searching of His understanding" (Isaiah 40:28).

He Who takes special care of the birds He has created, how much more does He take interest and time, including investing into each child He has fashioned in His own image?

Each day and each moment He gently surrounds you with His love and Presence as He tenderly refreshes you each morning with His touch of grace. He delights in bringing out the beauty and fragrance of the rose, despite the many thorns. This is what He also yearns to do with each one of us despite any thorny circumstance or experience we may find ourselves in.

With God surrounding, upholding, and enabling us, we can have the assurance that nothing evil can touch or harm us, for our God is above all. Just as He cares for the birds and supplies their needs, so much more will He do also for us. Likewise, the lilies of the field and the violets of the forest are arrayed in splendor befitting royalty. How much more than these flowers will our Heavenly Father care for you and me, as He ensures our needs are met on a daily and sometimes hourly basis?

PRAYER: Lord Jesus, I choose to trust and believe that You will care and provide for me continually. You are not like man, so prone to fail, but You take special care of even the birds and flowers. Help me to entrust my life, healing, and future into Your divine hand and all-knowing wisdom. It is so hard to trust when even Your own people have rejected and hurt me repeatedly. I choose to forgive and release them to You, and I choose to believe You are different from what fallible man has represented You to be. Please help me and hold my hand one step at a time as You cause the sunlight of Your love to enfold me in Your undying grace and care. Amen.

APRIL 23
READING: EXODUS 23:20, 23

When The Angels Sang

It was midst the shades and shadows, of a life's dark, tattered strands,
When my heart in pain was crying, that I heard the angel bands—
In great wonder, through the darkness, I glanced all about the shades,
But could see no source of music from eternal everglades.

In that tolling midnight hour came the strains of matchless worth,
As the corridors of heaven brought new faith and hope to birth:
For "Each step I take my Savior goes before me all the way,
With His loving hand still leading, He gives joy for ev'ry day!"

Thus the symphony from heaven sang their midnight chords of love—
At the ending of the chorus they returned to heav'n above;
But forever I'll remember vibrant messages they sang,
In a harmony of beauty, as with hope my bedroom rang!

Then through all the heart-sore shatters of rejection's disregard,
I then heard the voice of Jesus echo past the broken shards:
"This, dear Child, is My own promise which I bring to you this night:
For I've planned you for a purpose, and each day for you I fight!

Ev'ry step I go before you leading on to higher ground,
And My plan I am perfecting, though the battle's all around;
My dear Child, I'll never fail you—though some folks can't understand,
But midst pain and tribulation I support you by My hand.

So press on, My Child, be strengthened in My promise made this night
Through the message of the angels which they sang with truth and light;
I have called you for a purpose, though the way seems long and hard,
And though others fail, I'm with thee, and surround with angel guard!"

APRIL 24
READING: REVELATION 5:8-10

Angelic Encouragement

There are times in our journey when God performs miracles and shows Himself strong on our behalf as He encourages us along the way. This display of love, intervention, and grace is divinely inspiring to one's inner being and our upward travel.

It was during a time of receiving severe judgment, assumption, and condemnation from some of God's people for pursuing healing that the Lord stepped in. Each night I fell asleep in tears as I repeatedly cried out to God: "Please help me to choose Your love, no matter what is said, thought, or enacted against me and the work You are doing. I choose to forgive and release them into Your hand, Lord Jesus, along with every preconceived idea and misunderstanding. I reject every attempt of Satan to instill bitterness, but I choose Your love instead. Please bless and guide each individual who does not know or understand the truth of my situation and great work of healing that You alone are performing."

This one particular night when I was crying out in pain and choosing to forgive again, I was suddenly stopped short, just after midnight. I suddenly heard a group of male voices singing in the corner of my bedroom, though there were no males even in my house.

"Each step I take, my Savior goes before me, and with His loving hand, He leads the way. And with each breath, I whisper I adore thee; Oh what joy to walk with Him each day! Each step I take, I know that He will guide me, to higher ground He ever leads me on, until one day the last step will be taken; each step I take just leads me closer home." The music and singing slowly faded away at the end of the chorus, but the presence of Jesus was now right beside me. He assured me in loving tones that no matter what happens around me, or what others say or think, He is here "for keeps" to walk with me every step. Jesus also made it very plain that He will never stop the work of healing He has begun regardless of how man may perceive or disannul the work He is doing. Christ then enfolded me in His arms as I fell asleep for the night, resting in His love, promise, and presence.

PRAYER: Lord Jesus, I thank You and praise You for showing Yourself strong on my behalf through the singing of this song. Thank You so much for caring and standing by me regardless of what others choose to do. Give me grace, strength, and wisdom for whatever You have for me in the future. In Your name I ask it, Jesus. Amen.

KETURAH C. MARTIN

"Lord, Thank You For Fire"

"Lord, thank You for fire, which You guide us through—
Though painfully hot, Your dear Presence is true;
As gold in the fire is fully refined,
Just so You restore us for Your work divine.

The flesh would recoil from the fire's pained heat,
But Christ asks that we would cast all at His feet:
His purpose of love we may not understand,
But it's for our best to leave all in His hand.

How precious the fire that burns up the dross,
Refining His children as they bear His cross;
Not one degree hotter the fire will be,
Than that which is needed to purify me!

How loving the time that the dear Father takes
To purge and prepare us for His own name's sake;
Our Father can see just what each child doth need,
And through fire's anguish supplies grace indeed!

The hurts in our life are essential to be
Ingredients used, as the Father best sees,
Which shapes to the plan that He holds for each soul—
Becoming like Jesus, our ultimate goal!"

So don't fear the fire that's used by the Lord:
For He stands beside you while grace is out-poured;
His will is perfected, His name glorified
When you wholly trust Him and stay at His side.

Tried By Fire

It is very seldom that one would find a volunteer to literally walk through an actual fire, although firemen risk their lives every day, saving lives and putting out these fatal flames. However, when it is the Lord Who calls us through fire, it is generally a fire which He controls. It is designed to purify our inner being from the muck and dross that may have been picked up in the daily pilgrimage of life and to refine us in the areas He sees need such purging.

When God calls us through fire and/or difficult adversity, it is important to join Him hand in hand and walk each step with Him beside us as our Guide, Shield, and Protector. There is nothing to fear when He is beside us, even though to the flesh it is not comfortable to be in the fire's heat or the intense pain. Those who are unwilling to walk beside the Master through the purifying fire will unwantedly open themselves up to something far worse than a mere purifying process. Often the attempt to escape pain and refining results in one falling into the enemy's fire rather than walking through that which the Lord has planned they endure beside the Savior. The Lord loves and cares for us deeply, but the enemy's only goal is to snare, deceive, and ultimately destroy us eternally.

Just as the potter shapes vessels of clay and then puts them through fire in the kiln, even so the Lord also works on our behalf to create a vessel of honour which He can use. The potter's vessels are strengthened by fire and all the impurities are burned out by the heat of the fire. When the clay pot withstands the heat of the kiln without cracking or breaking, it is nearly to the stage of being identified as usable through the glazing process.

The Lord seeks to work through each off His children for a specific job in His kingdom. They must, however, be willing to go through the fire in whatever way He chooses prior to extensive use, or they will be unprepared for the strenuous work that lies ahead. Refining by fire need not be feared or abhorred, but welcomed joyfully, knowing that the Lord Jesus loves you enough to take the time to refine and strengthen you for His divine service.

PRAYER: Lord, I choose to place my hand in Yours and walk wherever You lead, even outside my comfort zone or through the fire. Cleanse me from all impurities as You prepare and strengthen me through fire for Your service. Amen.

KETURAH C. MARTIN

"Keep Your Eyes On Jesus!"

"Keep your eyes upon the Master when the billows rage and roar,
Though the surges swell unbidden and would drive away from shore;
Look beyond the waves of slander which the skeptics have launched forth,
Past the winds of misconception that howl in from all the north.

Keep your focus on the Savior, Who still pilots your frail bark:
For He understands completely, even though the night is dark;
Though misunderstanding rages through the fog of night or day,
Yet explicitly He knows you, and the truth of all your way!

Jesus holds your chart and compass as He guides your ship aright,
And will steer you through the darkness, which enshrouds you in the night:
For though most lack comprehension of all your ship's endured,
Yet your Captain knows completely: for survival He ensured!

When the timbers groaned and shuddered with the impact of death's blow—
Christ your Captain held the anchor and His triumph did bestow;
And when pirates did beset you and attacked from ev'ry side,
'Twas the Master Who preserved you and remained your constant Guide!

So when through the raging waters, you, My Child, are called to go,
Still no flood shall overtake thee and your bark not overflow:
For I've called thee by thy name, Child, and your life have fully planned,
So the waves and winds around thee, just entrust into My hand!

Do not view the dashing waters—hearken not to tempest wild,
But just keep your eyes on Jesus, with the knowledge *You're My child!*
Through deep waters I have called thee for a purpose you must fill,
As you rescue pained souls sinking—and I the storm will still!"

A Word From Your Captain

"Sometimes, My Child, you may face tempestuous storms while on this journey toward complete healing. No matter how the surges swell or the billows roar, as long as I the Lord am your Captain, you have nothing to fear. "There are many boaters out there on the voyage to eternity who have not encountered the type of storms, injustices, and attacks which you have. The waves of slander and winds of misconception such individuals may launch against you and your ship is not from Me. But as Captain of your ship, there is no wave, fog, or wind that can cause you to capsize when I am at the wheel.

"I know the truth of every detail of all that you and your ship have suffered from abusing shark attacks, pirates plundering, and the very impact of death that has often surrounded you. It does not matter what the unknowledgeable observer and skeptic may say or think, but only that I as your Captain and Savior hold your chart and compass and remain in full control of you and your ship in this voyage to healing.

"Satan, your enemy, will use anyone possible to enforce opposition against you and the work I have begun in you. But because he is defeated before he ever started, so also is anyone whom he attempts to subtly use in this stormy sea, who would try to stop My healing work in you. I am your Captain, Child, and there is no one who can stop My plan and the work I have begun!

"I understand you, Child, and acknowledge all you have endured. It matters not that others can't comprehend, for when you have Me, you have everything! Commit the pain of rejection, misunderstanding, and verbal attack into My hand, for I the Lord will fight for you and bring you into My desired haven, regardless of the skeptic, judge, or scoffer—I am the Lord! Just as I stand with you through the fire, so I will stay beside you through the storm. To prosper you and give you an expected end is My plan, and no man or situation can deter Me."

PRAYER: Thank You, Jesus, for being the Captain of my ship, life, and future. Thank You for being in charge of my healing journey and for salvaging my life from the ruins. I give You complete control of the wheel, chart, and compass and ask You to deal with all the roaring waves and those riding them. Thank You for Your love, protection, healing, and divine presence. Amen.

"Lord, Lift Me Above And Beyond"

"Lord, I cannot see—will You please be my eyes?
For darkness engulfs me; my heart always cries;
When tears blur my vision, one step I can't take—
Lord, please guide my feet for Your glory and sake.
I can't understand, Lord, the whys of this pain,
Nor how midst the tatters You salvage some gain;
When tears flow like rivers throughout the night, strong,
Lord, show me just where in Your plan I belong.
Dear Father, myself, I cannot understand,
But I must believe You hold all in Your hand;
The agony complex, in splinters and shards,
When given to You—to bring healing's not hard.
Lord, I see no value remaining in me,
And know not why I have been chosen by Thee,
To fit in a plan that just You alone know—
Midst darkness and anguish Your will, Lord, please show.
Lord, polish away all the dross and pained night,
Reach down through the shatters and shreds with Your light—
Restoring whatever has value to You—
Despite ruin's rubble, dear Lord, make me new.
Oh, Lord, though I'm sinking in anguish and woe,
This is not the life I desire to know—
Please lift me above and beyond depths of pain
That I can then serve for Your glory and gain!
Dear Father, I plead that You use all pain's tools
With which I'm afflicted in suffering's school,
To teach me just how to relate to pained hearts—
To empathize truly, when teardrops may start.
For most folks cannot understand depths of pain,
But I seek to learn midst this anguish that rains,
That I may be schooled by Thy hand to relay
Your hope, love, and healing to pained souls each day!"

The Truth Of The Matter

There are times in the healing journey where everything seems dark and the inner agony surpasses what any words can describe. Healing from a shattered life is not a package of instant mashed potatoes, but is usually a long and agonizing journey, which very few can understand unless they have been there. One's eyes may become clouded to the point that they cannot see themselves as having any value to God or man and feel despair at even the thought of taking one more step.

The enemy may use these times to inject lies that imply *how hopeless it is to pursue healing.* He may also want you to believe his condemnations when he relentlessly whispers, "You are just wasting your time trying to get to complete healing and are not worth even a fraction of the time it will take. You would be better off to just shove it all under the carpet and pretend that everything is all healed and in the past."

The enemy also uses people—even God's people—to verify these lies in attempt to persuade the healing survivor to just throw in the towel and take the route termed easy, which is enshrouded in denial, deception, cowardice, and fear.

Stop, my Fellow Sojourner! Do not even taste this bait of the enemy regardless of what godly person may have been used to bring it to you! Renounce the lie of the enemy and flee for refuge to the arms of Jesus Christ Who walked the road before you. Christ validates you and all you have experienced. He also offers you free of charge everything you will need to relinquish the foe and cross the finish line to complete healing. The Great Physician, Jesus, will never let you down, but holds your hand and guides you even when the darkness hides His face. Jesus understands as no other how Satan is just waiting for you to bury it all so he can create hidden footholds in your life as he plots your ultimate destruction through buried shame and pain.

RENUNCIATION: I renounce every attempt of Satan to plot my destruction through his lies, condemnation, and speaking through those who may claim to be a child of God. I claim the blood of Jesus to cover me, and I choose to walk hand in hand with Jesus through every obstacle until I cross the finish line.

The Potter Of Ruined Clay

The Master of Potters sat down at the wheel,
Within His scarred hand, I His touch could scarce feel;
A lump of hard clay, He had found me so prone—
Cast out and forsaken, and dying alone.
The Savior wept long o'er the ruins He found,
And tears of His love started healing profound—
They moistened the clay which was hardened by pain,
So trashed and misused by abuse that did stain.

The Potter then worked through the vast lump of clay,
Removing the pain shards He found in the way:
So gently He pulled out each anguishing piece—
Poured in oil and love that the agony cease.
The Master then viewed all the jagged, broke glass—
The remnants where cutting rejection had passed;
Each sharp, biting piece He extracted in love:
For He had a plan that none else yet knew of.

The dirt and defilement of violent abuse,
The shame, lies, and horrors of grimy misuse,
Was placed by the Potter beneath His own blood,
Where He wrought a cleansing of clay in that flood.
The Master of Potters then held to His breast
The lump of cleansed clay that could feel His touch rest;
The wheel of the Potter began then to turn,
Upon salvaged clay which so long had been spurned.

I've yielded my all to the Potter's own hand—
All pain, past and horror to transform as planned:
For He views a vessel that's shaped, cleansed and whole,
Through which He pours love on each hurt, needy soul.
To be held and fashioned by His divine hand—
Be shaped amid pain, though I don't understand,
To be shaped and molded for His divine praise—
This is my heart's yearning for all of my days!

Ruined Clay

Have you ever felt like a hunk of mucky clay, which had finally been tossed into a garbage bin after years of being unwanted and just tossed around out of the way? If you can at all relate, this is a message just for you!

When I was writhing alone and rejected in the rubbles of the trash heap, it was Jesus Himself Who stooped down and retrieved what appeared to be a hard lump of dirty, useless clay. As He gently picked me up, I saw He was weeping as He repeatedly said, "I never meant that you should be cast out to die by those who cannot understand, My Child."

As He sat down at the potter's wheel, I could scarcely even feel His touch, except to know that it was gentle rather than ruthless, as so many others had been. As He wept over me, His tears began to soften the hardened, trashed clay, which He worked over tenderly and patiently as it began to soften. Once softened, Jesus began to remove the shards of excruciating pain that had been violently embedded into the clay. For each piece He extracted, He poured in His love and oil where it had previously lodged. As He viewed also the countless shatters of rejection that pierced jaggedly from my heart's clay, He gently removed them as He wept with me in the anguish.

"I have created you for a special purpose, My Child, but there are so few of My people who are willing to be bothered with one who has suffered so. I will never give up on you despite what is found in this lump of clay. Every scar of abuse and misuse I intend to use as an example of what My power and love can do in a child who was cast out to die."

The dirt, defilement, and horror's shame were all brought to be washed in His own blood, as Jesus, the Potter, vanquished all the injected lies of the enemy that outlined my worthlessness. Finally the wheel began to turn as the Master guided, shaped, and molded me into a vessel that somehow fit into the plan that He had for me. Flourishing under His loving hand, I yielded myself into His hand, for it is Jesus alone Who can salvage, heal, and restore a trashed hunk of clay. Though one may not always be treated as valuable by man, yet Jesus can never fail!

PRAYER: Lord Jesus, I thank You for seeing enough value in me that You preserved my life and took time to dig through the ashes to find all the broken pieces! Even though I can't see any point for my life right now, I thank You for Your ability to know and see just what purpose You have for my life and future. I surrender it all into Your complete control for the exaltation of Your name and glory. Amen.

The Healing Process You Must Tread

If you were in a tall high-rise relaxing, marv'ling at the skies,
Just where would you be likely bound if all went crashing to the ground?
In heaps of rubble, concrete vast, splinters of lumber, piercing glass,
Appliances, people galore—they'd all with speed crash to earth's floor!
Destroyed would be the building, high—so many wounded, some may die,
And if by chance you'd be alive, would you midst injury survive?
For bones are broken, bruised and sore, and from your body blood may pour-
Your skull be fractured, one eye lost, internal organs gored and tossed.
And tell me, friend, how would you feel, while there encased in trash and steel,
Should able-bodies pass you by, as there so trapped you feebly cry?
In hopelessness you'd writhe in pain which nearly drives you to insane,
Your value seems to melt away: for no one helps you through the day.
As people view your desperate plight and race away in panic's fright,
They leave behind a dying soul devoid of help upon death's shoals:
They likely do not understand just how to lend a helping hand,
But God in heaven knows it all and He will hear you as you call!
But tell me, wouldn't just a prayer restore your body, heal, repair?
If in Christ's blood you'd be immersed, would all your pain then be reversed?
No, your condition, critical, would put your life on hold—would stall:
The doctors, hospitals, true care would be a 'must' if life be spared.
Outside a wonder from on high, the healing road you can't pass by.
Much time and patience this includes—from others' help you can't elude;
Just so, survivors of abuse who've suffered years of filthy use
Have been demolished to the core—destroyed to shards behind closed doors.
Yet many folks will pass them by, can't understand their desperate cry—
For none can sound the pools of grime which suffocate—putrid and prime:
But rather offer band-aids small to cover wounds and welts o'er all,
Emotions battered may avoid, not knowing how they are destroyed.
Let's seek to know and understand the filthy pit in which they stand,
Their loss immense to validate, which none can truly estimate;
Bear patiently in this their cross and seek to understand their loss:
Remove the rubble piercing sore, that truth so pure is seen once more!
Commit them wholly to God's hand for He alone doth understand,
To them live daily Jesus' love, and He will bless you from above!

The Healing Process

Jesus openly and tenderly invites all those who are hurting, burdened, lost, and needy to come to Him for hope, healing, and help. There are many people in this world who do not see their need for help, healing, and/or salvation. Jesus is the answer to all these needs, whether one knows it or not. The healing process is something that many people try to steer away from for many different reasons and/or excuses.

For the survivor of abuse and rejection, the healing process may feel scary and look hopeless. Trust has been so shattered that it does not seem possible to even trust God, especially if His people have in any way inflicted spiritual abuse or rejection.

To be trapped as in the previous scenario is the condition some find themselves in; and I too can speak from first-hand experience. Many survivors of abuse and trauma are so encased in the deadly effects of daily abuse or the aftereffects of it that it literally feel as if they are dying and crushed to death. However, very often, the people who call themselves *Christian* are busily attempting to ignore or turn a blind eye to the reality of those who may be trapped, bleeding, and dying right under their very noses. Though the carpets may often be humped with rotting things shoved under, there is always room for one more item.

Jesus never turned a blind eye to anyone in need or pain. He gravitated to those languishing in agony, death, and/or rejection and always gave His assistance even to the outcasts of society. He never told someone to *just forgive and forget and get on with his life.* Rather He put into action agape love and went out of His way to get right to the heart of the matter. He loved with an everlasting love, which incidentally was also infiltrated with self-sacrifice. He did not believe in administering band-aid solutions; He was/is in the business of healing heart issues. He never turned away even the faintest cry; nor did He care what the religious leaders thought of Him. Rather His goal was to glorify His Father in heaven and finish the work He was sent to do. Jesus always loved, accepted, and understood the broken, dying, and needy with no thought to His own comfort or reputation. Jesus is our only Advocate Who will never fail us!

PRAYER: I choose to forgive and release every individual, church leader, husband, and/or counsellor who has turned a blind eye, judged my painful plight, or outright rejected and abused me. I ask You, Jesus, to give a blessing to each one that has chosen to pass by the need, scorn me, and cover up the truth. Amen.

Tools In God's Hands

How could we be bitter for all we've gone through?
When we understand not what God wants to do:
For when there is suff'ring, rejection, or pain,
We then can be sure God is planning a gain.

We need not be angry for suff'rings untold:
For they are but tools to refine purest gold,
But rather embrace them as "gifts" from above,
Whereby the Lord seeks to expose His great love.

Our God uses testing and suff'ring immense,
E'en though it's unbearable, pained, and intense,
To further His goal for each life He has planned:
For just what we need He can best understand.

When God allows suff'ring, our thanks we must give:
For He has a plan for each day that we live;
He uses these tools to build Jesus within—
To draw us still closer, away from death's din.

So cry out to God amid anguishing pain—
He wants to assist you and bring you a gain,
To show you His power and strength from above,
That Satan's foul plans be destroyed with Christ's love.

Thank God for the tools whereby He builds your soul,
For testing and suff'ring beneath His control—
Equipping those yielded with pow'r from on high:
For He has a purpose and hears ev'ry cry!

The Father gives strength for each step that you take—
Amid your afflictions and all that's at stake,
His grace is sufficient each hour of the day
And turns pain to triumph as with Him you stay!

Bitter Or Thankful?

The human body and mind is a mortal being that does not enjoy suffering or the experience of physical pain in any way. The fact that God made the body with the ability to detect pain is a safety feature He built into it. This makes it possible that when the nerves feel pain, they send a message to the brain that something needs to be checked out to avoid further danger or harm. The emotional system God put within each human feels pain from the inside out rather than the outside in. Emotional suffering can often be far more agonizing than anything physical. To make it even harder to bear, it is not something that can be seen or treated with medicine, so therefore, the sufferer may be very misunderstood by the very people who should be supportive. There is a lot of emotional suffering involved with the survival of every type of abuse one may have endured, but there is abundant hope for a beautiful outcome.

The Lord's presence and willingness to walk each step of the painful journey with you is not dependent on whether any other human has the heart to care, understand, and accompany you. It is because of the presence of Jesus to walk alongside us that we are given the opportunity and possibility to give thanks rather than destroy ourselves in bitterness and anger.

It was not God's will that any one of us was abused, trafficked or degraded, but it is His will to take that abuse and all of its aftereffects of unspeakable pain and filthy shame and turn it around for our eternal well-being. What Satan meant for our destruction can be surrendered into the hand of Jesus so He can turn it all into tools by which to build and prepare us for greater service. The very destructions waged against us by the enemy can become powerful tools in the hand of Christ by which Satan is defeated in his own game, which he initiated. To become bitter or angry at God about our experiences will play right into the hand of Satan, causing him to score. Bitterness will eat alive anyone who engages therein and, ultimately, destroy every potential of God turning our circumstances and past into joyous opportunities of healing and exaltation of the love and power of God.

PRAYER: Lord Jesus, I choose to give You the agonizing experiences, abuse, and aftereffects and ask You to use it all to defeat the devil at his own game. I renounce all bitterness and choose to thank You for preserving my life and for Your ability to turn the pain into tools of blessing for Your glory. Amen.

Through Tempests Of Pain

When the body throbs in agony, midst writhing stabs of pain,
While the tears may flow unbidden and one can't see any gain;
Then I turn my eyes on Jesus and look fully in His face:
For my Lord is ever faithful and supplies sufficient grace.

Then His dying wounds come into view while hanging on the cross,
Where my Jesus suffered, bled, and died, to save me from death's loss—
He has suffered more than tongue can tell, to rescue my own soul:
For my Savior paid my ransom debt and filled redemption's goal.

Then my heart goes down to Calvary in gratitude and praise
For all Jesus suffered in my place, and loud thanksgiving raise;
Then my Savior draws so very near—I see his nail-scarred hands,
He so sweetly fills my heart with peace, and now I understand.

"Oh, my Lord, I now embrace the pain, despite how sore intense:
For when I am weak You then are strong—my Refuge and Defense;
I do thank You for the wracking pain which turns my eyes to Thee:
For my pain's an opportunity for You to work in me!

When You call me through the tempest or through waters of great pain,
I must turn my eyes on Jesus, while assured You plan a gain:
For the pain of body, mind, and soul are tools within Your hand,
To build, refine and strengthen me—though I don't understand.

So I choose to kneel before Your feet, surrend'ring pain and will,
And embrace the path You've marked for me, though painful, dark or still:
For it's You alone Who is my Light, my Guide, my Strength, my All,
And I praise You for sweet suff'ring's tools, through which on Thee I call.

I now yield them all into Thy hand to use as tools divine,
To perform in me Your perfect will, that glory may be Thine;
Your sufficient grace each breath I claim—I bow, Lord, at Your feet,
I surrender life into Your hand, as You Your work complete!"

Jesus, My Strength Midst Pain

When we truly stop to consider to what inhuman degree that Jesus actually suffered on our behalf, it becomes easier to stop our internal outcry against our own pain. We can begin to see how our sufferings are as nothing in comparison to His, even though our agony may be extreme. Because of the abuse Christ suffered which ultimately resulted in death and then His resurrection; He can understand, empathize, and assist all who come to Him. In fact He can turn the ashes of filth, pain, and hopelessness into strands gold and vessels of honour if we only choose to let Him have full control of all the tangled shreds and broken shards.

To choose to thank God for allowing this suffering and for His ability to transform the pain into tools that can build your life and the lives of others is the key that opens the door for God to begin His transformation of the pain.

It is only through the power, love, and presence of Jesus that we can truly thank God for our agonizing situation or aftermath of abuse.

When we can see how weak we really are and how much we need the help of God; that is when Jesus becomes our strength, our sufficient grace, and begins the process of transforming pain into value and beauty through which He alone is glorified. When it is all placed unreservedly into the hand of Jesus, He becomes our Refuge and Defense to such an amazing extent that it no longer matters what other around us say or think of us; because if the Lord is in charge of our healing, nobody can stop Him. He will complete all He has set out to do in us regardless of the lack of understanding around us, for Jesus is Victor and He comprehends in full our every need and heartache.

PRAYER: Dear Jesus, I thank You for suffering and dying on my behalf so there would be a way for me to be saved and healed. I am so glad You never gave up on me as so many others have. I ask You, Jesus, to take charge of all my tatters and anguish and transform them all in a way that will skunk the enemy and his attempts at my life. Please use the pain to make me into something with value that You can use and that will exalt Your love, mercy, and grace to all who suffer. Please be my Light and Guide as Your strength is perfected daily in my weakness. Amen.

Take No Thought For Tomorrow

"My Child, you are chosen—I've called thee by name—
To purchase salvation, for this cause I came,
As out on Golgotha your ransom I paid:
For there on the cross in your place I was laid.

Take no thought, My Child, for the raiment you wear,
Consider the lilies that grow without care:
For I have arrayed them in glory unknown,
And I'll do much more for My chosen and own.

If I the Lord God clothe the grass of the field,
And care for its growth and abundance of yield,
Much more for My children will I clothe and feed—
Supplying in love for their every need!

The birds of the heavens do not fret or stew,
But know that My mercies each morning are new;
The heavenly Father doth feed them each day—
My Child, are not ye so much better than they?

The kingdom of God, My dear Child, do seek first:
For He satisfies that deep spiritual thirst;
His righteousness seek and pursue every day,
As He then provides for your needs all the way.

My life I invested in you, My dear Child,
So now I will care for you though life seems wild;
For I walked before you the path you now tread,
And give stores of grace for whatever's ahead!

I know, Child, the trial, your need, pain or loss,
And I walk beside you to help bear your cross;
Commit to the Father your needs, tears, and care:
For He will not fail you, but always is there!"

In The Presence Of God, Part 1

It was a summer day in 1988, and I gazed out the window of the Vancouver General Hospital to the street far below. I had many questions about tomorrow's scheduled brain surgery, but my greatest fear and sorrow was that of losing my hair. Following years of multiple abuses, rejections, and mocking, I felt inwardly stripped and shamed, and losing my hair seemed only an addition to the buried shame and pain within. However, I was willing to go through anything, with the help of God, that I might be free from the three to twenty daily epileptic seizures and the 24/7 deadly throes of depression that resulted from each seizure. The top neurologist of epilepsy in the world, Dr. Juhn A. Wada, had discovered that the scar tissue on my brain, which caused the seizures, was located on my mood center, which in turn produced massive, life-threatening depression beyond all control to suicide proportions.

That evening three doctors came into my room to verbally prepare me for the major surgery in the morning. I asked them to please tell me in detail what would actually happen in the operating room. They seemed unsure of whether I would be able to handle this, but one, after sizing me up, proclaimed, "She looks as if she is made out of tough stuff. I think she can handle it." They explained that I would be shaved as shiny as an onion, after which my head would be clamped into a vise while two or three holes were drilled through my skull as a section of my cranium would be laid on the table in preparation for the surgeon's most delicate procedures. The neurologist would then hook up some wires onto the surface of the brain, induce a seizure, and watch the brain seizure, and finally instruct the surgeon what part to remove. After this would all be complete, they would put everything in place, sew me up, and call it finished.

After the doctors left, I felt a little more concerned about the morrow beyond the hair issue, and felt the need to put it all into the hands of Jesus to look after. As I came before Him in prayer, I surrendered my body, will, life, brain, future, surgery, and the doctors into His divine hand and asked Him to preside as Great Physician in 100 percent control above all the doctors. I also asked Jesus to give me some promise that He would accompany me into and through the surgery in the morning. As I picked up the Bible, it immediately fell open to Joshua 1:9: "Be strong and of good courage, be not afraid, neither be thou dismayed: for the Lord thy God is with thee whithersoever thou goest."

With great joy in receiving His confirming promise, I wrote this verse on my right hand with an ink pen in hopes that people on the medical team could also be encouraged tomorrow when they work over me. Then I went to sleep.

KETURAH C. MARTIN

Rainbows After Rain

So oft of God, we question "Why?"
Through storms of darkness we pass by;
It's hard to understand or know
Why through such hardship we must go.

The Lord, for us, knows what is best,
And why He calls us through each test;
He knows the stormy trials, wild,
Above the storm says, "You're my child."

God sees our life from start to end—
For inner growth dark storms may send;
True beauty comes just after rain,
So all we suffer brings some gain.

The storms of life Christ understands,
And holds the fury in His hands:
The rain and tempest He controls—
Through cloudy darkness guides our souls.

Christ in these storms His hand will lend,
To hold us up and to defend;
In darkness we can't see Him there,
But He's close by, the pain to share.

The sun again in time will shine,
And stormy days be left behind;
As rainbows, bright, come after rain,
So peace and rest will follow pain!

In The Presence Of God, Part 2

That last sleep with my long hair was abruptly interrupted by a nurse quite early in the morning. At 6:40 a.m., my Dad walked in unexpectedly with Mom, and we were together for twenty minutes before the nurse came to take me away to the operating room.

As I was wheeled away, I looked at the verse on my hand again and felt the divine presence of Jesus as I once more placed my life, body, and all into His hand and control. When I came face to face with all the huge lights, lasers, equipment, tables, and the many green-garbed medical team, fear attempted to rule, but was quickly banished as I looked at the verse of sweet promise still written on my hand. Immediately I was encompassed by the presence of the Great Physician with His assurance of loving care enfolding me to His breast as the anesthesia took over and I knew no more as the 12 ½-hour surgery began.

However, even though I was out all those hours and knew nothing of the occurrences in the operating room, the Great Physician, Jesus, was very obviously there overseeing it all as He stood beside me. In His great love to me during those long hours, Christ very graciously displayed the promise of Joshua 1:9 onto the wall in one-foot high golden letters. All I knew during those hours were the wondrous words of His promise, the bright light that encircled them, and the confidence of His presence near me! The words burrowed deep into my heart and memory and have never since been forgotten. This was all I needed and I could literally feel the courage, peace, and assurance of my Master though I knew nothing of the prolonged surgery that ended at 7:30 p.m.

To be in the presence of the Great Physician and be fed by His promise while my head was literally in pieces on the operating table was the richest blessing I had ever experienced to date. To Jesus be all the praise and glory! I was told later that during those long hours of labouring over my open head and brain, the doctors took note of the verse written on my hand, took courage, and experienced renewed strength. May God be exalted and glorified! It is always important to remember that God will never lead us to something if He does not intend to walk through it with us. "For the Lord will not cast off His people, neither will He forsake His inheritance." (Psalm 94:14) The pain, afflictions, and sorrows we face in life can be blessed tools in the Master's hand if we but choose to surrender it all into His control so He can freely use the adverse circumstances to mold us into a vessel through whom He can pour His love on others.

My Jesus Has Power

My Jesus has power, no limit it knows—
Whatever the need, it sufficiently grows;
The enemy flees at the sound of His name;
The fiercest of storms His great power can tame!

The most blackened sinner can come to the cross—
The blood of my Savior can cleanse each vile dross:
For He paid the ransom for each soul He formed—
Whoever will come, through Christ's blood is reborn!

My Jesus can pick up a life most defiled—
Can transform it wholly and make it His child:
From ruined trashed rubble He fully restores,
Brings healing and cleansing as power He pours!

Though one may be threatened with death or with harm,
Be stalked or misused by a mere mortal's arm,
No force can be victor when God's hand is there:
For He will surround with His power and care!

The life that is stung by rejection's pained loss
Is fully received by my Lord at the cross—
Despite the dark history one's life may assail,
My God is a Father that never can fail!

The bruised, mangled heart that is broken in shards—
My Jesus stoops down and says, "It's not too hard
To mend all these tatters of agonized pain:
For I have a plan of most infinite gain!

I see not one's life as a mortal may see,
But I the Lord know what the outcome may be:
The ruins and rubbles of lives shattered sore,
My love, grace, and power can fully restore!"

The Armour Of God

We as Christians are in a spiritual and invisible war wherein the enemy and his armies are fighting against our souls and position in Christ. We do not fight against Satan, his demons, and his warfare *for* victory, but rather we fight *from* the victory that is already won by Jesus Christ through His death, blood, and resurrection! Jesus, our Conqueror, has the keys of hell and of death—Jesus has all power over Satan and the demons of hell! Because of Jesus, we as God's children are equipped to win the war!

There is a sense of urgency in the command to "put on the whole armour of God," which must not go unheeded if we would claim the victory that Jesus has already won for us. God has graciously provided His armour for us to use in combat against the schemes and attack of Satan and his demons, and we are responsible to put it on correctly, completely, and to actively maintain all six pieces of it. We must use the armour God gave us to the fullest potential with His help and by the power of the blood of Jesus to obtain full, personal victory.

The first three pieces of armour are used in a defensive position in the unseen war, where we hold our ground in Christ in daily living.

The Belt of Truth is the first and most important piece of armour, for without truth, there is nothing for the other pieces to attach to. The majority of the Roman soldier's armour pieces were positioned in place by being securely attached to his belt, which stabilized the armour as a whole.

The enemy will use adverse life experiences to create lies and false beliefs that many Christians battle with. Satan's greatest tool against us is deception, and he is very subtle in his attempts to this end. When there are lies, deceptions, and false beliefs ingrained into the Belt of Truth, the pure truth of God is smeared in a confusion of camouflage, and the enemy gains direct advantage. Other armour pieces cannot be securely connected to the Belt of Truth when the connecting points are all clogged up with the grimy lies of Satan, which serve to feed unbelief and doubt. If the belt is not purged by the blood of Jesus from all the untruths that have soaked in and replaced with God's truth, defeat and disaster in the war zone are inevitable, making victory impossible. The way to keep the Belt of Truth on and stabilized is to be filled daily with the Word of God, with a humble heart and openness to learn and follow His perfect will.

"You're My Chosen Treasure!"

"My Child, you are loved and so precious to Me—
No words can express all I've meant you to be;
Before this whole world had been spoken in place,
I had you all planned in the time span of grace.

Despite life's dark billows, or midst sunshine bright,
I never, My Child, have been out of your sight,
Although from your view I have oft been concealed—
My rainbow of promise to you is revealed.

Full confidence, Child, you must have every day,
That I have been working in you all the way:
The time I've invested and work I've begun,
I'll surely complete when life's journey is done!

The pain you have suffered will not be a loss
When you bring it all to the foot of the cross:
For I specialize in resolving its throb—
Defeating the foe, who just kills, ruins, and robs.

Compassions each morning are rained down anew:
For I understand everything you've gone through;
My heart cried with yours in your darkest of night,
And carried you through, giving hope, help, and light!

You're My chosen treasure—I've called you by name,
And fully restore you from dark, broken shame;
Your true value lies far beyond mortal eye,
Where, for you, I'm making a prize in the sky!

Breastplate Of Righteousness

Every piece of armour that God has provided is important for the Christian to wear. For those who are addressing heart issues and the pain they have experienced due to abuse, it is doubly imperative. Satan will do everything possible to stop you on the healing journey, and repeated attack is imminent. The darts and arrows poisoned by lies will be aimed directly at the heart as he does all in his power to keep you in his bondage.

The Breastplate of Righteousness is attached securely to the Belt of Truth. God desires to protect the hearts of His children from all the fiery arrows of the devil and his army and has made provision for this critical area also. The Roman soldier's breastplate was made of bronze or chain-mail and covered him from just below the neck down to the thighs. For clearly obvious reasons the breastplate was called "the heart protector" and this is God's desire in our breastplate armour piece also.

The Breastplate of Righteousness does not mean that one goes about seeking to be righteous by doing good deeds. Rather the child of God is clothed in the righteousness of Jesus and lives by His power, a life that reflects in daily living the Truth of God and His Word. It entails aligning our will to God's will and being completely honest with Him, ourselves, and others while applying His Truth to our life with the help of His Spirit. If we do not have the Breastplate of Righteousness in place, we are deceived, unprotected, and openly vulnerable to the enemy's attacks.

Condemnation is one tool Satan commonly uses against the Christian in attempting defeat and downfall within the heart. There is a true guilt and a false guilt, and the child of God must be able to discern the difference by applying the truth of the Word and crying out to God to search the heart by His Spirit of Truth. If indeed there is sin shown by the Spirit, then 1 John 1:9 must be followed through on, but if none is shown, then one must claim Romans 8:1, using these truths on the defeated foe.

PRAYER: Jesus, please teach me how to wear the complete armour You have provided at all times. I renounce every attempt and lie of Satan that is designed to hinder my healing. I claim You, Jesus, as my Lord and Captain. Amen.

Vessels In His Hand

As children of the heav'nly King,
We're called by Him, each day to bring
Ourselves as vessels in His hand,
That He may use us as He's planned.

Self must be always cast aside—
The carnal nature crucified,
That Jesus Christ through us can shine—
To others show His love divine.

A vessel yielded in His hand,
By grace, through Christ, on Him must stand:
Filled with humility and love,
That God be glorified above!

So many people on this earth,
Are tired, hungry, face some dearth,
Discouraged, lonely, sick or such,
Whom God in heaven longs to touch.

Before the King, how can I stand,
When I reach heaven's borderland,
If I close up this vessel's lid—
Refuse God's use as He shall bid?

A lowly vessel in God's hand,
Assisting souls to help them stand
Is minist'ring to Christ above—
Extolling Him by His great love!

When through a vessel God comes near
To bless our heart and home, bring cheer,
We'll give Him glory and the praise
For show'ring love upon our days!

The Gospel Of Peace

The third piece of armour God has provided is the shoes for our feet with the Preparation of the Gospel of Peace. As born-again believers we have been delivered by the blood of Jesus from sin, Satan, and death, and therefore we are bearers of the good news of life and freedom in Jesus! The Roman soldiers' sandals shielded their legs up to the knee; there were knobs protruding from the bottom, and often there were nails coming out. This gave the soldier a firm foundation to stand on in the face of battle, which is very similar to what Christians have been provided with in their suit of armor. Without a firm belief and foundation that supports the Belt of Truth and the Breastplate of Righteousness, we become more susceptible to the enemy's attack—not only through the subtle deceptions and accusing condemnations but also through the doubt he casts onto the very basis of God's grace, goodness, and salvation, which can boil right down to denying the Gospel. Sharing one's faith is one of the greatest faith builders ever, as we share what Christ has done; and we must always be ready to run with the Gospel. The Christian must be alert, prepared, and deeply grounded in Christ as he faces the foe, both in the subtle attacks and also on the frontal battlefront when hand-to-hand and face-to-face combat is unavoidable. It is very important that the Christian remembers that God has completely defeated Satan and all his hidden and obvious agendas. God has delivered us from sin's penalty and power through the death, blood, and resurrection of Jesus (when we choose His provisions); and in the end, He will deliver us from sin's very presence. However, in the interim, we are facing guerrilla-type warfare with the demonic forces of hell and must continually be alert, ready, and fully equipped with the entire armour God has provided, taking complete responsibility to put it on fully.

PRAYER: Lord, I want to be fully armoured and equipped to face the enemy and maintain victory over him through You. I surrender myself to Your Lordship and ask that You would fight the enemy for me by the power of the blood of Jesus. I renounce every attempt of Satan to cause me to fall and I claim Your presence, blood, and power in my life. Amen.

By Faith Persevere

How goeth the travel in your life today?
What obstacles, friend, do you find in your way?
Do boulders and brambles loom harshly and grim?
Obscuring your vision as all grows so dim.

Do dark situations approach from all sides?
Attempting to hide the dear Savior Who died;
Dear friend take new courage and run to the cross
And persevere fully that there be no loss.

By faith cling to Jesus, despite what befall,
And hold to His hand, Who has power o'er all;
He'll bear you above all the rocks at your feet,
As near to His bosom your rest is complete!

Press forward and upward one step at a time—
Keep focused on Jesus and heaven's bright clime;
The winning is yours only as you keep on:
For joys are awaiting just inside the dawn!

The wounded and wayfaring, bring to our Lord.
By faith persevere, though they're tattered and gored:
For Christ paid the price to redeem every soul
And bids you to bring them to His sweet control.

Our Lord holds all healing and grace in His hand—
He helps the blind see and makes the lame stand;
Through Him we shall conquer all sin, death, and hell,
So press on in Jesus and all His love tell!

Shield Of Faith

The last three pieces are used in an offensive position, wherein we are right in the thick of battle and must engage in hand-to-hand war in order to extinguish the enemy's flaming missiles in his frontal attack.

Above all, we are commanded to take the fourth piece of armor, which is the Shield of Faith, by which we are enabled to quench all the fiery darts of the wicked one and his army. The Shield of Faith has a direct connection to the Belt of Truth, for without the truth of God, there is nothing to substantiate faith in Jesus as our Commander in this unseen war against the enemy of our souls. Faith is our absolute confidence in God, His promises, His power, and His program for our lives and future. This faith is different from the saving faith of our salvation (though it is grounded therein), but speaks rather of a current total dependence and faith in Jesus Christ for victory over Satan and all the demonic hosts of darkness. Using the Shield of Faith is to trust God's character, claim His promises, and apply God's truth, as the shield is held up against the attack of the defeated enemy.

The Roman soldier's shield was about four feet high and two and a half feet wide and was made of iron. Over the iron were two layers of wood, with linen over that, and on top of it all was a leather cover. They left a little opening in the shield—just a gap—where there was a pocket of air. The purpose for this: when the enemies would take their arrows, dip them in tar, light them, and shoot. When the arrow hit the shield in this small opening, it would extinguish the flames on the missiles, defeating any further damage.

It is of utmost importance to ensure that our Shield of Faith has not sustained any holes from the devil's boring shafts of doubt and unbelief. Paving the road with deception, doubt and/or unbelief will cast dark, ominous shadows on the truth of God's Word, His promises, His salvation, and the gracious provisions He has enabled us to be partakers of through Jesus Christ. The presence of doubt and unbelief will most assuredly hinder and completely halt the believer's progress in his walk or connection with God (and also in any healing journey from past hurts or rejections, etc., that he may be on), as he becomes a sitting target for the fire of the enemy's deadly aim.

PRAYER: Lord, I choose to put my faith and trust in You despite the storms. I renounce all doubts, and ask You to show me how to wear the shield of faith. Amen.

MAY 21
READING: 2 CORINTHIANS 10:4, 5

"I Will Not Let You Fight Alone"

"My Child, do come closer, for I hold thy hand,
Despite what may happen beside thee I stand:
For I know explicitly what you can bear,
And ev'ry dark trial thy Lord with thee shares.

Do not fear the fire, though hot be the flame:
For I walk beside thee, the tempest to tame—
With My Presence near you thou shalt not be burned,
But into cool paths by My grace you'll be turned.

No flame will I suffer to kindle on thee,
But close to still waters thy Shepherd shall be,
To lead thee and guide thee through heat and distress,
That I, thy own Shepherd, may comfort and bless.

Though fire, dear Child, may be painful and grim,
And misunderstanding may aim at thy brim:
My Child, look beyond all the arrows that fly,
And rest in My cleft till the storm passes by!

For I will not leave thee alone in this night,
But seek to expose all the truth and the right;
My Child, I will never, no never forsake,
E'en though through the valley, My Child, I shall take.

My ways and My thoughts are much higher than thine,
And I will preserve thee, for Child, you are Mine;
In My perfect time you will then understand
Just how ev'ry hardship enhances my plan.

When burdens are heavier than you can bear,
And night is so dark that one step you don't dare:
My Child, don't lose heart for I'll see you safe through—
Within My own arms, I thy Lord carry you!

Attacks In War Zone

The smoke is thick in the war zone where the dreaded foe is attacking, and there are doubtful items lodged behind the Breastplate of Righteousness in the believer's heart and mind. If this is so, it will cause the enemy's darts of confusion and arrows of destruction to fire right through the bored holes in the Shield of Faith and result in massive spiritual devastation and disconnection from God. It is the devil's goal to break the believer's fellowship with Jesus by casting doubt, manufacturing unbelief, and condemning harshly. But always bear in mind that he is still defeated by Jesus. Even though our Shield of Faith has been damaged by the shafts of doubt and unbelief, there are obstacles everywhere, and our relationship with God feels all screwed up, our Commander has the power to restore the shield and the relationship to what He intended. You must choose to renounce every doubt lodged within and request cleansing or forgiveness from the unbelief in the name of Jesus by the power of His blood. Then it is important to embrace the truth of God's Word along with His grace and empowerment to live it, as you align yourself and your will to His divine will and plan. It is highly likely that you will have to make a conscious choice above your confused feelings and the hurling doubts and warfare of the enemy when you attempt to crucify these unbelieving doubts at the cross of Christ. It is important to fasten your eyes on Jesus, His truth, and the cross and to claim His blood despite the war around. There may be some circumstances where deception has crept in through these inroads of doubt to a severe extent. Then God may use one of His children to rebuke and cast out the forces, power, and influence of Satan by the blood of Jesus. The obstacles to believing can be vanquished and sight once again restored when all the sources of doubt are obliterated. As long as the intense spiritual blindness resulting from unsounded depths of doubt or unbelief is present, it is extremely difficult to get free alone. Often someone who is free in Christ needs to take spiritual authority over Satan and his demonic agents by the blood and name of Jesus, for it is impossible for doubt to cast out doubt (Matthew 18:14-21, Romans 14:23, Matthew 21:21, 22). It is important to learn from our Commander how to hold up the shield with faith in God in the face of Satan's flaming attack so his fiery missiles can be deflected by the power of the blood and resurrection of Jesus.

Committed To Serve Him

My friend, are you grounded in Jesus today?
Committed to serve Him, though dark grows the way?
For Christ our Foundation can never be moved—
Throughout all the ages has fully been proved!

There's no other way to reach heaven above,
Except through the door of the Savior's great love,
Who loved us enough that He died in our place—
To save us from death, in His mercy and grace.

A love that would die for the foulest of men
Is greater by far than our minds comprehend:
In face of such love I can do nothing less,
Than yield Him my "All" with an absolute "Yes!"

Though friends all around may the Truth try to sell,
And weaken convictions, yet this I know well:
My Savior left heaven, His life freely gave—
He shed all His blood that the world He might save!

So therefore I choose to give Jesus my all,
At home and abroad, despite what may befall:
For He is my Anchor, my Refuge and Light,
My Hope and Redeemer—dispelling all night.

His footsteps will walk beside me all the way,
As long as I choose 'neath His Lordship to stay;
He's promised He never His child will forsake—
I too must be faithful each step that I take!

The Helmet Of Salvation

The fifth item of armor for the Christian to put on is the Helmet of Salvation. This does not refer to obtaining salvation, but in maintaining the hope of our salvation and assurance in Christ, which the enemy ceaselessly attempts to destroy. The helmet, which was made of bronze and covered with leather, was the last piece of gear for the Roman soldier to put on. It was obviously the most important because it protected the head, and if the head is injured, there is not much left. The Helmet of Salvation is the certainty of present deliverance from sin and attack and the ensuring of the protection of our minds in the thick of the battle that the enemy is waging against us. The vast majority of Satan's warfare against the believer begins in the mind. This battle can literally turn into a raging war zone as the foe injects thoughts, words, sights, and/or doubts.

If these injections from the enemy are left unchecked and are not dealt with immediately, Satan will use and magnify them against our position in Christ, and a massive spiritual devastation can occur as the powers of darkness begin building strongholds and false beliefs in the mind.

The Helmet of Salvation gives protection against these onslaughts in the mind, but must be used simultaneously with all the other armour pieces also, as the truth of God's Word is honestly lived and applied.

When the devil and his cohorts hurl missiles of fear, doubt, lust, despair, unforgiveness, bitterness, etc., in an attempt to get into the mind, the Christian must refrain at all cost from even dialoguing or reasoning with him or the item lurking. Rather one must immediately cry out to the Commander, Jesus, claim the power of His blood; renounce the enemy and his suggestions/lies; and immerse himself in the Word and promises of God as the enemy's thoughts, temptations, and deceptions are cast down through the power of Jesus in prayer. To give Satan even a moment of time or discourse in either the subtle or the frontal attack gives him advantage and makes it more difficult to dispose of him and his purpose of attack, as he seeks to build and/or fortify a stronghold in the mind. Once he gains control of the mind—be it ever so gradual—it doesn't take long until he controls the body and heart also, as he attempts to strip the spiritual armour from his controlled and now vulnerable prey.

"Jesus, I renounce every lie, scheme and attempt of the enemy against me, and I choose to make You the King and Lord of my life, will and future."

More Than Conqueror!

That mountain, ahead, we can conquer today,
Because Jesus died and for us made a way;
We're heirs to His power, His triumph, and lead,
Since Christ conquered death and is risen indeed!

There's naught that can separate us from Christ's love,
No peril or trial nor angel above:
Though dark tribulation or death be in store—
His love never ends and His grace is yet more!

All things work together for our best and good,
Despite all the pain that we may have withstood:
For God in His love is still in full control—
Midst fiery trial He purges our soul.

Let's go climb that mountain with Christ by our side:
For we've got His power, whatever betide;
We'll conquer and win by His power, divine:
For He has redeemed us and whispers "You're Mine!"

We'll scale that high mountain with Christ in the lead—
Amid tribulation, with Him we'll succeed:
For we have all power through Christ as our Guide—
He triumphed before us and now walks beside!

We're more than just conquerors—we shall attain
Emerge beyond vict'ry with infinite gain:
For our light affliction and mountains to climb
Work for us through Christ, weights of glory sublime!

The Sword Of The Spirit

The last article of the Christian's armour which he must always wear and/ or use vigilantly is the Sword of the Spirit, which is the Word of God. Usually the Greek word for sword of the Spirit is *logos* (meaning "entire word of God"), but here it is *rhema*, which means "spoken word or words given by the Spirit of God" to do close, hand-to-hand combat against the lies, deceptions, doubts, and outright attack of the enemy. This sword is both an offensive and a defensive weapon, which holds great power against the enemy and his every attack, and it must be used in both the subtle and frontal attacks of Satan. When the truths of God's Word are applied to the specific attack at hand, this is called resisting the devil, who like a coward, will then flee away (James 4:7).

Often when God is preparing His children, either individually or corporately for a great work in His kingdom or ministry, the *demons of hell make magnified attacks on the ones involved as *they attempt to destroy God's agenda that He seeks to accomplish through His chosen vessels. Very often we can know God is up to something because of the severe spiritual attack on us as the unseen war brings us into the front of the battle, face-to-face with the enemy and his demonic forces which determine to stop the believer God has chosen to minister through for His glory. The unseen, dark world very often sees more of what God is preparing to do in or through His children than what we can and will wage intense attack against His eternal plans.

As believers, we are children of the King of kings and Lord of lords. He has invested His authority in us to take power over all the defeated hosts of Satan and hell through the power of His blood, Name, and Word! Our "badge" is the "position we hold in and through Jesus Christ," Who has secured both the original and the ultimate victory over the enemy of our soul.

Every demon of hell must believe, obey, and respond to the authority of the child of God who uses the weapon of God's Word to shoot the bullets of truth to specific issues of attack and claims deliverance through Jesus and His blood.

Jesus said, "I beheld Satan as lightning fall from heaven. Behold, I give you power to tread on serpents and scorpions, and over all the power of the enemy: and nothing shall by any means hurt you" (Luke 10:18, 19).

KETURAH C. MARTIN

We Have The Power

We have all the power in Jesus' own name,
To live in full victory o'er Satan's foul game:
For he is defeated through death on the cross
And Christ's resurrection has spelled out his loss.

So freely we access God's power divine
When we use the weapon He gave for war time:
For there is an army which seeks our defeat,
But Christ our Commander has vict'ry complete!

When warfare we're faced with and peril is near,
With Jesus beside us there's no cause for fear:
For we need but call out Christ's name to the foe,
Then he will retreat and in cowardice go.

The weapon of prayer we can use any time—
Connecting to God, or in battlefields prime;
Unlimited power is ours if we ask,
And God in His truth will the devil unmask.

The armies of Satan cannot touch our heart,
When we use this weapon of prayer with each dart;
For we've got the power in Jesus' own name,
And He's true and faithful, forever the same!

PRAYER: Lord, I choose to embrace and walk in the victory that You have already won over the enemy of my soul. I ask You to walk with me each day and cover me with the power of Your blood and resurrection. Amen.

Intercessory Prayer

The Christian has been given a secret weapon that must accompany the proper use of the provided armour we wear in the unseen war we are engaged in against the demonic realm of Satan and his armies. The most powerful and strategic weapon in our warfare is Intercessory Prayer; both on a corporate and an individual level (Ephesians 6:18). Prayer gives us direct connection to God where we not only speak to God, cry out to Him in great need, express our thanksgiving, or intercede on behalf of others, but also listen in quietness to the voice of God as He shows us His will, work, answers, and/or promises, etc.

Prayer holds the armour pieces together and causes them to work unitedly to their highest potential. Intense, strategic, and consistent prayer is the most powerful and effective weapon in the war against the enemy, causing him to retreat as he pulls his troops in utter defeat. Deliverance is as close/far away as one's mouth, which must be opened and used to renounce the enemy, to cry out to God, and to shoot the bullets of Truth at the defeated foe before us to ensure that he remains defeated.

The missing ingredient in most churches and Christians is strong, Spirit led, and biblical prayer, which when present, will result in God doing supernatural things to the glory of His name as Christ is exalted. When God's people get into His Word, the demonic forces sit up and come to attention, but when they begin to pray strong, strategic prayers under the Spirit's direction, the demons shudder in terror. Prayer has a direct impact on the spiritual warfare we are engaged in and provides or assists in the deliverance of others who may be trapped in bondage, are facing demonic oppression, or are undergoing subtle or frontal attack. The power of God falls in supernatural ways where intense, consistent, strategic, and specific prayer prevails as the Holy Spirit directs.

We do not need to fear the demons of hell, but must learn how to wear the armour of God properly and also engage in strategic, specific, and consistent prayer against the schemes, attacks, and invasions of the enemy. We have all of heaven on our side when Jesus is the Commander of our life, and through Christ we have full victory and unlimited power! Praise be to God!

KETURAH C. MARTIN

But Jesus Is Victor!

Oft Satan strikes war and attempts to destroy,
His weapons of war will with cunning deploy
To smite down the servant of God with a blow,
And hinder the work which the Lord would bestow.
He trembles in terror when God is at work,
And at every bend he will steal, prey, and lurk—
Attempting to fog up the body and mind,
While shooting vile darts as he seeks to make blind.

The truth and the light he in vain wildly fights,
Opposing exposure and seeking black nights:
For he loves the darkness where sin he doth hide—
He authors confusion whatever betide.
When God uses vessels some captive to aid,
The enemy's fury cannot then be stayed;
He kills and destroys to maintain his vile hold
And obstacles, many, will raise up so bold.

But Jesus is Victor! And He holds control
Of all His dear children—their heart and their soul;
When Satan comes in like a flood to attack,
God raises a standard and then holds them back.
The demons of hell like an army may fight,
Attacking in anger the Way, Truth, and Light;
But when Jesus' blood they shall glimpse in the fray,
They tremble in weakness and hasten away!

For through Jesus' blood is assured their defeat—
Christ renders them powerless—each foe He's beat;
Although they oppose the Lord right to the end—
Christ Jesus still reigns and cannot break or bend!
Our Lord has all power—He's conquered each foe;
He gives grace sufficient though tempests may blow;
Through His blood and name we the power have got:
For from Satan's death grip our soul Jesus bought!

Stand Guard

Very seldom do we consider the formidableness of our opponent, Satan, and his demonic army, and that is to his advantage in his warring attempts against us. When we do have just an inkling as to who he really is, then we can better understand why prayer is never easy and why he fights to try to hinder or halt it. We are up against unseen evil power that destroys this dark world and against the spiritual agents from the very headquarters of absolute evil. Without intense, consistent, and strategic prayer, deliverance in warfare is absent. When it's in place, life-long strongholds will be pulled down, and territories of Satan in one's life will be retrieved by God as He takes control of them. Demonic bondage will be broken, miraculous deliverance will take place, and healing will abound. God will freely do supernatural work as we wrestle in prayer against the forces of darkness by the power of the Spirit.

Even though Satan and his army know they are defeated through the finished work of Christ, they fight unceasingly against the believer in their hatred for God. They seek to drag as many as possible to the doom of absolute misery that awaits them in eternity. However, if we are cleansed of all sin, follow God's instructions, wear and use the provided armour as directed, and consistently use our secret weapon (1 Thessalonians 5:17, John 14:12-14), we will win the war through Jesus' blood, as we claim victory in our walk with God!

Satan's darts are intended to cause us to take our eyes off Jesus and shift our faith and dependence from God to someone or something else. When the enemy is attacking, the truth of God must be claimed and applied to the specific missile as the shield is held firmly before us while our eyes constantly stay fixed on Jesus and His cross. To meet the enemy in either the defensive position or in hand-to-hand combat without the protection of the armour being fully in place will result in certain defeat and possible capture by our formidable foe.

Since Satan's battle is for the mind, we must continually focus on Jesus and the Word so that our mind can be daily renewed, and we can know and understand what the perfect and acceptable will of God is. We do not have to become a prey to Satan, for he is defeated by Jesus already, but we have to put forth the effort of putting on and using the armour of God correctly if the victory Jesus won is to be ours personally.

RENUNCIATION: Lord, I renounce every attempt and scheme of the enemy to capture me or build strongholds in any way, and I announce that I choose to embrace Jesus Christ as the Lord of my life from this day forward!

Rest In My Unfailing Grace

"My Lord, can You show me just what You have planned:
For I this affliction cannot understand;
Please teach me Your purpose: for I seek to be
Surrendered and yielded, my Father, to Thee."
"My Child, I invite you, come to My embrace,
And patiently rest in My unfailing grace:
For I hold you close to My bosom of love,
And plans so divine have designed from above.

Do not dread affliction or pain, My dear Child,
And be not dismayed when the billows are wild,
The fires of trial, My Child, do not fear:
For I am thy God, and each step I walk near.
My strength is made perfect when weakness enfolds,
And midst the hot fire I bring forth pure gold;
When life's situations bring hardship and pain—
Dear Child, be assured that I'm planning your gain!

My grace is sufficient for trials intense—
Expands with the need amid mountains immense;
Each step that you take, Child, I still hold your hand,
Perfecting My purpose just as I have planned.
So Child, be assured that My hand holds you tight,
And for you each step against Satan I fight;
My power upon you so freely doth rest,
And when all is yielded to Me, you are blest!

My presence shall go with thee both day and night,
Enfolding in grace and illuming in light;
My dear Child, take glory in thorny paths now—
Enriched by My power, with grace on thy brow!
For all of the suff'rings that here one may bear,
With riches in heaven can never compare;
In light of eternity, Child, I build you,
And in My own arms I will carry you through!"

Hearing From God

While God and I were addressing the life-long lie that "I am 'too bad' to be loved, helped, or understood," Jesus brought an answer to my cry, which set so much of it straight despite the need to look at some deeper things further.

His reply: "I planned you before the world began and have loved you with an everlasting love. I have understood you since the time I was forming you in the womb; and it is because of My presence, sustenance, and divine aid that you survived everything adversely painful throughout your life. Though man has not always understood or known how to love and help you, yet I the Lord can never fail you!"

"Lord, why in all these years did Your people not love, help, or understand my shatters and agony, but rather judged and condemned me?"

His reply: "Because My people are human, they have often misrepresented Me and My love, relying on their own understanding instead of Mine. Only I the Lord have seen your bruised and bleeding heart so ripped and torn by the experiences of abuse and rejection, and only I have understood. I have walked the road before you, but none of these others have come close."

"Lord, I choose to renounce the lie that I am too bad to be helped, loved, or understood, and I acknowledge that You have done all these things for me. Lord, will You break this lie by the blood of Jesus and take back all the ground given to Satan through it, and Jesus, will You break all the effects this may have had on my children and husband and retrieve that ground also? Please, will You forgive me, Jesus?"

His reply: "My Child, I will forgive you, receive you, and reclaim all the ground that the enemy stole. I will also exchange the lie for My divine truth, which is 'I have loved you with an everlasting love, I have drawn you with the cords of love, and I will keep thee as the apple of My eye. Though weeping has endured many nights and years, My joy comes in the morning!'"

"No Greater Love"

The love of Christ Jesus, no tongue can expound
The bountiful depths to which it does abound:
He gave up His life blood in anguish of soul.
To pay our full ransom from death was His goal.

Now we've been adopted through His love's design—
Joint-heirs with our Savior by His grace divine;
In love through His blood, Christ transformed us to be
His sanctified servants to spread His love free.

Agape love daily in us seeks to live
The love of our Savior to others—hope give:
To represent Jesus to all that we meet:
For love that's not lived is not ever complete.

A love sacrificial, dies daily to "me,"
Desiring the hands of Christ Jesus to be:
Uplifting the downtrod, to needy give aid—
The lowest of low, to assist unafraid.

True love careth not what the skeptic may say
About love's true efforts as lived out each day
But seeks to personify Jesus alway—
Do just as He'd do if He walked earth today!

Love gives time and efforts to those in despair,
No judgment will pass, but just showing we care:
For some are so steeped in deep bondage and pain
That just one more step they alone can't attain.

To lay down one's life for the sake of a friend,
To die in his place who's caused pain to no end,
To die to self, daily, as God's love you live—
This highest of love is the greatest to give!

JUNE 3
READING: 1 JOHN 3:10-19

What Is Love?

What is actually the truest definition of love? To some people, love is the scariest thing on the planet and always involves a risk. This happens when the people who should love them or even may proclaim love will actually turn around and hurt them verbally, emotionally, physically, or in any other way. Whether the recipient is a child, an adolescent, or an adult, the effects are very confusing, painful, and destructive.

However, Jesus Christ is the only perfect personification of love in its truest sense. Not only did Jesus die in the place of His friends and family, but He died to save the very men and mob who crucified Him with the criminals after beating Him brutally.

THINGS LOVE WILL DO:
- Give up its own agenda in order to help another individual
- Follow the example of Jesus no matter what the cost
- Speak only what is true, kind, and necessary
- With open heart and mind extend itself to help the hurting
- Serve selflessly, expecting nothing in return
- Go the second mile to show kindness to one who has hurt us

THINGS LOVE WILL NOT DO:
- Seek after self's agenda first and foremost
- Judge according to appearance or spread slander
- Discredit the brokenhearted and turn a blind eye to their pain
- Condemn the survivors and tell them to "get on with your life"
- Avoid reality while basing beliefs or opinions on assumptions
- Pretend that abuse and its aftereffects are not real

PRAYER: Lord Jesus, will You please teach me the truth about love and give me Your wisdom to identify every counterfeit of love and reject it. Please touch me Lord with Your divine love and make me a living vessel through which to pour Your love on others. Amen.

KETURAH C. MARTIN

My Cry From The Ruins

"Lord Jesus, I come to the garden of prayer,
And ask by Thy grace that You'd come meet me there:
For I long to pour out my heart and my soul
To Thee, Who in love has all things in control.

Dear Master, I seek to in full understand
Just what in this aftermath You may have planned—
The ruins and rubble so vast meet the eyes,
With limitless pain where the heart always cries.

I thank You, Lord Jesus, that You preserved me,
Yet question why brethren opposed seem to be
About stark reality that I'm alive—
Project condemnation that death I survived.

Dear Lord, was it "my wrong" that I was abused?
Just how do You view these vile ways I was used?
Please search me, my Savior, and see if there be
Some wicked way lurking somewhere within me.

So often I ponder 'Just why it must be
That he who destroyed us can run around free,
With never a consequence for his vile deeds,
While children so wounded are broken like reeds?'"

"My Child, never fear, for My hand is on you,
And I have a purpose for all you've come through—
No pain will be wasted—no tear goes unseen,
For I am your Savior and fully redeem!

I'll take every tear drop and each shard of pain
Creating true beauty with infinite gain,
No suffering is wasted, no tear lost will be,
For you, My Dear Child, are most precious to Me!"

Re-writing Your Life's Text

Often when people have faced painful circumstances, rejection, or abuse, they find themselves in depths of despair and hopelessness, not knowing how to even begin to climb up. The enemy takes advantage of their plight, ruthlessly taking delight in preying on their vulnerable brokenness while seeking their further destruction.

However, even in the darkest hour, Jesus has not forsaken us, and He never writes us off regardless of how destroyed or hopeless we feel, or may be. Rather He understands completely the pain of abuse, rejection, and even the agony of violent death itself. Yet these things He suffered did not destroy or devastate Him, but rather were the means by which God procured our salvation and rescue from death, sin, and Satan. Therefore He is able to save to the uttermost those who come to God through Him, and Jesus lives to make intercession on their behalf.

It is the desire of Jesus to re-write the text of your life. The things that Satan instigated against you and meant for evil Jesus can turn around for good if you let Him. Whether it is shame, inner agony, domestic violence, ritual abuse, or abandonment that you may be experiencing, Jesus is just waiting for you to place all the heart-shreds and shatters into His hand. Once there, He will take them one by one and begin re-writing your life text into a beautiful script of miraculous transformation.

Even though some of the tatters and shards of agony committed to His hand may be blood-soaked, defiled, or tear-stained, there is nothing too hard, torn, or demolished but that Christ can bring complete restoration. Jesus specializes in defeating every attempt Satan has made through others to destroy you and your future. Every strike he made against your body, mind, and soul through abuse, Jesus can turn into golden strands within the new text and life description He is re-writing. These anguishing experiences, after His healing touch, become items of blessing and bounty in your life and those around you, as Jesus is glorified. But you have to choose to be better or bitter.

PRAYER: Thank You, Jesus, that there is nothing too hard for You to heal and restore. I choose to give You the wrecked pieces of my life and ask that You would transform it all into something of value to glorify Your name! Amen.

KETURAH C. MARTIN

The Savior Responds To The Ruins

"My Child, I the Lord can the full picture see,
And understand wholly each thorn come to thee;
My perfect will was not that you were abused,
Nor yet midst pained anguish that you are accused.

I've salvaged thee, Child, from the rubbles galore,
And brought you new life when you'd come through death's door:
For I have a plan that's exclusive for you,
But great tribulation you first must come through.

These strands of deep agony none comprehend,
With purest of gold I am weaving a blend,
By which you may empathize, feel, and help bear
The pain of My children who have none to care!

The dark persecutions so subtly sent
Is one more attempt which the enemy vents—
He seeks to destroy you and healing to halt,
Lest I should soon use you, My name to exalt!

Though many are closed to the truth of your state,
And see not My plan, amid pain none can rate,
Yet I'm in control and have chosen a few
Whom I seek to use and who see from My view.

The misunderstandings, the pain and the past,
With each word of slander, on Me you must cast:
For I will accomplish the plan I've begun,
Regardless who counters the work I have done!

I've chosen thee, Child, and will never forsake:
For out of the ruins, a treasure I make!
No person or foe, though they don't understand,
Can hinder My plan and the work of My hands!"

"Come And Hear Me, Child"

"My dear Child, you are My chosen possession and the prize of My workmanship. The infinite value that you have in the eyes of your Creator and Sustainer of life is priceless, which is why I preserved you again and again.

"If there are any individuals who cannot understand your life, survival, and future, it is because they have only mortal eyes with which to see and understand. The worth you have to Me cannot be altered or extinguished just because there may be those who do not understand, who falsely accuse you, or who invalidate the truth of your experiences. I know and have a plan for you that the lack of knowledge and understanding from others cannot deter, for I am the Lord.

"I never make mistakes, and even though the mistakes of others can potentially damage you, yet I the Lord am there to walk alongside you and carry you through. I will restore the years that the locusts have eaten and bring you into a land of healing and plenty. All the attempts of the enemy to destroy you through the pawns he chose I will reverse, and his curse and destructions I will turn into blessings and a cord of love that is My preservation.

"Though sometimes it is hard for you to understand how people who caused so much hurt and brokenness should be living with no adverse consequences for their actions of abuse, yet you must surrender them completely into My hand. I desire to teach all who suffer at the hand of another to learn to see them through the eyes of Jesus, Who died for all men. What Satan used them to do to you was not right or blessed by Me, and it is in the line of My justice to hold them accountable for it. However, it is not your concern or duty to ensure that they receive justice, but only to choose to forgive and release them into My hand for Me to deal with. When you make this choice, the freedom that you will experience will surpass anything you have previously known, and this individual will no longer have control over you through bitterness.

"Though you, My Child, cannot see or in full understand, you must choose to believe that I the Lord am making a prize of great value out of your life, despite the ruins I found you in. There is nothing too hard for Me to do, even if the majority around you may not want to be involved. I will complete the work I have begun in you, and will turn the shatters, shame and pain into a vessel of honor, to shine for the glory of My name!"

KETURAH C. MARTIN

Satan's Underground Abuse Agents

His agents are bound in deceptions of night,
Who often rely on satanical might,
But this they can gain only as they succeed
In crippling the helpless while power they feed.
They strip down their captives so direly complete
In spirit, mind, body until at their feet
Their victims are bound in destruction's vile name,
While writhing in agony's filth and dread shame.
The captives are threatened with death if they tell
Of sexual perversions midst porno's dread hell—
They may never speak of the blood-flowing scenes
Where Satan is honoured in rituals obscene.
The shame of filth's night 'neath the carpet is swept—
They feel they have power, though victims have wept:
For they are addicted to pow'r and control,
That's gained through abuse and destruction of souls.
Their victim survivors are shattered and torn—
Most folks cannot fathom just what they have borne:
For eye cannot see the emotional shreds,
The trashed inner being, the threats to make dead.
With Christ at our side, through His eyes let us look
At Satan's used agents, who truth have forsook:
For they are but pawns in the enemy's hold,
Through whom he wreaks havoc—abuse, stark and cold.
These pawns are but human, and if you look hard
Deep into their hearts, you will find them all scarred
By pain and rejection in their childhood days,
Who in rage have chosen all Satan's dark ways.
We must choose forgiveness, releasing complete
Our ev'ry abuser, all pain they did mete—
Surrender it all to the Lord's hand, divine:
For out of the ashes He'll make beauty shine.

JUNE 9
READING: ROMANS 5:1-8

A Look Through The Eyes Of Christ

With the divine help and sustenance of God, it is very important in our healing journey to allow Jesus to teach us to see things through His eyes. This includes specifically to view our perpetrator through the eyes of Christ.

The human nature of every suffering survivor may cry out for revenge, justice to be served, and personal rights, etc. This however is not the route to freedom, healing, and wholeness. Should the law take it in its hand to prosecute an offender that is its God-given authority to do. Likewise we cannot cover evil-doing to protect the one hurting us. However, it is the matter of the heart and attitude that we as survivors must address personally within ourselves.

Join hands with Jesus while we take a walk together as He shows us the truth as seen through His eyes. Rely on His strength to see what He shows you, even though it may be painful.

"My Child, I have seen all that you have suffered, and I am delighting to heal and restore you to fit the plan I have for you. Now I will show you a picture of the one who was used to hurt you. Always remember that Satan is the instigator of abuse and all of its aftermath and agony. The individual he attempts to use to do his dirty work is often just a hurting little boy trapped in a man's body. Though I hold every person responsible before Me for his personal choices and actions, yet you must also acknowledge and understand that I died for the abuser as well as you. I love you both equally: for there is no respect of person with Me. I do not love or condone the sin, evil, and abuse, but I love and care about the hurting person who has been persuaded by the evil one to be a pawn in the devil's hand. The abuser and the evil he committed must be separated, for I also died for this individual so I might free him from evil and the instigator thereof. Though the perpetrator may now be camping in the enemy's territory, that does not mean that he has no value to Me. The power of My blood can cleanse and transform the most evil and abusive person and wipe his slate clean if he comes to Me in genuine repentance. If he does not want My help and forgiveness, I will never force Myself on him, but I will extend grace while time stands. Likewise, I love you, Child, and saw all that you wrongfully suffered as I stood by you through it all. I will continue to guide, protect, and bring full healing to you! The ashes which surrounded you will be transformed into treasure untold!"

PRAYER: Lord, I choose to surrender my abusers and their evil deeds into Your hand to deal with. Amen.

KETURAH C. MARTIN

How Can I Help A Soul In Need?

How can I help a soul in need whose troubles seem to far exceed
The things that I have known or felt—the like of which I've never dealt.
How can I know just what to say? How can I brighten up the way?
That anguished turmoil makes no sense when I have no experience.
Arise, take courage and rejoice: for love divine will aid your choice—
The power lies within your hand to tread one down or help them stand.
A soul of trauma longs and pleads, for one to listen to their needs
With open ear, unjudging heart—a hand to hold when teardrops start.

These hurting souls need patience kind, true love's support for heart and mind;
And they must have your trust so true, to know their words will stay with you.
Do not deny their anguished pain, the broken heart from horror's strain,
The gunpoint scenes of grief, filth, shame—judge not—accredit all that came.
Survivors of traumatic deeds your understanding always need:
For flashbacks, unawares, come up, where guns, threats, filth, again they sup.
Do not discount how tortures ruled, midst which the victims are thus schooled:
"You're useless, damned, accursed, and more—rejection only is in store."

Don't ever judge their shattered state, of which no soul can estimate:
For had their mind in one piece stayed, just hopeless death would be their aid.
They hunger to be understood, and just be loved as Jesus would;
The skeptic's views they do not need—on criticisms need not feed.
Discredit not, how memories real o'er body, mind, and soul oft steal,
Where writhing pain is not obscured, but throes of suffering are endured.
Just walk beside them—let them know that you will share their pain, tears, woe:

Before you act or say or do, for one mile walk and wear their shoe.
DO NOT show pity for their pain: for pity reeks and brings disdain;
Leave all condemning far behind—through care and time grant nurture kind.
Just be a gentle presence near, give calm assurance midst their tears;
Stand firm beside them, be a friend—be kind and true right to the end!
Compassion, gracious, show each day—the love like Jesus live alway;
Bring them to Christ, the Healer great: for only He can save midst fate!

Helping The Wounded And Rejected

1. How to help the wounded:
   A. Accept without judgment
   B. Understand without judgment
   C. Care without judgment
   Note: If judgment is present in any form, it is not possible to proceed to step D, and "safety is absent for survivor."
   D. Bring person and pain to Jesus, Who fully understands and is capable of bearing the load of pain, rejection, and/or shame, etc.

2. In the process of doing all of #1, the following must coincide with it in order that Jesus may be reflected through us to the hurting:
   A. Validate their pain and feelings resulting from the abuse, rejection.
   B. Never condemn, but allow the Spirit to do the convicting where needed.
   C. Do not show pity, but only compassion, as you become an extension of the love of Jesus, seeing the wounded through His eyes.
   D. Always under every circumstance, keep the person and the problem or pain separate. Otherwise the whole attempt to minister to the hurting may revert back to human reasoning rather than seeing the wounded through the eyes of a loving Father—God Himself.
   E. Never pressure a wounded, abused, or rejected individual to "be healed" or "get through the healing process." This can cause severe hindrances or reverses in the healing journey. Healing is in the hands of God, Who can see all the areas needing healing and which are often unknown to the observer or even the survivor.

3. God cares about the emotional pain and damage we carry in our heart and He longs to speak peace to each shattered, bleeding heart. He is able and wants to put all the broken pieces together again, if we let Him.

Cont.

Rejection: To be rejected can cause life-long damage if it is not brought to Jesus for healing. When an individual is rejected or abused by a father, it becomes nearly impossible to trust or connect to God: for the father image has been destroyed, and the result is a fear of God the Father.

In like manner, when God's people reject and ostracize an individual, they are misrepresenting the Father heart of God's love to a wounded individual, and they may become guilty of being used by Satan to drive away a broken life from God the Father.

Roses Midst The Thorns

Though my path lead through the roses,
Where thorns may pierce me sore:
When stark anguish 'round me poses—
I can't take one step more . . .

Then my Jesus comes beside me,
Midst shades of gath'ring night,
"My dear Child, I walk beside thee,
Upon thy path shed light!

Though sharp thorns may hem thy pathway,
And trials bring great pain—
Though the storm clouds make a dark day,
Sufficient grace doth rain.

For the rainbow of My promise
Above thee, Child, I raise,
And will span each darkened abyss,
As grace crowns all thy ways!

Look, My Child, beyond the thorned trail
To roses fair and bright—
Look beyond the shades of dark vale,
To sunshine of My light!

For midst thorns, there's blooming fragrance
Of beauty, grace, and love;
Through the valley's painful entrance,
My hand guides from above!

My dear Child, I'll not forsake thee,
Though thorns may pierce thy feet,
Thy eternal best your Lord sees—
His work in thee completes!"

KETURAH C. MARTIN

Roses Or Thorns

We are the center of God's focus and love, and it is in His own image that we were created. He sees you as valuable and cares for each area of your pain. He feels each thorn you feel, and Jesus has experienced it all before you. God never designed us to have to carry the heavy pain of thorns, rejection,

or abandonment. He is waiting to take the complete load and bring healing to the core issues behind the pain that is suffered. Each thorn which pierced the very core of your heart He can extract and pour His healing oil in. In its place a rose of beauty can grow as you allow Him to infiltrate all the cracks of your life with His love which others avoided or passed by in judgment.

Thorny pain and rejection is a disguised blessing which can be used by God to prepare us for whatever work He has for us to do. The enemy wants to use our pain and life-shattering experiences to destroy us and our faith in God, but the Master can turn them into something beautiful which glorifies Him when they are given entirely to Him for healing.

The following are some points for us all to remember and take courage from:

- "The depth of pain, abuse, rejection, and dirty shatters one carries *does not reflect in him a lesser value than any of God's children.* Rather it reflects a greater potential to understand and minister to the wounded with God's help and healing. It also shows the magnitude of the love and power of Jesus, Who specializes in putting together the impossible and agonized shatters of one's life."
- "There is *nothing too hard for Jesus* to understand and fix, if we let Him."
- "If God brings you to it, He will also lead you through it."
- "No one can ever truly change or heal a heart, but Jesus alone."
- "Jesus will never waste your pain, but can turn it into eternal gain when it is all surrendered into His hand of divine healing."

PRAYER: Lord, I choose with Your help to see the roses and the beauty of them, rather than the thorns which their stems are encased in. I choose to give You every thorn in my life and every abuse that has shattered me and ask that You bring me to complete healing through Jesus. Please, will You take the pain, and in its place plant the Rose of Sharon—Jesus Himself—where it had been. Take all my past, Lord, to build a transformed future where Jesus is exalted and the world may know that there is nothing too hard for Him to fix! Amen.

Hope Near Slippery Slopes

My friends, we are chosen by God in His love,
Through pain and past anguish preserved from above;
Christ went on before us to map out the way—
Was tempted in all points as we are today.
Along this our pathway an enemy hides,
But we must evade him whatever betide;
He's out to deceive us about who we are—
Lays slippery lies that can zoom us afar.
The lies and false guilt we may grab for dear life,
Which have been glossed over, but slice like a knife;
With arms and legs flailing, one slides in distaste,
And grapples for something to break slippery haste.
While gathering speed down the dark, slippery slope,
To break that momentum may seem without hope,
But do not despair for the Lord saw you go—
He's right there beside you, His way He will show.
The webs of dark lies that are sticky and grim
When put to the test of His Word grow so dim;
The hammer with which we ourselves may beat down,
He gently replaces with Truth which abounds.
He whispers, "My Child, do come closer to Me:
For I am thy Father, your Helper will be.
My Child, when you're hurting, so weak or alone,
When near slippery slopes you feel utterly prone—
My strength is made perfect in weakness, dear heart,
And My grace, sufficient, is there from the start.
So call out to Me, Child, before the incline
And be not entangled with enemy's twine;
Before you will call Me the answer is there,
And I walk beside thee to show you My care:
For you are My treasure, My joy, and My prize—
I seek to escort you to heaven's bright skies!"

KETURAH C. MARTIN

Hope On The Slope

There are times when survivors may find themselves sliding hastily down some unwanted slope, not knowing where they may stop or end up. The healing journey can be scary at times like this, but it is still worth it! Don't despair despite where the slide may dump you! Such rides do not mean that hope has flown or anything else the enemy tries to tell you. Nor does it mean that all is lost.

It is very mandatory in such times to cling to the hand of God which He is offering you. He understands our weariness and the subtle craft of the enemy at such times. Always get up again! It is the getting up again that will always count. The enemy would suck you into the bog of despair, but not if you get up again and grasp the hand of God that's there!

PRAYER: Lord help me to rise to new heights with You in full control! Amen.

READING: MATTHEW 18:10 AND MARK 10:13-17

"Will Somebody Listen?"
(Written on behalf of helpless children)

"Will somebody listen? Oh, please hear my cry!
Can nobody hear me? I'm ready to die!
I cannot get free from this dark, scary place,
Where I'm just a toy for bad men to efface.
It feels like my heart they have thrown on the floor,
Then jumped up and down till it's broken and tore—
My heart hurts so bad—can't you see how it bleeds?
For it like a sponge soaks up all their bad deeds.
So often the devil I see in their eyes,
Which tell me I'll never escape despite cries!
It warns me that pain without limits is due,
With no one to save me or find out what's true!
They strip all my clothes off, so that 'I'm so bad'
And if I refuse them—Boy, do they get mad!
He makes me so dirty, I cannot get clean—
Am told I deserve it because I'm obscene.
Those dark, dirty tatters and rags of despair,
Oh, can you not see them? Does nobody care?
Is there not some way that this vile night can end?
Must I live and die without hope, without friend?
I always am scared and there's no place to cry—
Nor may I e'er speak, or I'm told, "You will die!"
Inside me all things are just blowing apart,
And I hurt so much that I can't find my heart!
I am not allowed to step over the line,
Which others can't see, but which marks my confines—
If outside this circle I drag my vile pain,
Then they'd crush and kill me with nothing to gain.
Oh, can you not hear all the little ones cry?
While bleeding and dying without a friend nigh;
Will anyone dare to come rescue from night?
And bring helpless children out into safe light?"

PRAYER: Lord Jesus, please surround every trapped and hurting child with Your divine Presence and protection. Deliver each one and hold them to Your heart of love. Amen.

KETURAH C. MARTIN

JUNE 17
READING: LUKE 17:1, 2

Identifying With The Children

This is especially for the children who are trapped, silenced, threatened, and/or have no place to turn or escape from the abuse. It is written to all other survivors of abuse as well, including the little children where there is DID (Dissociative Identity Disorder) involved. I commend each one of you, and in prayer I bring you to the arms of Jesus.

You are all important and very valuable to Jesus, and also to me. I feel God wants me to tell the world what is happening to little girls and boys, because some of you are not allowed to speak and are too scared to tell anyone what is happening. You are not alone. I too suffered greatly when I was little and felt all alone all the time, even with lots of brothers and sisters. The fear of the bad man was everywhere.

Years later, when I brought Jesus the rags and dirty tatters of pain, I was crying and asking Him where He was when the bad men were hurting me. His answer made me cry with joy because it was so wonderful!

"When someone was hurting you I was always there. Sometimes I stood between you and him or put My hand in-between so it wouldn't hurt you so bad. There are times when I would just hold you close to My heart and carry you through all the yucky stuff that was done to you. What happened to you was so bad that you likely did not always know I was there. But if I had gone away and not helped you, you would have died. The angel of My presence saved you every time, and I was hurting with you during all the times you were being hurt inside and outside. I have a plan for you that just you can do, so I want to heal you from all the bad things that hurt you! Are you ready to let Me help and heal you?"

PRAYER: Dear Jesus, thank You for holding me close to Yourself when I was being hurt, so I wouldn't die. If You can get rid of all the yucky stuff inside me that hurts so badly, I will gladly give it to You. Can You please take the dirtiness and shame that makes me hate myself? And, Jesus, my heart hurts so much that it feels as if it is broken in pieces and stomped on by the bad man. Can You please take all that pain and fix my heart again? Will You make it to be happy again and take away all the scaredness I always feel? If it is not too much to ask, Jesus, could You give me a clean white robe in place of all the yucky stuff I had to wear for so long? Thank You for loving me and keeping me alive. Please live in me and protect me and help me, Jesus. I love You, Jesus! Amen.

Trust Each Step To Me

When life like a jungle is tangled and dark,
With no path apparent—no trail that is marked,
One then may feel lost, so deserted, alone—
May fear the unknown, and to dangers feel prone.

But in the deep tangle of untrodden maze,
When darkness surrounds or stark pain crowns thy days—
Look up then, dear soul, for the Lord is so near,
To clear you a path and to dry ev'ry tear.

My Jesus delights in impossible things—
Midst rivers of sorrow makes brooklets that sing;
In tangles of pain, amid under-brush dense,
His grace is sufficient, His love is immense!

For He sees the path that He's laid out for you,
Although to your eyes it is hidden from view;
Through brambles, o'er mountains, He cuts a clear trail—
Fulfilling His purpose: for He never fails.

He sees far beyond all your life's darkest night,
When it's like a jungle and gone seems the light;
Christ never will leave you alone in despair,
But through the dense trials, He says, "Child, I care!

When you see no path where your next step shall tread,
Or may be concerned where shall come this day's bread—
Just cling to My hand, Child—trust each step to Me:
For I create paths where blurred darkness you see.

My Child, it is I Who shall lead you each day,
To guide you each step and to show you the way;
No path remains hidden when I am thy Guide:
For I lead to heaven whatever betide!"

KETURAH C. MARTIN

Trusting Amid The Darkness

There may be times in our journey to healing where the path cannot even be deciphered and is all grown over with painful obstacles. Often the darkness of doubt and fog of skepticism may obliterate the trail completely, and to take one more step feels impossible. Often God may allow us to face all sorts of obstacles just so He can teach us to place our hand trustingly into His and let Him lead us through the darkness, pain, and obstacles. He always has our eternal best in mind even though we cannot understand what He is doing or why He leads us as He does.

Trusting anyone outside of our control can be a very scary procedure: for so many people have hurt us when we dared to trust. There are many times where God's people and leaders may have caused a lot of pain and rejection in one's life. This magnifies the obstacles of learning to trust God, for if His people have caused hurt and written off the broken-hearted, then what's to say God won't do likewise?

It is very important to always remember that "God is not a man that He should lie, nor the son of man that He should repent" (Numbers 23:19). Any time that His people have failed or hurt us in any way, they did not drag God down to their level. Rather they failed to measure up to His standard of love and His expectations for them, and ultimately, they failed both you and God through their lack of following His blueprint. Since God said He would never leave or forsake us, we can have the full assurance that He means just that. The Lord is always true to His Word, character, and promises regardless of how man chooses to respond to the love mandates of an unfailing God. To place our hand into His in our darkest night is the absolute safest way for us to get through it in one piece. Because God has our way planned perfectly and He has a purpose for us, what better Guide could we possibly dream of ever finding? He only asks that you hold His hand and take one step at a time, and then He can guide you through.

PRAYER: Lord, I choose to trust You to lead me one step at a time, even though so many have hurt, failed, and rejected me. I choose to believe that You cannot fail, even though some have misrepresented You. Take my life and future into Your control and help me to trust You with them completely. Amen.

The Master Designer

The Master Designer approached me one day,
When He found my shatters of pain by the way;
He gave me His hand and He lifted me up
Above all the ashes, midst shame in my cup.
"My Child, I have never designed you to be
All shackled in pain and such dark misery;
I never designed that abuse should destroy,
But I have made you for My own praise and joy.
I never have planned Child, that you feel filth's smear,
Nor that your own body you hate midst pain's tears,
But in My own image I fashioned your whole—
For My praise I made the mind, body, and soul.
It was not My plan that you be harshly used,
Nor have I ordained it that man would abuse,
But I am your Father, and, Child, I made you—
A vessel I've chosen to pour My love through.
I did not create you to bow down to fear,
All bound up in fetters right up to your ears,
But, Child, I designed it that you should be free,
Enlightened and vibrant with Jesus in thee!
My Child, I designed as a temple for Me,
Your body and all that I've made you to be;
Your value to Me, Child, can never be told,
And I will refine you as purest of gold!
I fashioned you, Child, that to Me you relate:
For I seek relationship none dissipate;
My Child, I designed that we walk hand in hand:
For only My power ensures you will stand.
But you must remember, My Child of great worth,
Despite any circumstance faced on this earth:
'Though Satan attempts to destroy one to chunks,
Yet I'm your Creator and never make junk!'
So yield to Me, Child, all the lies you believe,
Which may come from feelings midst hurt you've received;
Surrender all pain to My transforming hand:
For you are My own with a value I've planned!"

KETURAH C. MARTIN

Merciful Kindness

Looking back over my life to date, I can only praise God for being so completely gracious, loving, and full of mercy! Why would He ever have bothered to stop at the pile of worthless rubble just to dig through and find all the broken pieces of my life? How could He seemingly waste His time fixing a life trashed by years of abuse and rejection? Why is it so hard for us to see what He can obviously see, that He could be bothered to dig through the garbage bin just to find the little girl crying and dying all alone in thousands of pieces?

I still do not know God's thinking, nor do I understand all the answers to these questions. It is very clear, however, that God has seen value when it was completely unseen by all others. Also He took action to rescue me and redeem my life and future before I expired in destruction and death as was subtly programmed by some of the pawns used to destroy me.

We serve a marvelous God Who has an undying interest in each one of us. He intricately designed every detail of our being and has a unique plan for each life created. He wants to use each of us to fit the design and purpose He created us to fill. Though Satan fights God's design for us, yet even from the ash heap that the enemy put us in, God can restore and completely disannul the enemy's destructions, turning those attempts into tools which can further the plan of God. That is, if we choose to invite Him to take control of our pain, past and shatters, so He can bring beauty out of the ashes.

The Lord also has a heart of compassion for His children, and when someone is suffering wrongfully, His heart is hurt worse than the one being crushed. He sees and understands every type of abuse one may suffer; and if the angel of His presence would not be present, the victim would often die. He knows where all the broken pieces are, and through the suffering and stripes of Jesus we can be completely healed.

God knows when enough is enough and often will take drastic action to rescue His suffering children in His perfect time. "For the oppression of the poor, for the sighing of the needy, now will I arise, saith the LORD; I will set him in safety from him that puffeth at him" (Psalm 12:5).

PRAYER: Lord, I don't see and understand everything about myself as You do, but could You please continue to sanctify me and perfect the work You have begun? I surrender my past, present and future to You, and ask that my entire life be fashioned after Your blueprint that You be glorified through it. Amen.

A Trapped Victim's Cry

"Oh, why is there none who my plight understands?
How is it they see not the wall's massive bands?
Oh, why can't they fathom how thick they do rate,
Which mind, thought, or effort cannot penetrate?

The fences around all my life they don't see,
And understand not that *I'll never be free;*
The threats of dark death loom forebodingly near,
When next to these bounds I attempt to appear.

Folks tell me *Just run from the ones that hurt you,*
But they cannot fathom that this I can't do;
My life is at stake if I cross the dark line,
Which no one else sees, but sends chills up my spine.

For many have died when they tried to escape
The horrors and rituals, the filth, blood, and rape,
The fence they would climb or the wall that they'd scale
Became a dark trap through which death did prevail.

Am I beyond saving, and bound in death's curse
With no hope or help in this vile world, perverse?
Is there not just one who could lend me a hand?
Perchance there's a God, just where does He now stand?"

"For the Lord your God, He it is that fighteth for you
as He promised you!" (Joshua 23:10)

PRAYER: Jesus, I believe that You have all power to free me from captivity and to protect me from my captors and all threat of harm. I surrender all to Your control and ask You to protect me daily, and bring me complete freedom. Amen.

Invisible Walls And Fences

To endure abuse takes tremendous courage, but to survive it requires the divine intervention of God Himself. This is my opportunity to validate every survivor out there and commend you for your courage and perseverance! Most of all I give God the credit for your current existence, even though you may feel completely shattered and reduced to nothing. The very fact that you are reading this is a living proof that God has a purpose for your life, although it seems hopelessly destroyed.

Sometimes it feels so useless to be alive if we must live through the aftermath of all we came through. This becomes much more challenging when those around us do not understand what they cannot see or feel as we do. Others cannot even begin to comprehend those invisible walls that are only seen by us, but the Lord sees and knows all about those unseen fences and threatening walls. He understands the extreme terror pounded into those walls and anyone daring to cross them. He knows how thick and foreboding they are, and He cares about that crying little child inside you who just wants to find a safe place to rest. God in His great love has also provided Someone Who can break down all those walls and gates, regardless of how immense they may be or what threats they may hold.

It is Jesus Who longs to enfold you in His bosom where there is safety, peace, and loving protection. He has the power to deliver you from the deepest pit and from behind the thickest walls. You may wonder, "How could He care about a trashed thing like me?" But let me tell you that "Jesus has invested His life into you and all of us when He willingly died in our place as He took the death penalty for our sin." He came specifically to earth to save and restore broken and destroyed lives by His power and outstretched arm, no matter what has been done against us or how high the walls of terror have been built around us.

PRAYER: Lord Jesus, will You please come to me, past all the walls which are so terrifying, but nobody else can see? I choose to believe the promise that You can deliver me, and I place my life, body, and future into Your hand, for You alone can save me. Thank You, Jesus, for hearing my cry. Amen.

Jesus Answers A Victim's Cry

"My Child, I have seen all the horrors you bore,
And stood right beside you when death seemed in store,
Should I have withdrawn in thy anguishing night,
There would have been far greater darkness and blight.

Invisible walls that the world cannot see,
I understand clearly when I look on thee:
I know every stake that they pounded within—
Each nailing lie used to engrave their cruel sin.

But, Child, there's no fence—be it ever so high,
No wall that's too thick, but that I can pass by;
Though man may not help you escape your pained plight,
My blood paid your ransom and for you I fight!

My blood has defeated each demon of hell,
I've conquered the devil—each horror you tell;
I offer salvation, hope, freedom, and light,
And I give safe refuge by day and by night.

Child, bring me the tatters that few understand,
Bring Me the dark threats, unseen walls, and demands,
The vile, bloody rags of filth, force, death, and pain,
I'll take it all, Child, and exchange with My gain!

And Child be assured that I'm building for you
A mansion in glory that's peaceful and new—
Here pain is all past and there never comes night,
And near to My side you will bask in My light!"

KETURAH C. MARTIN

An Invitation From God

"When you feel all alone and that nobody can even begin to understand the unseen fences surrounding you, I invite you to come to Me. I was there holding your hand when the threats, danger and brutality ruled the stage.

"I understand, Child, the terror and horror that began that day to encase you day and night whenever you permit yourself to even think about freedom from the threats, terror, and yet pending doom. Come to Me, Child, and let us walk beside still waters and safe, green pastures. My love and power surpasses by far all the terror and evil power of those who have threatened you; and I can set you free in body, soul, and mind.

"Some people may think and proclaim that you should just walk away and forget about everything that has hurt and destroyed you. They do not understand the place you are in, nor did they see or experience the nails that were driven into the invisible fences built around you. Those who cannot comprehend your experience of utter pain, filth, and horror are in no place to offer concrete solutions, for they know not what they speak.

"I have loved you, Child, since before the foundation of the world when I planned your existence and the place you should fill in My calling for you. On the cross of Calvary, I suffered agony and abuse beyond description so that I can ransom and free you from the pit of ceaseless pain and filthy horror. Satan, the enemy of your soul is out to steal, kill, and destroy you, but I have defeated him through My death and resurrection from the grave. It is he who is using his selected people to destroy you, My precious lamb.

"Come to Me, Child, and I will give you rest in your body and soul and protect you from all the forces of evil while breaking down every unseen wall and fence so violently encased around you. I am the Lord, and I cannot fail you!"

PRAYER: Lord, it is so scary to trust, or to even think of taking one step toward Your invitation. Please, will You help me to find rest and hope, and freedom from the invisible fences? I choose to come and implore Your help, presence, and protection. I renounce every lie, threat, manipulation, and evil horror used to bind me, and I claim the blood of Jesus over each one, in Your name. Bind Satan through Your blood, Jesus, and help me to be free. Amen.

Peace, Like A River Serenely Sings

"My Child, come away with Me, resting awhile:
For I am your solace and strength for each mile;
Do not let your heart, Child, be troubled or drear:
For I am thy Lord and will always be near.
Come walking with Me, Child, beside peaceful streams,
Where you can relay to Me hopes, fears, or dreams:
For I know thy heart and each trial you face
Though burdens grow heavy, there's always more grace.

The dark, stormy clouds which you don't understand
Commit them, My Child, to My all-knowing hand:
For though lightning strikes and the thunder may roll,
I always decree what is best for your soul!
Come drink of Life's river, so tranquil and sweet
Your worries and burdens cast down at My feet:
For peace is unceasing when you yield control
And place in My hand your mind, body, and soul.

Take sweet rest, My Child, 'neath the shade of My wings,
Where peace like a river serenely now sings;
With cool waters here will I bathe your sore feet,
As you are embraced in My solace complete!
The greater the trial or burden you bear,
So grows My rich grace that is freely your share;
My strength is made perfect when you may feel weak
Brings power and courage where once all was bleak!

I fully delight and I specialize, Child,
In things thought "impossible," trying or wild;
From out of the tempest I bring peace and calm;
Midst tatters of pain, I restore healing's balm!
Rest, Child, on My bosom and make My will thine:
For your life's broad picture I see and refine;
I walk right beside you for life's journey through,
And, Child, I'm preparing bright mansions for you!"

KETURAH C. MARTIN

Come Walking With Me, Child

To have the opportunity to rest in safety under the almighty wings of God Himself is a blessed privilege indeed! Where else could one abide in such abundant safety from everything and everyone who could cause potential harm, including Satan and all his destructive forces that are out to steal, kill, and destroy?

To walk with the great Creator Himself through His creation and experience divine protection near His heart of love and under His wings is more than our human minds can truly grasp. But this is what He is offering to you as His heart yearns to enfold you and bring healing for every anguishing thing in your life.

You have great value to Him—so much that He sees you as a crown of glory and a royal diadem in His own hand! (Isaiah 62:3) When something is of great value to someone, he will go to extensive lengths to protect, cherish, and hold it. God has invested the life of His Son in you, and He will go to great lengths to keep you covered under the shadow of His wings while wrapping you in His undying love. There could be no greater love and protection to bask beneath than under the wings of the Almighty Himself as He cares for your heart. If God be for us, who can be against us?

There is no need to fear Him or worry that your past will repulse Him, for He knows it all and yet is inviting you to walk with Him, rest in Him, be protected by Him, and find new life and healing through Him.

INVITATION: My Dear Child, I invite you to come walking with Me, that we may traverse together this healing journey right to the finish line. I gave up heaven's Best, My only Son, to redeem and restore you from the ashes. Come, let us walk together over impossible mountains, across languishing rivers and through life's fiery trials that I may sustain you with My Presence, uphold you by My power, infill you with My Spirit and surround you with sufficient grace each step of the way! I am the Lord your God and cannot fail you!

PRAYER: Father in heaven, I accept Your invitation to walk with You. I want to experience the safety of being sheltered under the shadow of Your wings. If You can keep me safe and help me to be free, will You please help me and walk with me? Everything is so scary, but I want something better for my life than this prison of terror and shame. I choose to accept Your invitation to walk and learn of You. Amen.

Transformed By The Potter

The Lord is the Potter behind the great wheel;
With vast lumps of clay He in love daily deals:
Each lump He doth fashion and shape at His will,
As they remain waiting, so yielded and still.

Sometimes there's a vessel deformed or so marred—
By life's situations been broken and scarred:
Yet God never trashes these vessels of clay,
But shapes and transforms them in quite a new way.

They first must be softened through pressure and pain—
Subjected to moisture amid stormy rain;
The Lord knows the shape of each vessel He makes,
Exerting love's care for His own glory's sake.

God's hand holds the clay as the wheel spins around,
And guards it from falling away to the ground;
He shapes and He molds it precisely and clear—
Producing a vessel of honor, so dear.

The scarred, broken past of the vessel grows dim,
And now bears the touch and the image of Him
Whose daily compassions are new every morn—
The Potter Who never throws out those so torn!

The vessel now molded awaits His desire:
For He must refine it within the kiln's fire;
Though painful and trying, close by He remains—
Ensuring His strength and eternal, rich gains.

The vessel, transformed, by the Potter now stands—
The dross all consumed and refined by His hand;
So yielded and waiting for His use and praise,
To pour out His love in the future always!

KETURAH C. MARTIN

At The Potter's House

With Jeremiah, I went down to the potter's house to observe how all the different vessels are made and see the various stages of becoming a usable vessel. Off in the corner was a large bag of mucky clay, out of which the potter scooped a big handful. Fascinated I watched as the wheel whirled around and the lump of clay began to take some shape. Suddenly the potter took the half-formed vessel and reduced it to just a lump of clay again.

"Why did you do that?" I queried in a surprised voice as I became all ears and eyes.

"It was worn too thin on one side and I have to start over and make it stronger," he replied knowingly.

At that moment I noticed another bag of hard, broken, and unfinished pottery that had some water in it.

"Whatever do you keep this junk lying around for, sir?" I asked with obvious interest.

Turning, he replied a bit sharply, "Nay, my friend, you must not see those pieces as worthless junk to be tossed out and forever trashed! They are very valuable to me and will be fashioned into very usable vessels of great worth. Before I had put them through the fire, someone broke in here one night and deliberately broke those waiting to go into the fire in the morning."

"Is there actually some hope left that they can be fixed and restored to something worthwhile?" I asked unbelievingly.

"Aye, my friend, that there is," replied the potter with twinkling eye. "These broken pieces are some of my favourite projects. They remind me of my Heavenly Father Who picked up all the broken pieces of my life. He could have tossed me out to the trash bin as worthless, just as many of His people had done, but He saw value when nobody else could. With the right moisture, care, and work, this clay can be made whole, pliable, and usable again. God never gave up on me, but continued to work, heal, and restore my life out of the shambles because He saw the hidden value. I too salvage from the ruins whatever possible, just as the Master Potter has taught me."

PRAYER: Thank You, Jesus, for salvaging my life with vision and purpose to bring healing and restoration. Thank You for loving me. Amen.

Fellow Soldiers, Wounded

Life's a battle, fierce and raging—
Good and evil troops at war:
Gallant soldiers pressing forward
Midst the warfare thick and sore.

Our Commander Chief is Jesus,
To His voice we needs must hark,
If we want to claim the vict'ry—
Triumph at the finish mark!

Why do Christians shoot their wounded
Who are victims in life's fray?
How can they say Christ is in them
When they shoot and wound all day?

Why do they tread down the smitten,
Strike and gash them o'er and o'er,
Their combatants, pained and injured,
Stab and wound them yet some more?

Why are fellow-soldiers battered,
Judged and treated as the foe?
Why, though shell-shocked, does their squadron
Launch against them, strike a blow?

How can Christians toil as snipers
With their cannons, bombs and dirks?
Shooting down fellow combatants—
Their Commander's love they shirk.

When a fellow-soldier, wounded,
On life's battlefield we find—
Waste no time to solve pain's prelude,
But just show Christ's love—be kind.

KETURAH C. MARTIN

Battle On The Battlefield

As we take a somber walk out onto a foreign battlefield, what exactly might we find? The smell of death is everywhere, and there are wounded men all over the ground. Some appear to be dead, and others are in delirious pain crying out for help, while some are entrapped in the trenches. As we proceed, we come closer to the battlefront where we see men falling like flies in the name of *dying for their country.* Bloodstains are everywhere, and the sound of whistling bullets fills the air as hatred swarms thick and fast in every direction. Dead and wounded men are being carried off the battlefield on crude stretchers as commanding officers shout out the orders.

Suddenly I am horrified at what is taking place! Right before my eyes, a group of soldiers are deliberately attacking men from their own battalion of officers! I witness them stomping on a soldier's already-broken leg; shooting an additional bullet through another's already-bleeding shoulder; kicking the head of an unconscious fellow soldier, and literally killing their own countrymen. Sick at heart, I turn away, repulsed by the actions of war's heartlessness.

"Why is this happening?" I cry out to no one in particular.

Then a still, small voice replies, "My Child, this is what so often happens among the people who are called by My name. There is a war happening between good and evil, wherein Christ is the Captain and Commander of My children fighting against the devil, all his armies, and those who choose to join them. However, I have wept many tears when some of My soldiers are found wounding the wounded and destroying further those who are already bleeding and dying alone in agony. It is not the job description of My soldiers to decide whether a wounded soldier is worthy of help, hope, or healing, but only to take action to bring help, love, and support. My soldiers are all equally important, whether wounded or not, and have great value in My sight. Those who have been wounded and receive the healing I can bring them are just as useful in My kingdom, or more so, than those who have rarely received a scratch. I would that My children would always view each other through the eyes of their Commander: for with Me there is no respect of persons, nor is an abuse survivor of any less value or importance than anyone else in My kingdom."

JULY 2
READING: 1 JOHN 3 AND JOB 3:16

Live God's Love

God's shown His love so full and free,
By sending Christ for you and me—
On Calvary for us He died
To save our souls—make us His Bride.

God shed His love within our hearts,
That by His grace we may impart
Love's cheering ray to pain-filled souls,
To lift them up to Christ their Goal!

When God's great love is shown so free,
To needy ones in agony,
It brings true courage, hope, and cheer—
Assures that soul that Christ is near!

So many souls at whom pain tears,
Have never known love's tender care,
But when God's people live His love
Hurt souls are touched by Christ above!

Christ's love in us will lend a hand,
Will hear one's pain and understand;
It won't condemn or judging be—
Loves constant, unconditionally.

Let's live God's love from day to day,
Assisting souls along life's way;
Christ's love let's show to all we meet:
For love not lived is not complete!

KETURAH C. MARTIN

A Living Love

The children of God are expected by Him to be representatives of Him in daily action. To put it in simple terms, our feet become the feet of Christ, walking only to places He can bless. Jesus seemed to always be walking toward the very people and places where someone needed help or His touch of love. His feet led Him to the blind, the lepers, funeral processions, the poor and beggarly, the brokenhearted, the captives and many others in need.

Our hands are to be governed by the overruling factor of doing what Jesus would do with His hands. The hands of Jesus were nearly always busy— not doing things for His own gain, money, fame, or guarding His time, but He was out helping those in need. With His hands, He lifted the dead girl up and gave her new life; He gathered the little children near and blessed them with His words, His touch, and His presence; He helped the young man out of his coffin; and He washed His disciples' feet. In nearly every account about Him, Jesus was serving and ministering to someone, leaving each one in better condition than He found them.

Jesus did not make any pretense to avoid those who were suffering in emotional and mental agony, but nearly always made a point of gravitating to them so they could feel His healing touch of love and words of acceptance. He was never ashamed to be seen with the lepers, the outcasts of society, and those who were oppressed by demonic forces. The leaders thought He should steer clear of all such people, but they were condemned by Christ's actions of love to those who were the lowest in value according to the Jewish traditions.

Let us rise up and truly become representatives of Jesus Christ—the One who died in our place to redeem us! In order to effectively do this, we must daily ask the Lord to crucify our selfish, human nature so that Jesus can live and radiate from within. Only when self is crucified can we truly represent and live the love of Jesus in His strength!

PRAYER: Jesus, I thank You that You have left an example for us to use as a pattern to know how You want us to represent You to all with whom we come in contact. Thank You for loving the wounded, outcast, and the rejected ones who are a write-off to society. Help me to live Your love every day of my life. Amen.

Christ Gave Up His All

Christ went to Gethsemane, lonely and drear,
To seek out His Father when death loomed so near:
Forsaken by others, He went there alone—
In love He was willing my sins to atone.

He knelt before God in the gathering gloom—
Envisioned the cross and the death in the tomb;
He prayed, "Oh, My Father, take this cup from Me—
Yet not My own will, Lord, but Thine shall it be."

While there in the garden, He sweat drops of blood—
Engulfed in the anguish of man's sinful flood;
Three times He then prayed to His Father above—
Surrendered His will in His infinite love!

He yielded Himself to the soldiers, uncouth,
Yet nothing but love did proceed from His mouth;
He stood before Pilate in mockery's den—
Then death's condemnation He faced for all men.

His lifeblood He gave as He hung on the cross,
And died with the crim'nals—though death proved no loss:
For He paid our ransom to free us from death—
The world's sin He carried right to His last breath!

His body, midst sorrow, they laid in a tomb—
The earth was enshrouded in death's ghastly gloom;
Bur on the third day He burst forth from the grave:
For He conquered death and He lives now to save.

Christ gave up His "All" to redeem us from death,
He died in our place to secure living breath;
Lord Jesus, my "All" I surrender to You:
For You are my Savior eternity through!

KETURAH C. MARTIN

Alone In The Garden

When Jesus went to the Garden of Gethsemane, He went willingly because He loves all mankind enough to die in their place, and He knew His time had come. He went with His disciples (with the exception of Judas Iscariot) as they were often wont to do. As His time drew closer, Satan and all his horrid, demonic armies relentlessly attempted to get Jesus to just abandon the whole plan of giving Himself to die. Finally in the agony of the hour, Jesus went a little way off from the disciples and cried out to His Father.

There in the garden He yielded His will to the Heavenly Father as He cried out, "My Father, if it be possible, let this cup pass from Me; nevertheless, not My will but Thine be done."

Try to comprehend that He was beginning to feel heaped on Him the sins of the entire world, including before, during, and after His walk on earth. Then we can possibly get a glimpse of the horrendous load He carried in complete innocence. What a matchless and unfathomed love that would go to such degree of self-sacrifice, just to deliver sinful mankind from eternal death!

Because of all Jesus has suffered before us in our place, we now can come boldly to the throne of grace to obtain mercy and find grace to help in time of need. Heaven's storehouse of grace has a limitless supply for those who ask. We also can gain through Jesus the power to yield our wills, rights, and very lives into the hand of the Heavenly Father, just as Jesus did. The blessings that can be ours when we take this step are beyond human comprehension: for when we withhold nothing from God, He does not withhold from us! Our healing journey progresses much more speedily when our all is yielded to the Master's hands and control.

PRAYER: Lord, even though it feels so scary to relinquish everything to Your control, I want to choose to follow the example of Jesus. I choose to give You my will, life, and future and ask that You could make it into something of value to You. Thank You for loving me enough to send Jesus to die in my place, so that I can live and be healed. He sacrificed everything on my behalf, so I think I should be glad to give Him all I am or have, even though it is hardly anything. Please help me, Father, to be totally yielded to My Jesus! Amen.

Who Will Help The Children?

Do you hear the children crying
In the stillness of the night?
Stifling sobs within their pillows,
Lest some hear their dreaded plight?

Can you sense their spirits quailing
In a terror with no end
As they face the dreaded evil,
All alone without a friend?

Do you see their bodies quiver,
`Neath a load of pain untold?
Or detect their hearts' deep longing
For a loving hand to hold?

Who is willing for the Master
To go stand within the gap?
Who will offer love and safety
In the place of pain and slaps?

Who will break the solemn silence
Behind which the guilty hide?
And speak up for all the children,
Before some more have died?

Who will stand up for the children,
And midst terror hold their hand?
Who will span the gap for Jesus?
Break the silence in this land!

For my Jesus loves the children—
To each one His love imparts,
He has said we must be like them,
As He holds them to His heart.

KETURAH C. MARTIN

End The Deafening Silence

The enemy of our soul is as a roaring lion, seeking to devour whomever he can get his clutches on (1 Peter 5:8). Satan is very crafty and does not necessarily always pounce on his prey and immediately devour them in a few big, juicy bites. Rather, as "the father of lies," he will subtly get his potential prey sidetracked from pressing on in the narrow way by what may seem to be simply "stopping to look" at something he points out to observe. However, one can be sure he will always have some type of trap hidden which will spring without warning.

The devil's destructions against his prey very often begin with injections of camouflaged poisons into the mind where he attempts to either create a war zone or to build a stronghold through his subtle lies and deadly influence. He brainwashes his pawns to believe it is okay to molest or play around with that child in order to have a little fun, and in the end, lives are destroyed.

- It is Satan, the enemy of God, who convinces even God's people to keep silence about the horrific abuses going on behind closed doors.
- The devil has no heart to care how the little children and innocent suffer at his instigation through the adults he has deceived.
- Satan, in fact, loves to see the children suffer, in hopes that he can gain a foothold in the early years, which will give him some access to them in later years when he is least expected.
- It is the enemy who glosses over the despicable crimes of rape, domestic violence, human trafficking, and every other abuse and gets responsible citizens and even the church to turn a blind eye to the crying children and survivors.
- The enemy is the one who persuades church leaders to just sweep that unmentionable thing under the carpet so the whole church won't know and/or look bad to the community, while the children suffer.
- Satan is the instigator of convincing God's people that it is okay to turn away the brokenhearted and abused and/or refuse to help them, regardless of Jesus' teaching, example, and commandment.
- The enemy of God wants all those with sealed lips to remain quiet and continue the cover-up. But we will help and speak for the children!

Because Jesus Lives!

Because my Redeemer has died and now lives,
He's there to sustain me as power He gives;
The road up ahead He has charted for me—
Permits only that which His plan doth foresee.

Because Jesus lives, each new day I can face:
Each morn dawns accompanied with His sweet grace;
His life-giving power surrounds from on high—
Enabling vict'ry, despite what comes nigh.

Because Jesus lives, there is healing from pain,
And life that's eternal with heavenly gains;
There's help for the wounded and sight for the blind—
Supplies for all needs in our Savior we find!

When Jesus is Lord of our life and our All,
He walks right beside us and answers each call;
In Him, more than conquerors, now we can be,
Because Jesus triumphed in full victory!

Should Christ not have risen, all hope would be gone,
And vanquished forever our spiritual dawn;
Our faith would be vain and sure death be our fate—
Had our dear Redeemer not burst from death's gate!

But thanks be to God, Who through Christ can now give
His children full vict'ry, in triumph to live
Above sin's defeat and the bondage of death—
In Jesus our Savior we have living breath!

KETURAH C. MARTIN

Jesus Meets Me In The Garden

In the quiet of the morning, e'er breaks the dawning day,
I then meet my blessed Savior where roses bloom always;
Jesus meets me in His garden near lilies fair and bright:
For each morn He bids me enter to fellowship in light.
My Lord offers golden nuggets, derived from Holy Writ—
With each truth comes rainbow promise, with which His love is knit;
While beneath the rainbow's shadow, we have fellowship so sweet,
I gain strength in dear communion while sitting at His feet.
As we kneel beside the brooklet on dewy slopes of prayer,
Hand in hand we talk together, my longings with Him share:
"Oh my Lord, please draw me closer to heartbeats of Thy love,
That I may be lost in Jesus, extolling Thee above."
We discuss, among the roses, just what He's planned for me:
He explains, in tones so kindly, divine necessity,
That I must go through the fire to fit His perfect plan,
And assures of grace sufficient, though I don't understand.
As He plucks a rose of splendor and brings its petals near,
He reveals exquisite beauty and shows me truth so dear;
"The new life and fragrant beauty of this My chosen rose
Must first push beyond the briars before it blooms and glows;
So, My Child, despite thorned pathways where briars pierced thy soul—
Though pain's brambles oft encase thee—for thee I have a goal;
In My love I have preserved thee, My chosen Child and prize:
For I know My plans to thee-ward, which vision never dies.
Midst adversity's pained pathway, I've held thee in My hand,
Down the vales of anguished sorrow, My hosts with thee did band;
Through the floods of vast destruction, in love I held My child:
For I see the bigger picture, despite the tempests wild.
Tho' dark thorns have stemmed thy pathway and worse than death you've faced,
My dear child I've not forgotten, but send to thee much grace;
I've been pruning and refining midst darkest circumstance,
That true growth may be forthcoming and inner life enhanced.
My Child, push beyond the briars by My own strength and might:
For I seek to make a vessel through which I shine My light—
My own vessel, tried and proven, restored by grace divine,
Through whom I can touch the hurting and cause new hope to shine!"

READING: 1 SAMUEL 15:29 AND MATTHEW 19:26

Promises And Realities To Remember

1. "God specializes in things thought impossible."

2. "She/he that cometh to Me I will in no wise cast out."

3. "God is not a man that He should lie, nor the Son of man that He should repent."

4. "Doubt, unbelief, and lack of trust in God and His Word will result in a barricaded healing experience. Truth cannot be personally fully applied when these obstacles are present, whether known or unknown." (Psalm 62:8)

5. Anything of occultic origin in your life or your ancestors' will give Satan a back-door access into your life if it is not completely abolished through the blood and power of Jesus to the tenth generation.

6. Pain, affliction, and hardship become blessed tools in the hand of Jesus when we surrender it all into His control along with our will, life, and future.

7. "God will never waste your pain, but longs to use it to build you into a vessel of honour for His use and glory when you choose to place it back into His hand."

8. Satan is 100 percent defeated by Jesus, and there are more with us than with the enemy who wages war against us. We need not fear our foe when Christ is by our side.

9. We do not fight for victory in the spiritual war, but we fight from the victory that has already been won by Jesus Christ our Commander. Because of Jesus, we need only to claim His victory, blood, and power by faith.

10. "One pebble at a time, your insurmountable pain and past can be addressed and resolved, for with God nothing is impossible!"

Jesus said, "Behold, I give you power to tread on serpents and scorpions, and over all the power of the enemy; and nothing shall by any means hurt you" (Luke 10:19).

Lord, Why Must I Sup?

"Lord, why must affliction be here in my cup?
Dear Lord, it's so bitter, just why must I sup?
My heart is so anguished and can't understand—
Is suffering, Lord, what for me You have planned?

Lord, help me and guide me each step of the way;
Midst tears and vast sorrow, give grace for each day:
For I am so burdened, and strength I have none—
Lord, give me Your power—may Thy will be done!"

"My Child, I have bought thee and called thee by name;
My grace all-sufficient is each day the same.
I know of thy heartache—the pain in thy cross:
Affliction and sorrow shall not prove a loss.

As gold in the fire is proven and tried,
My children midst suff'ring are drawn to My side;
My arms everlasting abide under you—
Affliction's great fire, My grace sees you through!

Child, suff'ring's dark waters around thee may roll,
But I am thy Father, and I keep thy soul:
Thy hand I am holding—My strength is untold;
My children, refined, shall come forth as pure gold!"

PRAYER: Lord, I choose to yield all the pain and pieces to Your divine hand. I ask You to heal, restore and refine every broken piece of my heart so You can help me become a vessel of honour for Your glory. Amen.

Alone, Unlovely, But Preserved

Twelve-year-old Jana loved to be outdoors where the towering mountains always stayed the same, though everything within or around her might change or be so painful. Jana did not like herself very much because several times every day she had those horrible things her mom called epileptic seizures. They felt really scary inside just before everything would go black and she'd fall down into unconsciousness. No matter where she was or what she was doing, when a seizure came she would always fall in a heap of nothingness.

At the new Christian school, the children would laugh at her when she collapsed. Whenever she entered the room, everyone found some excuse to walk away. By now Jana believed that she was very, very bad because of all the seizures every day, which made her too despicable to own a friend.

The calves in her dad's dairy barn became her very best friends, and they always gave her a loud welcome. Often she would lie down on the straw beside them and soak up all the love and acceptance possible.

One day after getting a dose of love from the calves, Jana climbed the hay pile inside the barn loft. Sticking her head out an opening at the top, Jana looked down at the beauty of the valley and up at the splendor of the Rockies. Climbing out, she walked all along the top of the round-roof barn, which was one hundred feet long. Suddenly she felt a seizure coming on, but only had time to sit down on top of the round roof. Usually she went unconscious in five seconds after feeling this.

"Oh God, please keep me safe!" breathed the terrified girl from her lonely heart. Any second she expected to roll off the barn roof, unconscious, to her death below.

Ecstatically, she suddenly realized that God had heard her prayer and kept her from falling to her death! He obviously cared more about her than anyone else, except maybe the calves!

"I can't be a perfect or loved girl with these seizures," thought Jana "but maybe it doesn't matter to God!" He will take every moment of suffering, every stab of rejection and every heart shred of agony and transform it all into strands of pure gold in your life weavings. When the heavenly Father is in charge of our broken tatters and anguish, then the plans of the enemy are thwarted and a life is redeemed from destruction.

God uses broken people, likely more than those who seem perfect. Hardship, pain, and affliction prepare us for a higher calling in the plan of a loving Father.

KETURAH C. MARTIN

Destruction So Vast

The great devastation of earthquakes behold,
Where panic and terror midst death do unfold;
The earthquake results are so deadly and grim—
So many have perished, or been torn limb to limb.
The city and buildings have crumbled like dust,
Encasing their victims in doom's deadly crust;
The pleas of the trapped could at one point be heard,
But if rescue came not, their hope was deferred.
Just so the reality looms ever near,
Within the survivors of earthquakes right here,
Where violence, domestic, destroyed to the core
And victims were shattered midst crime's deadly gore.
Emotions are massacred—just left to die,
Amid pain so deep that the heart always cries;
The stench of filth's shame is revoltingly near,
But yet there's no rescue, despite death and fear.
The heart torn to shreds and pierced violently through
Is cast on death's heap 'cause none know what to do;
Though many pass by on the far side of road,
Is there not just one who will help lift death's load?
Avoiding reality spells out sure fate—
Intensifies suff'ring that no soul can rate,
It shackles survivors in chains of dark doom,
While writhing in anguish within death's lone tomb.
Survival is downtrod, condemned is the pain,
As Levites and throngs from the wounded abstain;
The darts of the judging are hurled through the heart,
And rivers of tears seem will never depart.
Survivors can never pretend all is healed
Though heart-shreds throb deeper than knowledge or field—
When pain is condemned and they're told, "Move along"
The anguish increases and just grows more strong.
Let's lift up the wounded—support midst pain's load
Assist with the aftermath, throwing down goads:
For we can't afford to just blindly pass by,
But, with Christ the Master, must heed each pained cry!

Bringing To God
Domestic Violence And Aftermath

"Lord, You know how it seems impossible to love and accept myself, and it also seems that nobody else has been able to either. Can you please teach me why this is and how to love, accept, and see myself through Your eyes?"

"I knew and planned you before the foundation of the world for a definite purpose that no one else can fill. Your value is so high that My only Son died in your place, and I accept you completely through His shed blood."

"Lord, why did so many Christians, criminals, and my husband abuse, reject, and destroy me if there is anything of value in me? Can You show me if I have done any wrong to any of them?"

"The internal damage caused to you through the choices of others since you were in the womb was neither known nor understood, nor could anyone understand the life-threatening implications of the medical conditions. Rejection and abuse resulted because My love and understanding was not sought after, but human reasoning, control, lust, and/or power prevailed."

"Lord, how can I love something that is unlovable?"

"I can see what you've come through, where I'm taking you, and My plans for you; and I see what you are in and through Jesus. Most of what you see and feel is the dirty, rejected, and pained shambles of what people did to you. You must look at what Christ did for you and is working in you, and finally what I seek to accomplish through you by Christ Jesus."

"Lord, what do You want me to do with the dirty, rejected shambles and ceaseless pain caused from what was done to me?"

"Jesus, the Great Physician, shed His blood for you that by it He might cleanse, heal, and restore you in soul, body, and mind. Bring the painful filth, rejection, and inner destructions to Him, along with all that I show you, and I will heal and transform you into a vessel of honour for My glory. What the enemy purposes and inflicts for evil, I can turn into your good and My glory, with a blessing. But you must surrender completely to My control the mangled womanhood, the pain, and all the effects of everything that you have experienced."

PRAYER: Lord Jesus, I choose to surrender to You and Your transforming hand, all my mangled past and the pain of my life experiences so You can turn it all around for Your glory and use it to exalt Your love and power throughout the earth. Amen.

Adversity Yielded

Affliction's dark waters by God are allowed—
The load may be heavy, the heart pained and bowed,
But God sees our lives from beginning to end,
Allowing those things which will beautiful blend.

The flesh would recoil from the pain and distress
Of this my affliction, its anguish and mess;
Infirmities seem to be cheerless and grim,
But God has rich blessings to spill from the brim.

Come kneel before Jesus and yield Him your load:
Adversity's briars, and thorns on your road,
The boulders of anguish, the pangs of deep grief—
The Greatest Physician can bring full relief!

Infirmities yielded of service can be,
As God's grace sufficient we faithfully see,
Assured that His power and love knows no bounds—
With strength He uplifts as His presence surrounds.

When all your adversity's yielded complete—
Surrendered, you wait at the Master's dear feet;
He then begins weaving the dark strands so grim,
To make something useful that glorifies Him.

The dark pain He blends with a beautiful gold,
Whose value, eternal, can never be told:
For when we in triumph pass through heaven's gate,
Earth's pain will be nothing—our joy none can rate!

And there before Jesus our past fades away,
As with Him we enter eternal life's day—
As joint heirs with Jesus forever we'll be
The Lord's sons and daughters, in heaven so free!

Unnoticed Diamonds

How can one ever truly look at affliction, pain, hardship, and/or abuse and find a way to in any manner have a willingness to be grateful? The human flesh literally recoils from hardship and any sort of trial or pain.

Just as a young tree grows stronger through winds, drought, and adverse surroundings, so we also need something more than sublime conditions if we are to mature into the image of Christ. Jesus suffered more than our human mind can comprehend, and He is completely sinless and perfect.

In order to be able to get to the place that we can be grateful for hardship, we must come before our Heavenly Father and totally yield our rights and our will into His hand and choose to make His will our very own. Although God never condones or instigates abuse, yet if evil men choose to go against His will, it then becomes God's will to use the experience in the survivor's life as a means to defeat the enemy in his own game. This can only happen if we are willing to surrender the horrors and painful effects of it to Jesus.

In all reality, a trial is the creative pressure that the Lord uses to form diamonds on one's heart. The degree of pressure or pain used may be a good indicator of the size of the diamond He is forming. He takes painstaking time and effort to produce exactly what He sees best and of most value, even though we may not understand. However, if we resist His work, the pressure/pain involved, and His divine plan, then He cannot work freely as He desires, for He never forces Himself. Some of the most beautiful diamonds in the world are found only after extensive chiseling away of the exterior matter all around it. Yielding to the blade of the chisel in the hand of the Master is of utmost importance if the true value is to come to the light or surface.

We are all diamonds in the rough, but in order for the true beauty to come out so it can glorify God, we must be willing and yielded to endure the painful chiseling and refining process with the endowment of the grace of God.

PRAYER: Lord, it doesn't feel very good to experience this pain and hardship, but I choose to trust that You know what You are doing. I choose against my flesh to embrace this cross, endure the pain, and to yield myself and the entire experience into Your hand and divine will. Please help me and give me the strength I need, dear Jesus. Amen.

KETURAH C. MARTIN

The Great Losses Involved

When one must depart from a spouse that's untrue,
That she might be safe and begin life anew,
Should one need escape dread abuse and vile shame,
By then she's so torn she may know just her name.
A partner is gone, though unfaithful was he—
A home is now broken, as all our lives be—
The grief wives encounter when such is the case,
Is greater by far than had death shown its face.
The loss of great magnitude none understand,
Is that she knows nothing of God's marriage band—
She knows not the love of a husband that's true,
But just death's control and abuse was her due.
She knows not a trust which is free from alarm—
Not knowing when children would feel deadly harm—
To be under care of protection so true,
Is something so foreign, and which she never knew.
The children know naught of a father's true love,
And mangled are concepts of God up above—
In agonized plight is the wife left alone
To fix broken children, so pained and more prone.
The wife in such cases has not the first clue
Just what it could mean to be cherished anew:
For worth was molested—from her fully torn,
As daily abuse made a shell so forlorn.
She has no provider for food or for clothes—
No shelter called "home," though the wild winter blows—
Though all of life's needs were restricted before,
Yet obviously now it is just a closed door.
To her it is only a tale that's untold
That husbands, to some, are companions of gold:
Experience taught her midst pain, filth, and death,
That he has control of her down to each breath.
The losses are greater than herein portrayed,
While inner destruction is writhing and frayed;
Yet God sees it all and my Husband is He—
He fathers my children and stands beside me!

Needed: Divine Strength And Intervention

The message contained on this page is specifically for anyone who, in order to remain in the land of living, had to be physically removed from an abusive spouse. It is also for those who are infused with enough of the love of Jesus that they are willing to help the fatherless and what is far worse than being a widow.

Regardless how abused or destroyed one may be in the deadly scenes of domestic violence, there is never any Scriptural reason for either divorce or remarriage. (See Mark 10:11, 12; Matthew 19:8, 9; Luke16:18; Mark 10:2-9; 1 Corinthians 7:10, 11;) According to 1 Corinthians 7:10 and 11, God in His all-knowing wisdom knew that there would be some cases in fallen humanity where the abuse and suffering would be so severe that an escape route would be necessary in order to survive. If there are differences, disconnections, and disputes in marriage, God desires that every possible avenue to reconcile be pursued and that everyone involved come under the God-ordained headship order as He defines it. If, after extensive attempts to bring peace and wholeness, life and safety are still at stake, God steps in to become the unfailing Husband, Protector, and Provider for the abandoned, abused, and/or destroyed woman. He becomes a Father to the fatherless.

When separation due to violence becomes necessary, it is far more devastating than if one's loving spouse had suddenly died. Death, despite the grief and loss, is more final than to be in a shattered state of agony. Often the survivor is also left with broken, abused children that need extensive assistance to work through their emotional destruction, in addition to her own remaining tatters. When someone is abused by the one whom God commanded to love his wife as Christ loved the church (Ephesians 5:25), the consequent demolitions and emotional excruciations are incomprehensible, but God is faithful.

PRAYER: Lord, I choose to forgive and release _____ for _____, and I ask You to take back all the ground in me that Satan may have gained through bitterness. I yield that ground to Your control, Jesus. Please will You be my Husband and a Father to my children? Please provide for us and keep us safe and in Your will. Amen.

Abolish Slavery

To be a slave I cannot dare, and must avoid its deadly snare—
An Abolitionist I'll be, and do away with slavery.
And I can never dare to stoop to hatred, or its bitter soup:
For then I'm choosing readily another man's own slave to be.

And I must always cast aside the bread of bitterness that's dried:
For just a crumb could poison me, and chain me as a slave, not free.
That tantalizing malice spread must not be buttered on my bread:
For that, too, seals my binding fate—enslaved in bondage none can rate.

The pastry that may look so nice, but binds one fast, as cold as ice
Is clanking unforgiveness chains, which makes real slaves and has no gains.
The slave owner just stalks around and preys on those who could be bound;
The overseers capture all who in their cruel clutches fall.

The bloodhounds sniff out every scent—ferocious frenzy oft will vent
When some poor soul from slavery flees through Jesus Christ escapes so free!
Old Satan owns the slaves (he thinks), but he's defeated—on death's brink;
And we can choose his slavery, or else a life in Jesus, free!

For Jesus bought us by His blood, so He could free us through that flood;
Let's not succumb to slavery, but choose forgiveness, love so free!
Forgiveness choices free us up, despite what pain is in our cup;
It places All within God's hand, Who in this choice by us will stand!

If we will dare to even taste a crumb of bitterness in haste,
We could be spelling our own doom and end in dark destruction's tomb:
Each day we must make conscious choice—forgive abusers in love's voice:
For Jesus taught us to forgive, and so we must if we would live!

Slavery Of Unforgiveness

To be abused and ultimately destroyed—whether physically, emotionally, sexually, spiritually, etc.—our human nature would see forgiveness as the last thing one would *feel* like doing. When violent abuse was so extreme that lives were being threatened or even lost, forgiving seems even more impossible.

However, something needs to be clearly understood by all, especially those surviving abuse. When we insist on hanging onto our right to remain bitter, angry, hateful, and revengeful toward the perpetrator, we are shooting ourselves in the foot and crippling all future healing and progress. Furthermore, we are willingly subjecting ourselves to the position of "slave," with the perpetrator becoming our slave owner! Why would any wounded person desire to remain in captivity to the very one who has deliberately caused so much inner agony and lifelong destructions?

Bitterness and unforgiveness, regardless of the offense, will eat one up from the inside out until there is nothing left in life but death. It is one of the most-used tools which the enemy attempts to launch against all who have innocently suffered the throes of agonizing abuse. Once his planted seed of unforgiveness takes root, it is only the power of the blood of Jesus that can fully reverse the damage and bring true freedom from these chains of slavery.

Bitterness brings with it no benefits and consumes the chained slave in life-long regrets. The imprisonment it brings to those who choose to remain bitter is a deadly cell of their own making, for Jesus set the example of forgiveness in its truest sense. It is Jesus alone Who can break these unforgiveness chains!

PRAYER: Lord Jesus, I choose to forgive and release _____ into Your hand, and I renounce every binding fetter of bitter unforgiveness in the name of Jesus. I ask You, Jesus, to take back all the ground Satan gained in me through my bitterness and take complete control of that ground. Jesus, please give me the same love You had for Your abusers when they nailed You to the cross. Amen.

Supporting Survivors

"Dear soul, if you're willing, it's all in your hand
To bear up the hurting and help them to stand,
Though you have not been there, you still can be used,
To minister love to the hurt and abused.
The greatest necessity with which to start—
Is validate all that has crushed the pained heart,
No matter how gruesome, how shocking or torn—
Accredit all details of each abuse borne.
The second importance which must be in place,
Before one can share the abuse and disgrace,
Is knowing for sure that you're trusted and true—
Assured all they share will stay strictly with you:
For they have been battered, betrayed, and denied—
Their trust is more shattered than what can confide,
Thus friends, confidential, is always "a must,"
Or hope, help, and safety will turn to pained dust!
Despite what you hear, don't stoop ever so low,
That midst intense pain, you some pity bestow:
For pity repulses and goes just skin deep—
A band-aid so dirty and ever so cheap!
Don't offer 'solutions' or 'fixes' so quick:
For you're not a doctor, nor are they the sick;
Take time when they're struggling to lend them your ear,
And give them your shoulder to soak up the tears;
Refrain from all judgments and using of goads—
Such billy-clubs only increase their pained loads;
Stop short, friend! Go walk in their boots for a mile—
And seek divine love, lest assumptions compile.
If ever in doubt about how to relate,
Assistance from Christ always seek at prayer's gate;
Think, speak, and live love just as Jesus would do,
And treat each survivor as if they were you!"

How Would Jesus Treat The Abused?

Jesus said, "Verily I say unto you, inasmuch as ye did it not unto one of the least of these, ye did it not to Me."

Often it is easier to gain a correct perspective and make a God-centered choice when we ask ourselves, "What would Jesus do if He were here in my shoes?" Since Jesus also suffered abuse of every nature, how do you suppose He would respond in the following scenarios?

- ✓ Rounding the corner in an alley, Jesus comes upon a five-year-old girl being brutally raped and beaten. *Would Jesus help and defend the helpless or just walk away and keep everything hush-hush?*
- ✓ Every night three scared little boys are found hanging in the balance at the supper table, as their dad attempts to make a reason why he can beat them and assert his authority or control. *Would Jesus say, "Oh, that is a real manly thing to do and you have My blessing"; or would He take steps to ensure that safety and protection come into place?*
- ✓ Jesus is entrusted by His Father to shepherd a church group. When an abused single mom and her broken children begin to attend this church, co-leaders advise to keep them at arm's length, invalidate what they have survived, and harshly reprimand them for not just forgiving, forgetting, and pushing everything else out of sight so all looks great. *Would Jesus follow the counsel of such input or would He bind up the brokenhearted in love?*
- ✓ An eleven-month-old baby is being beaten because she is expected to be quiet, and the perpetrator has vowed he won't stop until she does. She is becoming black, blue, and purple all over. *Would Jesus rescue the helpless and innocent, or would He say, "Sure, go ahead and do whatever it takes to break her will"?*
- ✓ Every night and throughout the night, a wife is expected to become a robotic sex toy for her husband while he violently gratifies his lust at her painful expense. Failure to be as a lamb in the paw of a wolf results in children being abused. *Would Jesus support treating a woman in such a circumstance in a way that he would actively encourage this treatment, or would He intervene and help make rescue possible?*

Cont.

Jesus expects us to support, assist, validate, and bind up the brokenhearted just as He did. Just because one cannot personally understand the depth of suffering someone has survived is no reason to discredit the happening or sweep it under the carpet. He will hold each of us accountable about how we represented Him and His love to the bruised, abused, and brokenhearted. What will you do with the wounded ones He brings to you?

Borne On The Wings Of God

In waste and howling wilderness—in desert land so dry,
The Lord looked down and found me, when He heard my desperate cry:
For all my life was barren, 'twas so wretched and alone—
I writhed in livid anguish, to dark danger, oh, so prone.
In love unknown He led me and instructed me each day,
Though sandstorms howled around me, yet He kept me all the way;
He guided me through trial and amid pain's darkening sky—
Within His hand He kept me as the apple of His eye!
As eagles stir their nest up and then flutter over young,
So God is watching o'er me—all my life on Him I've flung;
He flutters gently o'er me as He keeps me safe from harm,
Though storms may howl about me, I am shielded by His arm.

And when the night is raging with great pain and grief intense,
My loving God is near me and He spreads His wings immense;
He bears me on His wingspread far above the world below,
And carries me midst trial and through anguish none can know.

When soaring with the eagles, there upon the wings of God,
I'm safely kept from evil—from the devil's darts and prod:
For though the storms may gather and through trials dark I go,
The Rock of my Salvation will use all that I may grow.
When I am gently borne up in true love on wings of God,
Despite what hardships gather, He is there with staff and rod
To comfort, guide, protect me, and to fly me safely through:
He sees the fullest picture: for He sees beyond my view!
If I can find my refuge safe beneath the wings of God,
And feel His wings a-flutter amid lush or barren sod,
If He shall bear me safely on His wings of greatest love—
Though hell may try to shake me, I have got the Lord above!

KETURAH C. MARTIN

A Guiding Hand

In such an immense world with millions of people, why would the God of heaven take the time to worry about a little girl who was struggling all alone in a wilderness of abuse and rejection? Crying out to God for help, love, and acceptance since she was eleven years old, she hardly knew if that big God up in the sky had time for such *an insignificant thing as herself.* But what Sylvia did not realize is that the Lord of heaven and earth had cast His eye on her long before her birth and had a specific plan for her.

He kept, guided, and carried her through what at times was worse than death, always standing between her and the attempts of the enemy to destroy this chosen vessel He wanted to work through. But Sylvia could not see what all was happening behind the scenes while the hand of God preserved her. Had she been given just one glimpse of how lovingly God always preserved and sustained her very life amid unspeakable abuse and 24/7 physical affliction, she would have leaped for joy despite it all. But it was only years later after surviving abundant and additional trauma/abuse that God helped her to see through the glass more clearly.

Many times along the pathway to healing, the pain, terror, or flashbacks may be so severe or continuous that, in our basic attempts to just get through the day in one piece, we do not realize the power and presence of a guiding hand. It is in these times when we can barely put a foot in front of the other that God steps in, picks us up, and carries us for a while. He knows exactly how much His child can bear and fortifies her with strength and grace just step by step. Each step taken with the Master is one step closer home! And when He is by our side, no evil can touch us because the power and love of God by far surpasses all the evil of the world. To walk the healing path with God turns anguish into diamonds, crying into rainbows, and terror into trust! To attempt the journey without His divine healing and guidance is to take matters into our own hands because we think we know better and can make it on our own. This latter choice can potentially lead us down roads of unwanted regrets and additional ruins.

Prayer: Jesus, I choose to invite You to be my Guide and constant Companion throughout this healing journey. I renounce the lie that I can do it myself, and I announce that it is only with You that complete healing is possible to the fullest degree, with blessings to top it off! Thank You, Jesus. Amen.

Eternity In View

Each second of time that is given to you
Is grace from above midst eternity's view;
Let's use ev'ry moment of God-given time
To build for eternity in heaven's clime.

Most live for the present and view not beyond,
But place their main hope in their stocks, gold, and bonds;
They try not to think what will lie beyond death,
And live for the moment of each current breath.

The heart of the Lord is now writhing in pain,
As He views the millions that live in disdain
Of all the provisions through Jesus He made—
So many reject it as time daily fades.

Each day there are hundreds who fall o'er time's brink—
In Christ-less eternity, doomed they do sink,
For them, time is over—all chance is now gone
To make preparation for eternal dawn.

The Father's heart urges His children alway,
"Go tell the lost world that My own Son did pay
The price for their ransom from eternal death,
And riches in glory through Him are bequeathed

To all who accept the provisions I've made,
And trust in Christ's blood which for all sin was paid:
For Jesus alone is the Way, Truth, and Life—
He purchased redemption from hell's endless strife."

KETURAH C. MARTIN

How Do We View Eternity?

Unless they are 100 percent certain of where they will spend eternity, most people do not like to think about what happens after death. However, we need not be fretting and stewing about eternity until it gets here (unless we are unprepared), but we must be up and working while there is still time. The most important question we will ever benefit most from by preparing for it properly is *"Where will you spend eternity?"*

Once this question is answered and settled through Jesus Christ, we need to look further regarding our responsibility, especially toward those who are suffering and needing a lift. Just as Jesus had an undying passion about touching as many lives for eternity as possible, so we too need to be consumed with the yearning to be representing Him correctly to those with whom we come in contact. If our loving Master Who came to heal the brokenhearted, set captives free, and purchase salvation for all is not represented correctly to the teeming masses of hurting people, then there is obviously someone else's agenda standing between them and His love. He holds us accountable for misrepresenting His unconditional love.

- If Jesus would stand in our shoes to choose, would He stop to help the wounded, or would He pass by on the other side for fear of who might see?
- Would Jesus rescue and protect a battered little boy, or would He commend and justify the one abusing him?
- If Jesus, as Shepherd of the church, were allowed to shepherd the flock, would He make the widow and fatherless to remain on the outside looking in because they have been through too much, or would He treat them in love and on equal grounds?
- Would Jesus seek to bring healing to a wounded heart, or would He prefer to sweep everything away from the public eye and live in deception and pretense?

PRAYER: Jesus, please help me to live each day in the light of eternity. Forgive me if I have misrepresented Your love to any. I choose to forgive and release anyone who has not represented You as You really are. Please bring me complete healing through Your love, blood, and power and for Your glory. Amen.

He Healeth The Broken In Heart

In darkness and anguish a broken heart lay,
'Twas uselessly shattered—a vessel of clay:
Discarded and downtrod, just left there to die,
But Jesus in love with a purpose passed by.

"This life that the enemy tried to destroy,
I made for a purpose, for My praise and joy."
In love, so divine, then the Savior bent down,
And tenderly gathered each piece off the ground.

Although you feel hopelessly broken My Child,
I've come to restore you from all that's defiled—
The things which to you may impossible seem
The blood of Christ Jesus can fully redeem!

He poured out His love as each piece He retrieved—
Each one He washed fully as each He received:
Submerging them all in His healing divine
While graciously saying, "You, Child, are all Mine,"

The pieces all yielded, and now in His hand,
He shaped and restored to fit in His great plan:
A vessel of honor, united to be,
Of use to the Master, as He best shall see.

He healeth the bruised and the broken in heart,
He's there to uphold when the teardrops may start;
A life fully shattered, a heart bleeding sore,
My Jesus has power and love to restore!

KETURAH C. MARTIN

God's Love Letter To The Broken

"Before the foundation of the world I have planned, loved, and chosen you. Even though you may feel you do not know Me very well or at all, yet I know you, My Child, in an intricate way.

"Even the very number of hairs in your head are all numbered, and every member of your body in My book has been written. Because you are a part of My crowning creation and thus fashioned in My own image, therefore the devil does all he can to destroy you so he can get back at Me. But you are precious in My sight, and I keep you as the apple of My eye. The bounds that I have set around you prohibit anyone from going past My decree. When something adverse does happen, that is when I am holding you up and carrying you through, My prize and joy.

"When you may experience times of discouragement, flee to My arms for rest and solace, for I understand your mortal state. Even though you may not see or understand how the pieces of a broken heart and life can become a weaving of gold in My hand, yet I ask you to trust that part to Me as your Lord. I see the full picture and purpose before I have even begun, and I have a plan to use the broken pieces in a way which will glorify My name in all the earth.

"My love for you will never fail, dear Child, and I will never leave or forsake you. When the war of the enemy you feel, I want you to forever remember that his fight against Me to reclaim you will go on until I receive you into My very arms in glory. But there are far more with you than is with him, for he is defeated and doomed by the blood of the Lamb. My love will never let you go, and as you abide in Me, you are protected from the power of the enemy.

"Rest daily in My arms of love, dear Child, as I lead you safely through the refining and restoration process. You are Mine and I am yours, My precious Child!"

PRAYER: Thank You, Lord, for loving me, rescuing me, restoring me, and protecting me! Thank You for understanding and preserving the broken heart-shreds of my life, and I am so grateful that You can make something of value to Yourself with all the broken pieces. I surrender it all into Your divine hand. Amen.

JULY 29
READING: 2 CORINTHIANS 9:8

Strands Of Pain Bring Gain

The road up ahead may so oft appear drear,
With no open door which is handy or near,
Yet God is our Light and will show us the way—
If we will but choose to believe and obey.

Just take a step forward, your eyes fixed on Him:
For He'll surely guide you, though life's bright or dim—
The doors which appear to be shut, locked, and barred,
By God can be opened—with Him naught's too hard!

Commit to the Lord all you don't understand—
Each trial that comes as allowed by His hand;
The throbbing afflictions which may beset sore,
Surrender to Jesus right down to the core:

For He understands every tear that you cry—
His heart throbs with yours when you question, "Lord, why?"
How deeply He yearns to take your entire load—
Walk with you each step down this long, painful road.

His grace all-sufficiently showers each day,
To keep you so true despite what comes your way;
When days are the darkest and pain most intense,
The Lord holds you safely—your Rock and Defense!

The Master is weaving the strands of deep pain,
Which none comprehend, and where ne'er is seen gain;
Rich gold He can see from the upper-side view,
As gains so eternal He's working in you!

So do not lose heart though the way seems so long:
For Christ walks beside you to keep each step strong;
You'll praise Him unceasing for all of earth's pain
When heaven's bright shore you at last shall attain!

KETURAH C. MARTIN

The Lord's Storehouse

Despite what we are faced with, what we have been through, or what cross we may be called to carry, God is always faithful. When the time comes to meet our need, affliction, or deepest pain, the Lord does not stop to look at what kind of resources we have to meet the need. Rather He goes directly to His own divine resources in the heavenly realms. His riches in glory by far exceed anything our finite minds can even begin to comprehend.

Is it any wonder that we as humans often tend to view our plight as impossible, the cross unbearable, or the mountains impassable? It is because we can only see from our limited human standpoint and current pain. Humanly speaking, we do not have even a fraction of what it takes to get through some of the experiences or situations many of us may face. But God is not worried, for His Father heart knows that He has far more supply than we could ever use in a million lifetimes, and still there would be more!

His storehouse is exhaustless, His grace without limits, His love without measure, and His riches are guaranteed to never go bankrupt!

Why would we ever attempt on our own resources to get through our pain, affliction, or the devastating aftermath of the atrocities committed against us? The Lord has far more than we will ever need to get through or find complete healing, restoration, and peaceful purpose without measure!

Often the enemy of our soul is the one who attempts to get us to take our eyes off Christ and what He is waiting to pour out on us. He doesn't want us to tap into the heavenly resources or his hideous job becomes more difficult. His every lie, fear, and obstruction must be renounced as we claim the free and exhaustless riches of Jesus.

PRAYER: Lord, I never knew that You had so much in Your storehouse, just waiting to pour out on me! I renounce every lie and obstruction that the enemy uses to barricade my access to what You have to offer, and I claim Your love, grace, and measureless resources for my life and needs. Whatever I need to fix my broken life and heart, I ask that You would supply that from Your storehouse of love and mercy through Jesus Christ. Amen.

The Potter Of Pained Hearts

My pained, broken heart before Jesus was brought:
For He in compassion the ruins had sought;
The Master of potters beheld its crushed state—
So shattered in anguish, which no soul could rate.
My heart was so uselessly broken and cracked,
That His divine love could not fill up what lacked:
For often had pain lashed its cruel, heartless whip,
Which left wounds and cracks as destruction did sip.
The Master wept long and knew what He must do
Before He could heal and restore my life new—
He looked in my eyes and said, "Child, don't forget
That I have a plan—I'm not done with you yet.
The pain you endure, with My beauty I'll blend,
Enhancing My purpose and plan in the end,"
He then raised the hammer of circumstance grim—
Allowing pained blows which made life grow more dim . . .
Until my crushed heart lay in powder so still,
Subjected in full to the Potter's own will;
He sobbed, and the tears from His eyes freely flowed,
While falling like raindrops on ruins bestowed.
The Master worked over my heart-ruins in tears,
While holding my anguish and calming my fears,
Until my crushed heart became soft yielded clay,
Which Jesus, the Potter, could shape His own way.
The clay of my heart He then fashioned anew,
Creating a vessel as none else could do—
No longer were seen jagged cracks of deep pain,
But beauty imprinted by His hand attained.
There's no heart so ugly or scarred from the past
That can't be transformed with a beauty that lasts;
Impossible heartbreak, the Potter above,
Can change to a masterpiece of His great love!

KETURAH C. MARTIN

AUGUST 1
READING: 2 CORINTHIANS 1:1-10

God's Exchange Program

The Lord has an *Exchange Program* that is provided completely free of charge to us: for Jesus paid it all when He died on the cross of Calvary in our place. This is a place, down at the cross, where we can come and bring all the rags and the afflictions of our life and past and dump it all off with Jesus. Then we are given what He has to offer in place of what is disposed of at the foot of the cross.

Following are some of the *exchanges* that can be made:

Our sin........................... exchanged for...........Robe of His righteousness
Selfish nature.................. exchanged for...........Presence of Holy Spirit
Lies of evil one .... exchanged for...........Eternal truth
Bleeding heart .... exchanged for...........Restored vessel of honour
Pain............................... exchanged for...........Healing and wholeness
Terror .... exchanged for...........Love and safety
Emptiness....................... exchanged for...........Overflowing fullness
Abusive past .... exchanged for...........A glorious future
Defiled garments .... exchanged for...........Robes of white
Shattered dreams .... exchanged for...........A hope and future
Worthless tatters .... exchanged for...........Value beyond measure
Rejection's pain .... exchanged for...........Full acceptance
Raging warfare .... exchanged for...........All power in heaven
Judged repeatedly .... exchanged for...........No condemnation
Abused body .... exchanged for...........A new life
Horrific flashbacks .... exchanged for...........Heavenly visions
False accusations............. exchanged for...........Free exoneration
Abandonment .... exchanged for...........Adoption into God's family
Self-hate .... exchanged for...........View through Christ's eyes

PRAYER: Lord Jesus, thank You for paying the price for all these things, which can be exchanged for my filthy rags. Please help me to bring You all this junk and accept what You have to offer in its place. Thank You, Jesus! Amen.

All Things Work Together For Good

Our Father is waiting for us to just come—
Bring Him ev'ry trial that's so cumbersome:
For His ways are higher than our thoughts and ways,
And He has a plan for our life and its days.

All things work together for our best and good—
Though all may seem dark and there's naught understood:
For we have been chosen, called out, and made new
According to purposes our God doth view.

The Father will never a good work begin
Within His own children, whom He's saved from sin,
Except that He plans to perform and complete
His purpose in those, whom at Calv'ry He meets.

Though circumstance outward may darken the way,
Yet God has all power and He holds each day;
No storm, despite fury, can pass His command:
For He holds our future and good in His hand.

No person or power, no weapon or foe
Can separate us from our God Who doth know;
And if God be for us, against none can be:
For it is the Lord Who now fighteth for thee!

When sorrow may crush with such mountainous weight,
And burdens like iron just don't dissipate,
Yet Jesus will lovingly take full control
And work it all out for the best of our soul!

Yield all to the Master and place in His hand
Each painful affliction you don't understand;
His purpose is greater than we comprehend,
And grace all-sufficient He faithfully sends!

KETURAH C. MARTIN

AUGUST 3
READING: COLOSSIANS 1:27 AND ROMANS 9:23

Work Together For Good?

When we are in the middle of suffering or attempting to survive the darkest night of horror, the last thing we want to hear is anything about this *working into something good.* Nor can we fathom any truth in such idealistic thoughts when our inner agony is nearly killing us, and there is not even one soul around who can begin to understand.

After years of nearly continual abuse, shattered lives, and violent destructions, I would gloomily read the verse in Romans 8:28: "And we know that all things work together for good to them that love God; to them who are the called according to His purpose."

"It is impossible that this could ever apply to me," I thought hopelessly as my tattered heart bled ceaselessly. However, in my yearning for God to make something out of my shambled life, I would always try to tell Him that *if He could do anything to work something good out of the heart-shreds, then He should go ahead and try.* My faith amid the agony was near zero, but I did not want to slam the door in God's face if He was willing to take the time for one so devalued by mankind.

Although God is still working on me and weaving some of the remaining tatters into the golden strands of His own beauty, yet He has brought me to the place where I can give thanks to Him. I thank Him not only for His repeated assistance in assuring my survival, but also that He can indeed bring beauty out of ashes, joy out of pain, light out of the darkness, hope out of despair, and life out of death! There is nothing too hard for Him to do with a destroyed life! Jesus actually delights in foiling Satan's attempts to destroy and turning it all around to the devil's utter defeat. The very things that were meant to squelch the life and hope from us can turn into a blessing of triumph, everlasting joy, and abundant life as Jesus uses them all as tools to help others.

PRAYER: Lord, I cannot understand how this endless pain and vile baggage could ever be used for my good or benefit. I choose to give You an opportunity to work with all that is buried and all that which is painfully obvious. Please take it all into Your control and send Your Spirit to work in whatever way You see best, so that my life can be transformed and the enemy's attempts on my life be defeated. Amen.

Dig For The Gold

Within each believer lie roots of bright gold,
Which we're called to bring to the surface and hold;
We cannot afford on the surface to live:
For shallow relationships leak like a sieve.
Christ Jesus within us will dig past the rocks
In fellow believers, despite that which blocks:
Our mission to search for the gold down below,
Past stones, muck, and gravel be willing to go.

Discovering gold takes commitment so true,
Demanding that we stick with them right on through,
Past bedrock and boulders, through muck, dirt, and grime
We dig through the darkness to reach gold that shines.
And when you encounter the rocks as you dig,
Don't ever resort to a human flaw, big,
Of stacking the rocks on "observer's dread pile,"
Where spectators gawk as the tongues run a mile.

Through eyes of the Master, view always each soul
While "digging in love for gold nuggets," the goal:
For He sees the value of each soul untold
And He's the Refiner Who purifies gold!
We dare not be numbered with those who give up
On fellow believers despite what they've supped:
For God won't abandon the work He's begun—
So we as His children must dig 'til we're done!

Seek always to bring out the good in each life,
And don't be caught digging for that which makes strife:
For we are but instruments used in God's hand,
To bring forth the gold in our dear fellowman.
Delight in the brotherhood day after day,
Their beautiful nuggets lift up and display—
Exalting the Savior Whose throne is each heart,
Who always completes every work He doth start!

KETURAH C. MARTIN

Spiritual Gold-Panning

Back in 1849, there was a gold rush in California, and droves of people from every walk of life thronged to the West to get their stake in for a claim. The self-sacrifice, peril, and even death that individuals were willing to encounter in order to dig up some glittering riches were phenomenal. Often they would have to dig in unsafe conditions through rock, storm, or heat with very little to show for it. Many times bandits, murderers, and other greedy individuals would attack just to get what someone else had worked so hard to unearth. Panning gold was hard, dirty, and often mucky work, yet men gave their lives in the attempt to get rich quick.

How much more should God's children be all *fired up* about digging and panning for the spiritual gold in fellow believers? So often many of the people who are called by Christ's name spend more time slandering, assuming, and gossiping than they spend lifting up the golden nuggets in others. In fact, many do not even bother looking for gold nuggets in others—they are too busy looking for the rocks, mud, and boulders to hurl at another.

The Master's desire for His children is that we pan for gold in one another with the mind of Christ within us. Though there are individuals who have been through things we cannot understand, or their pain is something we cannot comprehend, yet beneath it all lies buried gold which the Master wants to refine. He asks that we never give up on one another and never write someone off as *a useless claim.*

Everyone has a value to God which surpasses the worth of all the gold in the world. Because He died for each and every one, we are all equally valuable regardless of what circumstances, pain, or abuse have shaped us. Even these anguishing tools can be used by the Savior to refine the gold or increase its value as He sees best. Digging for the gold in our brother or sister can be a blessed experience when we are armed with the love of God that shines for His glory, and view every potential claim through the goggles of Christ!

PRAYER: Lord, help me to never give up on anyone no matter what they have been through or how hard the digging may be. Empower me with Your love and the eternal vision of how You view each person and claim. Amen.

From Pits Jesus Rescues!

The power of darkness—what horror it holds,
It binds one in chains as to slavery they're sold:
The foul chains grow tighter each step of the way,
As master of darkness destroys more each day.
The power of darkness will strangle to death—
Eliminates wholly one's spiritual breath;
It squelches all hope and desire for God,
As cruelly one's beaten beneath Satan's rod.
Deception's grim web will entangle complete,
Until one is doomed in a constant defeat:
Its sly, sticky lies will like poison dart out,
And strike without warning with dark, deadly clout.
The power of darkness will suck you so deep,
That you can do naught, but to struggle and weep:
For daily those chains will their bondage increase,
Until they're encased in a darkness not ceased.
This power's oppression, more heavy than lead
Is filled with dark horror where terror is fed;
The spirit and body, emotions and soul,
Are pushed down in blackness beyond all control.
The master of darkness would have you believe,
That once in his chains, you can never receive
The freedom and cleansing through Christ's blood divine,
And whispers so subtle, "I've trapped you, you're mine!"
But God has redeemed me to shout out what's true,
Declaring what wonders my Jesus can do:
His power, unlimited, no bounds doth know—
He breaks every fetter—all darkness will go.
There's hope in the Savior through His blood divine,
From pits He will rescue, says, "Child, you're all Mine:
For I died to save you, My blood bought your soul—
The power of darkness cannot keep control!
When I rose triumphant from death and the grave,
I conquered the Devil, and live now to save;
Each stronghold and chain can be broken by Me
No bonds are too strong that My love cannot free!"

God Accesses The Deepest Pit

In a lonely Western valley, a young girl named Annika became an unwanted victim of someone in the community who was feared by all. Due to facing extensive rejection and abandonment, she was a vulnerable prey to such a predator. However, unknown to Annika, God was overseeing all the agonizing circumstances and ensuring His preservation of her life despite what came. It wasn't long until this lovely but vulnerable girl was being forcibly coerced through unspeakable traumata and torture. It was at such a time as this that the enemy of her soul dragged her into a black pit of horror during the very moments of her minimal survival and vulnerability.

Suddenly, one day years later, Annika was awakened by the noise of the dark wall beside her crumbling. Then there was light streaming into her dank prison cell as every shadow fled in unbidden haste. In a moment she saw Jesus standing before her offering a freedom unlike any she had ever known or dreamed of, as the fetters and chains of the enemy snapped in pieces. He led her up out of the miry pit and down to the cross of Calvary where her cleansing and freedom became complete.

Jesus has the power to bring freedom to every bondage, chain, incarceration, or slimy pit one may be bound in, whether it is spiritually, physically, or emotionally. Satan is very busy trying to ingrain his lies into those he holds captive, but I am alive today to share with the world that he is a liar and the father of lies. He is out to steal, kill, and destroy you; and every lie that is believed is one more dose of poison through which he attempts destruction.

Truth of God:
- God is not a man that He should lie, nor the Son of man that He should repent.
- No matter what you have experienced or what rituals you have been forced through, there is abundant hope, life, and freedom through Jesus.
- Satan is a defeated wimp who cannot stand before the blood of Jesus.
- Greater is He that is in us than he that is in the world.

PRAYER: Lord Jesus, I choose to renounce every lie of Satan and I claim Your truth that I can be free through Your blood. I renounce every experience where Satan could have got a hold on me. Break every chain, fetter, and stronghold in my life, Jesus, and fill me with Your presence and power. Amen.

Angel Of God's Presence

Affliction and heartache one's lot oft may be,
'Neath dark, stormy cloud-break or midst sunshine free;
God never forsakes us—He turns no blind eye,
Embracing arms take us to heights in the sky,
Lest in the deep anguish of pain or abuse

One's hope may all languish and feel death's dark noose:
For God is afflicted when we writhe in pain—

Grants grace unrestricted as He builds our gain.
Our Lord sends His Presence surrounding our form—
Delivers in essence from wildest of storm,
'So tenderly saving midst anguish untold,

Precisely engraving one's name in pure gold;
Reminding us always of His angel near—
Enfolds near His heart-rays the one He holds dear!
So never despair child, despite painful blows,
Endure all the wild winds, assured that He knows;
No evil can hurt you with His angel near,
Cause His love doth skirt you—His Presence is here . . .
Embraced in His arms is *a diamond so dear*!

PRAYER: "Thank-You Lord for having my back and surrounding me with Your Presence in every circumstance. Thanks for loving me with an everlasting love no matter what storm or trial may beat upon me. I invite You Lord to be the Captain of my life ship from this day forth and forevermore!" Amen.

Skeletons In The Closet

There are many accounts in history where various individuals tried in some way to escape their past or run away from it. It is not possible to truly get away from ourselves or any adverse circumstances we may have encountered. Even though we attempt to bury it all in some back closet of our heart or mind, we are really only hurting ourselves in the long run. To bury or try to run away from the pain, shattered dreams, or abuse of our past is actually cheating ourselves out of what could be a transformed life of freedom, fulfillment, and unspeakable joy. It is also limiting the power of God and what He wants to do in transforming the pain into diamonds of value.

The past never needs to dictate the future unless we choose to allow it to do so. By doing nothing, we are choosing to bury it, and by burying anything that's unresolved, we are choosing to become a chained slave to that slinky skeleton which many may not even know about. Ultimately, we are cheated out of experiencing the miraculous touch of God when He performs that which we assumed impossible! Then we are stuck with those abhorrent skeletons that are reeking with stench and repulsion, when Jesus wants to exchange them for something far better.

We do not have to live in the bondage, pain, and haunting horror of the past. Jesus has made a way that we can face the things of the past, regardless of how agonizing, abusive, or devastating it has been. He has defeated Satan and also every attempt and lie the enemy uses against you to get you to keep the skeletons for him to secretly feed on.

To do anything but face the past head-on and allow Jesus to deal with it is to willingly place ourselves into its shackling control. Then comes the hideous journey of being accompanied through life with the haunting skeletons of unresolved issues where the enemy secretly makes hidden strongholds. But we have the blood of Jesus and all of heaven's resources to work through it all and then leave it behind.

PRAYER: Dear Lord, I ask that You would search my life and show me if there is anything hidden there which needs Your touch of healing. No matter how painful it may be to deal with the stuff in my closet, I choose to be free, and I renounce every lie and hold of Satan on me. I claim the blood of Jesus on my life and future, and accept Your work of healing in me. Amen.

Just Rest Within His Arms

When the storm around thee rages,
And the sails are rent and torn—
Look beyond the gath'ring tempest
Which the eastern sky adorns.

For though waves may dash in fury
And your bark is threatened sore,
Yet your Pilot holds the compass,
And He'll guide thee safe to shore.

He will not allow the tempest
To control or overthrow:
For His child He safely carries,
And His vict'ry thou shalt know.

When the waves spill in around thee,
And o'erflow from your frail bark—
Jesus still remains your Pilot—
To His voice the storm must hark.

So don't fear the waves so violent,
But just rest within His arms:
For He holds the storm and future,
And He shields thee from all harm.

Through the darkest night He brings thee
To a dawn of hope so bright;
Christ your Pilot never fails you:
For He is thy Rock and Light!

KETURAH C. MARTIN

In The Midst Of The Storm

Very often when someone makes the decision to address with Jesus all the unresolved issues of pain, etc., that He's shown, then the enemy gets really upset and attempts to make war. Satan makes war because he is afraid he'll lose some ground in us, or that he may be exposed for what he really is. He gets really riled up if he thinks someone might blow his cover or expose his lies and deceptions.

In my situation the enemy has been angry about the in-depth help and healing I've received for a shattered life and also about the writing of this book. The war and tempest he has created is so extreme that at times my body has literally given out or my brain shut down. However, the devil becomes very cowardly when the blood of Jesus is claimed and always runs away, at least for a short time, with his tail between his legs.

When the tempest is raging and the oppressive waves are tossing about everywhere, cry out to Jesus. He is the Captain of your ship. Despite what Satan may claim or assert, Jesus will never let you sink in the waves and storm but is there to guide you safely through. When you cry out to Him, even if it is just His name, He understands the need and is there to rebuke the enemy and cover you with the power of His blood.

Satan knows he is defeated through the blood, death, and resurrection of Jesus. However, he wants to get his captives and those in pain or need to believe otherwise. He will go to great lengths to lie and deceive people in every walk and nation, just so he can gain an advantage over them as he plots to steal, kill, and destroy. The blood of Jesus, His Word, and His name are the three most powerful weapons we have against this deadly foe who continually seeks our destruction. When we engage in war against him and his lies with these weapons, he will flee as he becomes powerless before them. He is defeated and we need only to claim the victory which Jesus already won for us!

Prayer: Lord, I want to renounce every lie, deception, and attempt of Satan against my life and healing. I claim the blood of Jesus and the victory He has already won over all the power and schemes of the enemy. I claim Your presence and power in my life for Your glory, in Jesus' name. Amen.

It's All In My Hands

The future, unknown, may foreboding arise,
As on the horizon dark clouds fill the skies;
The thunder is crashing and lightning strikes low—
The ominous outcome one just doesn't know.

The Heavenly Father the universe scans,
And sweetly doth whisper, "It's all in My hands.
Child, leave all the tempest, so wild, in My care,
Assuredly knowing 'thy burden I share.'

I see all the future beyond storm and gales—
Each day chart your course and anew set your sails;
I guide you safe on past destruction's dark rocks
And spare you, My Child, from avoidable knocks.

Be still, My dear Child, though the waves dash and foam:
For I am thy Captain and I guide you home;
Your Refuge and Fortress I am in the storm—
In My love and care you remain safe and warm.

Though there be some stretches uncharted, unclear,
My Child, I'm beside you with light ever near,
To guide and sustain you, to comfort and hold—
I never will leave, My dear Child, in the cold!

My children I lead not through rocky terrain,
Except that I see it will bring them some gain:
All things I work out for your best, My dear Child,
And give grace sufficient amid storms so wild.

The homeport is Heaven for each ransomed soul,
And I steer your ship to this heavenly goal;
For your light affliction, like moments in time,
Works glorious weights in eternity's clime!"

Affliction And Sacrifice

Everyone in life faces some sort of trouble, grief, or heartache in a lifetime, but some people are destined to endure far more than the average. We often cannot understand why life seems completely unfair to some individuals, and others can just shoot through life as a gentle breeze over the sea. However, it is not for us to question *why* God allows extremely difficult things to happen to some but not others. From God's perspective, He can see our entire life picture from start to finish and has an exquisite plan for each one.

When God asks an individual to literally become a *living sacrifice* through the diverse physical sufferings she is called through, He has something unique and specific in His planning. Should one be called through such intense affliction that life seems like an agonizing restriction and constant suffering, God is still on the throne and carefully holds that life in His hand. The internal beauty He is creating in this particular life and those involved is something which He can see, but the suffering one cannot.

In these excruciating times it so important to cling to the Lord with the grip of faith—feeble though it may be. To surrender the situation and all of one's feelings that go with it is very crucial in order to prohibit the enemy from attempting to make inroads of bitterness, anger, or utter despair. The dark, black underside of our painful life's weaving to us may look completely useless, heartlessly cruel, and absolutely a waste of life and time. But God in heaven is viewing the upper side of your life's weaving. From His perspective, He can see where the pure gold came shining through every time your will, life and agony were surrendered again into His divine hand. How brilliantly it shines forth with the golden luxury of these heart-shredding strands which were repeatedly offered up to Him in soul-rending tears and cries. This weaving, linked together with the tearstained prayer of total surrender, is truly the most valuable and magnificent of all, and the loving face of Jesus Christ shines through its every fibre with the purest of gold. He will never fail or forsake you!

PRAYER: Lord, I cannot understand the unceasing pain, the black despair, and the feeling my life is wasted. I renounce the lies of Satan, and I claim Your truth. I ask You to take my will, the pain, and my life and make something beautiful which can glorify You in every way. Amen.

Jesus Loves My Heart

Jesus loves the broken heart,
Though it makes His teardrops start;
He can see its deepest need
And with grace will always feed.

Jesus loves the heart that's crushed,
Which so near to death has brushed;
He can pour in love divine
And restore this heart of mine.

Jesus for each piece doth care,
Of the wounded heart that's bare;
He can make the rivers flow—
Bind together shreds of woe!

Jesus never will reject
Broken hearts full of neglect;
He will never hush my cry,
When it feels I'm gonna die.

Jesus loves the tatters wild,
Of my heart that's been defiled;
But there is no strand too black:
For He gives true whiteness back!

Jesus never meant for me,
To be broke in misery,
So He wrapped His arms of love
All around from up above!

KETURAH C. MARTIN

The Love Of Jesus

Jesus specifically said that He came to heal the brokenhearted. This speaks of a true love that will not bypass the lives which many others may try to avoid, neglect, or bury under the carpet. The very heart of Jesus weeps more loudly than any other when He sees what the choices of self-centered perpetrators are doing to little girls or boys. As they cry out in anguish and terror, it is Jesus Who steps up and puts His arms around them as He tenderly preserves them in love. He has designed each child and individual for a purpose far beyond what can be comprehended. Regardless *what* or *who* Satan uses to try to destroy any one of His children, Jesus will never just walk away or leave His child in the paw of the lion. Rather, He holds them tenderly in His arms as He shields them from the very worst of their experience while shielding them from death itself.

There are cases where a child may actually die in the midst of extreme abuse and horror. I believe it is the mercy and grace of God that steps into a crime scene such as that and beholds that the agony and destruction is more than can be borne. Lovingly, before everything happens which He can foresee coming, He picks her up, holds her in His bosom, and wings her home to glory to be forever safe in His presence.

When Jesus comes across a broken heart or the tangled tatters strewn about, He stops and takes notice and then does something about it. He knows exactly who did this deed against His child and intercedes to the Father on behalf of His broken child.

There are many folks out there who want the suffering children and everyone else to just keep everything about abuse quiet so nobody looks too bad and they can avoid accountability. But Jesus never takes the cover-up route. Jesus spent a lot of time while on earth exposing evil and outlining something better. He alone is the Defense of the helpless, abused, and downtrodden; and He understands perfectly.

PRAYER: Jesus, I thank You for loving my heart even if it feels so yucky and bad. I want to give You all the pieces so You can make them clean and make me to be all white inside. I am so glad nothing is too hard for You! Thank You, Jesus, for Your undying love! Amen.

Depression

Depression's a reality that most can't comprehend or see,
Most often it's misunderstood—thought of as sin, which is not good;
Just as diabetes or bad heart, so this with illness shares a part,
But illness of the brain and mind is hard to see and be defined.
This monster, real, is in the brain—affects the mind and all thought train:
The concentration runs so low and victim's memory oft will go;
One gets upset for no real cause and often cries with little pause,
But often when the pain's too deep the tears are locked and one can't weep.
The sleeping patterns often change, and appetites can rearrange:
Some people lose a lot of weight, while others may increase their gait;
Digestive symptoms may occur—real pain severe one may endure,
Headaches are present most of the time, and racing mind will not unwind.
The body's actions may slow down—it's hard to talk or walk around,
They're tired, but they cannot rest—their mind's awhirl—black thoughts infest;
Enthusiasm often goes, int'rest in life one may not know:
The victims may not even care for those with whom their life they share.
Sometimes abuses of the past intensify its deadly blast:
Traumatic incidents and grief makes all look hopeless—no relief;
The victim often worthless feels, guilty, unwanted, with no zeal,
And in the cases most severe, don't want to live, of it won't hear.
Excruciations of the mind are agony—can't be defined:
So worthless, hopeless, in despair—to live at all one doesn't care;
Words can't express depths of despair, the ceaseless hurting one must bear—
The pain of future, present, past in guilt forever seems to last.
Oft Post Traumatic Stress and grief contributes to the "No relief,"
Abuse survivors who alone must stand, to this are far more prone.
The chemicals and all the brain are all messed up—must be retrained,
The mind gives messages unreal and tells the body how to deal:
For in the most severest kind, the victim copes as tells the mind—
"Life's hopeless horror I can't face," and without help, life may erase.
Some people think, *If you just pray, then all these troubles go away;*
A leg stays broke through just belief, so prayer alone won't bring relief.
It takes a doctor's kind, true care and understanding that is rare,
It may take counseling of sorts and from the patient, true efforts;
And then from family and friends—unjudging faith to prayerful ends
It takes the Great Physician's care to heal the shattered pain that's there.

If There's Life There's Hope!

People God Used

- ♥ Abraham lied
- ♥ Jacob deceived
- ♥ Aaron made an idol
- ♥ Moses disobeyed
- ♥ Rahab was a prostitute
- ♥ David spied from rooftops
- ♥ Elijah caved to fear
- ♥ Jeremiah was depressed
- ♥ Jonah ran away
- ♥ Zacchaeus didn't measure up
- ♥ Peter denied Jesus
- ♥ Thomas doubted
- ♥ Paul persecuted Christians

"I choose to believe that God can use me for His glory, and I surrender myself into His hand."

Depression

Depression is a thing that is very often misunderstood. As a result, those who suffer with it may also be discredited, judged, and/or not understood. Though sometimes depression may follow a life of sin, that is not necessarily always the case, and each case must be treated and understood separately. Often depression may be the result of suppressing abuse for months and years. In other cases, it can be a chemical imbalance, or it may be an entirely physical issue as was the case of the author. In such a case one can only cry out to God.

PRAYER: Lord, I cannot see or understand this horrible darkness and apathy, but please have mercy on me and take over completely. Amen.

Take Me Deeper, Lord Jesus

"Lord Jesus, take me deeper than I have been before—
E'en though it means dark trial, I want to love Thee more:
For Thou hast suffered greater than any tongue can tell,
To rescue me from Satan and save my soul from hell.
My Jesus, take me broader within Thy Word and will,
That I may know Thee better—more intimate yet still;
Grant me Thine understanding of all Thy Word portrays,
That it may feed me daily and guide me in Thy ways.
Lord Jesus, make me stronger through Thine own life and love—
Though it mean pain and hardship, to God draw me above:
For trial and affliction can strengthen my own soul,
When I yield all to Jesus and give Him full control.
Lord Jesus, take me higher, above the world's dark night:
For vict'ry will be absent without Thy blood and might;
With resurrective power, Lord, fill me step by step—
I need Thy strength and guidance that I be safely kept.
Lord, guide me through the brambles, despite sunshine or rain,
When Satan seeks to ruin me through unforgiveness strains:
For I have chosen fully to place within Thy hand
Each soul who wrought much suff'ring, though I don't understand.
Lord, take me through refining—midst fire's heat intense,
That I may see Thee clearly and know Thy grace immense:
For I desire wholly, that self be crucified—
Let dross be purged far from me, for praise of Thee Who died!
Lord Jesus, draw me closer to Thy heart's perfect will—
In Thine own Presence take me and with Thy nature fill;
Lord, though it may take suff'ring, or waters deep and wide,
I long to blend with Jesus—His heartbeat at my side!
Lord, take me through the valley, past boulders of dark pain,
Through floods and stormy waters—for, Lord, I seek to gain
A yielded understanding of Thine own plan for me,
And live in grace sufficient which You give out so free—
To be a vessel fashioned by Thy great hand of love
Which Thou hast healed and strengthened, midst fires from above:
For Thou Who sees my picture of life from start to end,
Has planned it for a purpose, and I with Thee must blend!"

KETURAH C. MARTIN

Take Me Deeper

Do you think it seems utterly absurd to implore the Lord to take you through deeper fire, storm, and hardship? Has someone completely lost it to request something so weird? This seems pretty unrealistic, I agree, after barely surviving insurmountable abuses for years.

However, when Jesus reaches into a shattered heart with a hand of divine love, miracles are bound to be happening! As more and more healing took place and the enemy lost huge amounts of territory, the presence of God became so meaningful that we could walk and talk in a manner as never before. The war from the enemy also increased to a proportion never before experienced, but the Lord became even more magnified as He fought the battle for me. In the midst of severe trial to literally feel the hand of God and feel drawn even closer to Him is a wonderful experience that I yearn to be the encounter of every survivor. To taste the Lord as I have after years of barely surviving is such a blessing it must be shared! There is hope for each one of you who may be hurting from something in your past or present. The same hand of love, mercy, and grace that has restored millions of shatters is just waiting to do the same for you!

There is no limit to His love and the power to put it into action for the best of your eternal well-being! His understanding is infinite, which means it can go far deeper than mortal man can even begin to desire. Mere men can often fail those who are drowning in the agonizing tatters within because they cannot understand the depth of the need and incidentally may grow frustrated. But God is not a man, and His understanding of you and all you experienced is comprehended better by Him than it is by yourself! This makes it feel a lot safer to come to Him for help, healing, and the touch of love that can create miracles of transformation in your life. He will never fail you, but yearns to restore all that evil has broken, as the power of His love is exalted.

PRAYER: Lord, I want to have such a complete healing that the pain and filth are gone and I can experience You for Who You really are in the fullness of Your love and power. I desire for You to fight the enemy for me and hold my hand as the victory of Jesus is claimed. Please help, Lord. Amen.

Rest In My Bosom

Lord, why is trial now crushing us sore?
Just what may the future still hold in its store?
The load is so heavy midst anguish and care,
And now I must ask You, "My Lord, are You there?"

"My Child, worn and weary, look up and behold:
For I'm by thy side and right now I enfold
You safe in My arms and tight close to My breast,
As in Me, midst sorrow, you find perfect rest.

My Child, I've designed you in detail complete,
From hair on your head to the sole of your feet:
I too know the future, My goals and My plans,
For which I created you, Child, with My hands.

My ways and My thoughts are above what you know,
But, Child, be assured that with you I will go
Each step and each moment to walk by your side,
And grant grace and comfort whatever betides!

When waters so dark sweep you off your worn feet,
Or fiery afflictions each day you may greet,
Dear Child, to My arms I invite you to flee—
Midst anguishing burdens I'll now carry thee!

I know, My dear Child, even better than you,
Just what you can bear, and in triumph go through;
In love I surround you, as Guard to your soul:
Each incoming hardship must pass My control.

So rest in My bosom of love so untold:
For I midst each trial thy hands safely hold;
Commit unto Me every detail of pain,
And I thy Great Refuge will fully sustain!"

KETURAH C. MARTIN

God Is A Safe Refuge In Trial

A life without trials, affliction, and hardships would be a life of shallow nothingness, and what many people may term as *a life of ease.*

There are many great masterpieces that have been made by various people, but in every case, whatever was being formed or created had to go through extensive pain, chiselling, cutting, and/or fire to come to perfection and usefulness.

Jesus promised that to follow Him would not be an easy road, but rather a very difficult one. He told us we would have persecution, sorrow, rejection, false accusations, betrayal, and many other things that would not be pleasant according to the flesh. In light of all the potential suffering His children may experience, He also assures them of His presence, love, and grace to accompany them in every situation. He offered Himself as a resting place for all who carry heavy loads and grim experiences. The safe resting place Christ has provided for us is at His bosom of love where we can always resort to no matter what we may be going through. He has suffered all these things before us so therefore is equipped to walk through it as a knowledgeable guide.

The trials and hurts God allows in our experiences are essential ingredients that He uses to build Christ-like character within us. It is up to each individual to give Him the *green light* to unrestricted access in their lives so He can work His perfect work through these hardships.

Pain and trials need not be viewed with fear and abhorrence, but rather as being much more precious than gold in the fire, being purified. Jesus also suffered for us, leaving an example that we should follow His steps.

A life without trials, pain, and afflictions is one that has not been subjected to very much shaping and preparation for usable service. When we are worn and in suffering, that is when the strength of God becomes evident and shines through with nothing of our human nature to restrict it.

PRAYER: Lord, even though I don't understand the trials and pain that are around me, I know You do; and I surrender it all into Your control. Help me to rest in Your bosom and permit You to do the work You desire in me through any hardship You allow. Prepare and work through me for Your glory, Jesus. Amen.

Take Self Away

Is God the Father Lord of all? Is He the God on Whom you call?
Or is idolatry your fate, where self is crowned and guards each gate?
"Self" crowned each day fares sumptuously with good companions: "I" and "Me"
Who work toward one common goal—"that they may stay in full control."

"I" sits enthroned within the heart, upheld and honored from the start:
Until the Lord is left no space—idolatry then takes His place.
"Me" seeks to govern, be in charge of all decisions small and large—
Opinions, choices, all must be just those that bring some gain to "Me."

Who has the charge of all your time? What governs where you spend that dime?
Is God's approval through each day, inquired after all the way?
Does Jesus have pre-eminence of daily life in ev'ry sense?
Or do you hide a secret room which Satan governs to your doom?

With "Self's" own nature all are born, yet from the heart "Self" must be torn:
"I" cannot rule a life in peace—"Me" governs future hope to cease.
"Dear Jesus, take and crucify imposing 'Self,' the 'Me' and 'I':
Dethrone them from my heart and life, and cleanse me from their selfish strife.

Lord, take me daily to the cross and cleanse me from all selfish dross,
Ensure the devil has no ground whereby he aims to keep me bound
For all his schemes I do reject that You alone I may reflect,
For You have rescued me from hell, that I Your love and pow'r can tell!

Lord, be enthroned and take control of all my body, mind, and soul;
With Christ, let self be crucified that I may live through Him Who died.
Lord, help me live from day to day while treading through life's pilgrim way,
A life that's dead to self and sin, which manifests Your pow'r within."

KETURAH C. MARTIN

Allowing God To Work

There may be many times in our journey where we might feel as if we are at a dead end or against a brick wall. We most likely won't be able to comprehend what is actually going on or what the obstruction is. Sometimes there are obvious things we can identify which may hinder our healing journey, but often they are undetectable.

The enemy is very subtle in his deceptions and hindrances with all God's people. However, when it appears to Satan as though someone who has been abused and trashed at his instigation may be on the right road to receiving hope and help, he will do everything possible to halt that process. The last thing he wants is for one of his captives to get free and go share the truth of hope and healing with the teeming masses of hurting people in his clutches. Then he begins an attempt at constructing barricades in the roadway which will stop or impede progress. He begins by injecting various lies and suggestions to the survivor. To even give a split second of time to the injection, *except to claim the blood of Jesus over it*, is giving him time to make the second injection. He will make every attempt to raise up *what your rights are in the whole painful mess* until self is the most prominent thing in the foreground, if one takes his bait. As soon as the ugly head of self is viewing the landscape, there is no room left for Jesus to continue His work of restoration, and the road is barricaded. It is very important for our carnal nature to be repeatedly brought to the cross of Christ and totally crucified with every injection of fear, lies, self-rights, bitterness, and desire for revenge. When these things and their relatives are present, Jesus the Great Physician has a very restricted access to work the miracles of transformation He desires.

PRAYER: Lord Jesus, I want You to have unrestricted access to my heart so You can change it from ragged tatters to robes of faith and righteousness. Please crucify every selfish motive, and bring every thought and lie of Satan into captivity under Your control. Make me into something clean and of worth for Your glory, Jesus. Amen.

The Cross Stands Between

Put your hand in the Master's, look up and rejoice:
For through Jesus Christ we can lift up our voice;
His child He is holding within His embrace—
Each step that she takes God enfolds her in grace.

Although she may tread down a dark, lonesome path
And someone may plot her destruction in wrath,
Yet do not despair, for the Lord is her Guide,
And Jesus is walking so close to her side!

No evil attempt past the Lord can get through,
Despite what the enemy thinks he can do,
But angels are camping around His dear child—
The cross stands between her and danger so wild.

The devil is bound when he faces the cross:
For through it was gained his defeat and sure loss;
His power is nothing where Jesus surrounds:
For Christ's blood spells "victory" on enemy grounds!

So take up your cross through Christ's power divine,
For He paid your ransom and says "You are Mine"
He carries your load and walks with you each step—
By His hand of love you will always be kept!

He'll carry you through raging waters and floods,
And always protect through the pow'r of His blood,
The cross stands between you and enemy bands—
As Christ leads you on to the heavenly lands!

KETURAH C. MARTIN

The Protection Of The Cross

Did you realize that the cross experience of Jesus on behalf of all mankind is not only the means of procuring our salvation, but through Christ and the cross we can also have divine protection? God never does anything half-heartedly, and this includes our salvation provisions. He knew that the enemy of our souls would be very angry with the escape route from sin and evil that was accomplished through Christ on the cross. Because of this outrage, God in mercy provided a means by which we can be completely protected from all the onslaughts of the enemy through the power of the blood and the work on the cross. Praise God! It is our choice to come under His protection and whether we remain there with His care around us.

Sonya was a twenty-five-year-old mother who was caught in a situation of domestic violence with a beautiful new baby. How she loved her new little boy, but she didn't realize the work of the enemy preparing battle in the next room. Sonya's husband became very jealous of the time that was needed to care for the baby and as a result became increasingly abusive toward her. Her mother heart was shattered in a million pieces when repeatedly he forcibly restricted her from going to her crying, hungry baby. In place of caring for him, she was forced through violent assault as a toy to feed lust, and be turned over to his vicious sex demons.

Years later when Sonya brought the unutterable agony of her heart to Jesus for healing, He was very gracious and full of mercy as step by step He led her to the complete freedom of choosing to forgive.

When she asked Jesus why the damage was not any worse, He replied, "I stood beside you through it all, and when it was enough, I would put the cross between you and the one hurting you. I took most of it for you."

This is a beautiful picture of God in His mercy actively helping the helpless and abused at the most crucial hour. He never turns a blind eye but is there for His suffering children. Jesus is the One Who actively ensures the survival of His bruised lambs.

PRAYER: Lord, I praise You for taking enough interest in me that You actively help me get through the hard times. I choose to remain under Your protection and ask that You walk with me throughout this journey. Amen.

The Dark Strands Of Suffering

"To Thee, my Lord Jesus, I must pour my heart,
Amid the dark sorrows that tear me apart:
For I know not, Lord, what for me You have planned—
This painful adversity can't understand.
Lord, how can this agony glorify You?
How bleak looks the future that rests in my view!
Lord, why must I suffer such anguish untold?
While all that's before me looks grim, dark, and cold.

GOD'S ANSWER . . .

"My Child, I am holding you in My embrace—
From heaven's own bounty enfold thee in grace;
My heart throbs with thine, amid pain none can know,
Yet through dark afflictions My Child can still grow.
Yield every dark sorrow to My hand divine,
And whisper with Christ, 'Not my will, Lord, but Thine'
The heart-shreds of anguish so dark that you see,
Will shine with pure gold in your life tapestry.
Dear Child, keep your eyes fixed on Jesus your King,
Lest Satan hide truth and dark lies try to bring;
I've counted you worthy, My suff'rings to share—
Each heartrending burden beside you I bear!
The dark strands of suff'ring in luster will shine,
When yielded completely to My hand divine:
For all that the enemy thought would destroy,
I'm using, My Child, for your eternal joy!
Your children and husband—your future untold,
Just place in My hand, that I may fully hold
Each life which I've planned to bring glory to Me:
For I am thy God and will not forsake thee!"

—Your Heavenly Father

Sufferings That Keep Us Kneeling

There are many people called to go through far more extensive suffering than what most can even fathom. This does not mean that they are being punished or any such thing, but rather, that they have been chosen to fill a spot which few can actually fill. To suffer day in and day out, whether it be physically, sexually, emotionally, or psychologically, takes a quiet spirit of submission and endurance that is attained through Christ alone.

Daily and sometimes hourly, or moment by moment, these jewels of individuals must repeatedly pray their way through the entire day or night in their internal distress. As they give their will, lives, and emotions to God again and again, the diamond of their soul is being refined into exquisite value and beauty by the divine hand of Christ Himself. Though the individual may not know of the eternal beauty which Jesus is imprinting on her heart and soul, yet the angels can see and rejoice with the marvelous work of God brought about by the tools of pain and surrender.

These trials that keep an individual kneeling before their lifelong assignments are never a haphazard thing, but an intricate plan for a work of art by the hand of God. He understands the pain and chiselling that will be involved and is there to weep with you in the pain and carry you when not another step can be taken. He will never forsake you in this painstaking project of eternal value. The fact that He chose you to take part in this assignment of infinite value speaks of His confidence in you to come through by the power of all He is pouring into you through Jesus.

You are counted worthy to suffer and build eternal treasures in glory, so hold on tight to the hand of the Almighty, for He will never let go of you!

PRAYER: Lord Jesus, I cannot understand this unbearable pain and suffering, but if You are willing to walk through it with me, I yield You my will. I choose to give You my hand and my heart to preserve for Yourself. I renounce every lie and attempt of Satan that tries to deter me or wants me to throw in the towel. Lord, I surrender my will and my rights to Your divine will and purpose. I claim the blood of Jesus over my body, mind, and soul; and I claim the victory that is mine through Jesus. Amen.

The Glorious Light

The Lord in His infinite love toward me,
Commanded His light to shine fully and free;
It pierced the stale darkness and shined in my heart—
His light, truth, and knowledge a work then did start.

He loved me despite all the guilt of the past—
From east to the west, just this far can He cast
The darkness and bondage, the blindness and night,
As His glorious gospel brings life changing light!

The image of God through Christ Jesus came near—
Illumined my night and said "Don't ever fear;
I never will leave or forsake you, My Child,
No matter what past on you may have been piled."

Then reaching down through all the anguishing past,
With eyes of deep love now upon me held fast,
My Jesus then showed me the truth of His love—
Forgiving my sin by His grace from above.

The glory of God in His face I have seen:
For He has transformed me from what I have been;
He rescued my soul from the pits of death's night—
Enlightened my path so I walk in His light!

I choose to embrace all the light of God's love,
For He has shown mercy from heaven above—
I pledge Him my life, all my future and time
To glorify Jesus in heaven sublime!

KETURAH C. MARTIN

From Darkness To Light

The all-encompassing darkness, horror, and terror that are subsequent to extreme abuses of specific nature are very difficult for the average observer to even begin to wrap his mind around, let alone to understand. But it is okay to not understand, because the main thing is that *the Lord understands 100 percent* and is a constant Companion, though all others fail. Just because people do not comprehend the truth or depth of one's suffering does not discredit the reality, or invalidate the facts of its source. It is the Lord Who brings complete deliverance, healing, and freedom through the death and resurrection of Jesus.

Landon struggled desperately in the tight chains which fastened him mercilessly to the stone wall. He had been shackled in this dripping dungeon at the time of that unspeakable incident of horror that he could never tell anyone. He had been told that if he told of that life-shattering abuse *he would be locked up as insane or even killed.* The darkness in this place was unbearable, but became much worse when he began sinking in the miry muck which was over most of the floor. One day as he was crying out hopelessly for mercy, the stone door was suddenly broken down and a great light flooded the dank area as the darkness fled. Then he saw that it was Jesus Who had entered and that even now was offering him His hand. Looking up into the kindest eyes he had ever seen, Landon grasped the hand of life with an insatiable desire to be touched by the Lord Himself. Jesus led him out of the dungeon's darkness and brought him to His cross, where complete healing and cleansing were granted to him for every need, horror, and pain he had suffered. Landon experienced a life altering freedom as one drop of Jesus' blood broke every satanic ritual abuse chain that had bound him for decades! Thank You Jesus!

PRAYER: Lord Jesus, You can see and understand all the shackles and darkness that nobody else can. Will You please bring me complete freedom and healing and bring light to the darkness so I can experience You just as You are in Your love and light? Amen.

The Master Uses Storms

When life's raging sea is rolling and the waves may dash so high,
Then the Lord looks down from heaven and He hears my desperate cry;
He extends His hand of mercy through the darkness, storm, and waves—
From the heaving sea He lifts me, as so tenderly He saves!

As in love He safely shelters me within His strong embrace,
Then He draws me yet still closer and enfolds me in His grace;
While beneath His wings I'm hiding, though the painful billows roar,
His sustaining Presence stays me and preserves me evermore!

For the enemy can't touch me when the Master is so near,
And the waves cannot consume me when I hold His hand so dear;
But the storm, though fierce and raging, by my Pilot can be used
As a tool to help me trust Him, and I need not be confused.

When the storm may grow still darker and His hand is all I know,
Then in utter trust I grasp it as His faithfulness He shows;
Then I know midst howling tempest, when I cannot understand,
That my Pilot is beside me and my charted way has planned.

And midst waves of dark rejection when the heart is crushed so low,
Though its tempest sweeps me under, yet my Savior's there I know:
For He holds my chart and compass—He's the Anchor of my soul,
And He's Master o'er the billows that can't pass His full control.

So I praise You blessed Savior for the foaming billows, wild:
For above their pain-filled lashings is relayed, *You are My Child*;
And for agony and heart-shreds, I do thank You, Jesus mine:
For it's on these broken pieces where doth rest Your hand divine!

Though I may not know Your purpose, and the storms can't understand,
Yet I know You are the Master and hold all things in Your hand;
And I thank You, Lord, for using all the pain that life may hold:
For when to Your hand it's yielded, You can bring forth purest gold!

KETURAH C. MARTIN

Save On Sea!

Far out to sea in a little lifeboat, Raquel drifted along helplessly in the tempestuous waters. Just ahead, the briny spray from the huge tugboat she was chained to was thrust mercilessly at her now-dripping form. The tugboat was owned and operated by a man who had forcibly chained her little boat to his when he found her adrift in a large seaport town. Once the chains were tight, she was informed that she could never again be free. Often she had to bail water just to keep afloat, as each day became stormier and hopelessly devoid of love, help, or rescue.

As she became resigned to her fateful lot, she was daily indoctrinated in the ways of this new life, and her spirit and emotions became more dead every day and hour. In time, life was done mostly as a trained robot—*a thing* with only the emotion of fear left; all else was dead.

The tugboat chugged through several seas and the storms grew wilder every time they developed until lives were often seen hanging in the balance. By this time Raquel was so destroyed within that she barely knew her name and could only utter one cry, "Help me, God!"

One day Raquel heard an unfamiliar drumming noise overhead as she bailed water and tears out of her boat. Looking up, she saw a chopper lingering over her little dinghy and observed three lifeguards taking in the situation. Suddenly there was a lifeline thrown to her as one of the rescuers chopped the ropes asunder which tied her to the big tugboat. As the line was pulled up hand over hand, Raquel was bathed in a bright sunbeam of hope as the filthy slavery and robotic use below came to an end.

We have a God Who never sleeps on the job, even though we sometimes think He responded in a late manner. However, He is always on time and has a wonderful way of working out everything in detail in a perfect way. Often He may send assurances and incidents of divine origin just to acknowledge His suffering children and give grace to get through another day or hour. His hand is not too short to make a complete rescue when the time is right.

"Who is like unto the Lord our God, who dwelleth on high? He raiseth up the poor out of the dust, and lifteth the needy out of the dunghill." Psalm 113:5, 7

Exposing Pornography's Hell

There is a dread enemy prowling this land,
Polluting the printeries, on foul demand;
It crawls along subtle, or blatant it cries—
By internet access, around the world flies.
It creeps in the heart through the lust of the eye,
And lust of the flesh it would then gratify;
But once it begins, on its own it can't stop—
Eventually drowns one in sin, death, and slop.
It is an addiction with death-grips of hell,
Whose magnified appetite daily doth swell:
Each gruesome perversion becomes more advanced,
And he who engages, with Satan has danced.
It's wrecking the homes and defiling the church,
While nations sweep downward in its filthy lurch:
For love is ice-cold where the porno life rules—
Relationships die midst this vile devil's tool.
The homes break apart where connections have died:
For porno is always the first satisfied;
The dear children suffer—the wife's brought to naught
When this tool of Satan is used, lived, and sought.
Pornography breeds out destruction and doom,
And captures the innocent in a vile tomb;
It shatters its victims in films, death, and greed,
Attempting this limitless monster to feed.
Abuse and pornography walk hand in hand:
For those there enslaved "must feed lust on demand"
Despite children crying in filth, shame, and fear,
They use them so lewdly while scorning their tears.
There's nothing too shameful, obscene, or perverse,
When Satan's chained pawns are a slave to this curse—
They buy, bribe, and sell at another's expense,
Whose shattered life pays midst this evil immense.
The devil would have you believe "You are trapped—
In porno's dread talons forever are wrapped;"
But Jesus' own blood is sufficient to free
Both slave and the victim: for He died for thee!

KETURAH C. MARTIN

"I Can't Remember"

By the time Raquel was rescued from the tugboat situation, she was terrified to live in a world where she didn't remember how to live. Always before, the dark tugboat had tugged her along, giving no opportunity or allowance for her to even think on her own, much less make any decisions. Terror of the boatman followed her like a shadow: for she knew that he had just lost the toy which was his main diet to feed his porno wolf.

For the first month, every few minutes and/or with each decision, she had to remind herself that she was safe now in this haven God had provided. She had to repeatedly tell herself that *it was not sinful to make decisions for her children and herself,* yet the terror of the repercussions haunted her night and day.

Raquel, like many others, had been severely brainwashed and internally destroyed while trapped in the deadly talons of abuse, porno, trafficking, and domestic violence. The confusion, misunderstanding, and excruciation when such is the case is very traumatic for these individuals. They desperately need to be surrounded by love and support as they try to understand how to live again.

God can potentially use these damaging and destructive abuses and ashes to build His child, using those very things to bring beauty out of that which is very ugly. His heart is grieved to no end when He observes how *the love of Jesus to the church* is being misrepresented across the nations, as abuse, trafficking, and pornography run rampant and lives are destroyed worldwide.

TRUTHS FOR THE RAQUELS OUT THERE:

- As long as there is life, there is hope, and God never sleeps on the job.
- God is not a man that He should lie, and He loves you ceaselessly.
- Those engaged in pornography cannot love beyond a 3 percent level.
- There is no abuse or destruction which is too hard for Jesus to fix.
- The man's porno addiction is not your fault.
- Porno addicts are never satisfied, even to the death.
- Pornography is the fire which fuels human sex trafficking, resulting in devastation and potential death.
- God will be your Husband when the earthly one fails (Isaiah 54).
- Safety and restoration from all the destruction is possible through Jesus.
- God specializes in things thought impossible—there's nothing too hard for Him, and He can't fail!

Riches Untold

I have an account in a heavenly bank,
And for this I only have Jesus to thank:
For He paid the price for an open account,
And now I can cash in for any amount!
When I must repeatedly choose to forgive
The one who destroyed all the life that I live,
I go to God's bank where there's riches untold—
Withdraw on Christ's love, that's worth much more than gold!
And then a deposit I place in His hand
Of every attempt from the evil one's band,
To sow seeds of bitterness, hatred, or wrath:
For I before Jesus must have a clear path.

So often it seems that I withdraw on grace,
But yet there is always some more in its place;
The heavenly revenue never depletes,
But needs great or small it repeatedly meets!

And when there's a load that's too heavy to bear,
I go to the teller at windows of prayer;
Where Christ the Lord gives me a full cash advance
Of strength that's sufficient my load to enhance.
He takes a deposit of pain so untold
By grace turns it all into nuggets of gold;
No pain's ever wasted when placed in His hand:
For He makes investments to use as He's planned.
"Of all that I have, Lord, I give You control,
And ask that You work for the best of my soul;
Invest in my life, Lord, as You best can see,
And fit me for life in Your eternity!"

KETURAH C. MARTIN

SEPTEMBER 4
READING: ACTS 20:32 AND PHILIPPIANS 4:19

Withdrawals From God's Bank

Daily, hourly, and sometimes continually, Raquel had to go to the heavenly bank to make withdrawals on her account for divine love, as she chose repeatedly to forgive the man in the tugboat.

The war against her from the enemy of her soul was tremendous, as he sought to implant seeds of bitterness, hatred, and revenge within. But God helped Raquel to understand that *to engage in bitterness at any level of thought or attitude would be playing right into the devil's hand, whose goal was to steal, kill, and destroy her.*

Again and again she prayed for Jesus to *please help her to choose to forgive the one who had been used by Satan to cause so much destruction and unspeakable pain.* Jesus never scolded her for withdrawing too much grace, love, and forgiveness from the bank account. Rather, He commended her for looking to Him for what was needed so that the enemy couldn't wedge in a foothold during this anguishing time. Often during the night she had to make withdrawals on her account as she cried out to God for the grace and strength to choose again to forgive as the limitless inner agony engulfed her.

Many individuals out there have the misconception that *one is supposed to forgive and forget and get on with their life—end of story.* However, Raquel knew that she had to remain vigilant against the devil, for he was relentless about getting a seed of bitterness started. Forgiveness toward an abuser is not necessarily a one-time deal, but very often one has to choose to forgive again whenever flashbacks and triggers are engulfing and Satan attacks in the midst of it all. Raquel also knew that *to forget what had happened* is not humanly possible, and, in fact, closes the door on God's plan to use painful experiences as tools to perfect His work of art. Her goal with the help of Christ was to come to a place where she could remember without pain, and that all she remembered would be used to help and understand others in similar plights.

PRAYER: Dear Jesus, I want to choose to forgive and release into Your control everyone who hurt me in any way. I place them into Your hand and ask You to bless them today in some way as You show Your love to them. Amen.

The School Of Suffering

The school of suffering can be grim,
Where grief may overflow the brim;
Oft pain and heartache seem all loss—
We know not why this is our cross.

But God above is in control—
Allows what's best to build one's soul:
When through pain's school you're called to go,
God plans for you a special role.

If never we knew grief or pain,
Had suffered not midst storm and rain,
We'd be hard pressed to understand
Another struck by suffering's hand.

When called through suffering, still God keeps
Us in His hand though He may weep;
Your anguished pain He feels and sees—
With arms of love He's holding thee!

Should you be called through suffering's school
By God's great grace, follow this rule:
"Trust all to God, on Him lean hard,
His perfect will don't disregard."

In wisdom He's preparing you
For work which only you can do;
To purify your heart and soul—
Come forth as gold—this is His goal.

So trust each breath into God's hand,
Who knows what's best and helps you stand:
His perfect strength will see you through,
And if need be He'll carry you!

KETURAH C. MARTIN

God Speaks To Suffering Ones

"My dear Child, when I see the extent of all you have suffered and are suffering, My heart yearns for you. It pains Me also to see My children in anguish, whether physical, emotional, or in any other way. My delight is not to see the suffering, but I take great joy in you, My Child, when you bloom and thrive after coming through the agony. There are always blossoms you bear for Me when you have brought Me your pain to heal and your will to surrender. I am glorified through My Son Jesus when you submit the tatters of your heart or life to His divine healing.

"I have a specific plan for you, Child, that cannot be fulfilled by any other, for there is no other designed just as I have designed you. I have designed each of My children to be unique to fill the specific work I have planned for each. Even though it may take some chiselling, shaping, cutting, and fire to prepare you for the service I have chosen, yet you need not be afraid. I will walk with you through every painful procedure and hold you close to Myself as we endure it all together. And do not be afraid of the fire, dear Child: for I will go with you and stand by you as the dross is consumed and the gold will remain for the praise of My name.

"My Child, you must also remember that the sufferings of this present time are not worth even speaking of when you compare them with the glory which will be revealed in you. The affliction and pain you face in this world for such a brief time is working for you such an exceeding treasure in glory, that you cannot truly comprehend its eternal value.

"So don't ever despair, My Child, but always trust your life, suffering, and future solely to My hand. I see the big picture and am planning the very best for your eternal well-being and for the time when you will be with Me forever in glory. I will keep you through everything, as the apple of My eye."

PRAYER: My Father in heaven, I thank You for showing me more clearly this path I must trod. I praise You for the love You have to me that You would be willing to walk this road with me, and that You are looking at what is best for my eternity. I claim the work of Jesus to bring me healing, grace, and strength for each step of the way, and I yield my will to blend in one with Your will. Amen.

There's Naught Too Hard

All things are possible with God,
As on life's path each day we trod;
There's nothing that's too hard for Him,
Though painful mountains loom so grim.

When dark affliction you must sup,
And overflowing seems your cup,
Yet God is near you and His hand
Is holding yours so you can stand.

When grief and heartache you shall know,
Christ Jesus understands your woe;
God's bottle now your tears doth hold,
As to His breast His child He folds.

To cups of sorrow, pain, and grief,
The Lord can bring a full relief;
No good from you will He withhold,
Nor will He leave you in the cold.

The mountains large He can dispel:
Affliction's torment He can quell;
Midst raging storms He gives His peace—
Gives joy and causes tears to cease.

There's naught too hard for God to do,
There's nothing He can't see you through:
Our God omnipotent is King,
Whose arm is strong in everything!

Midst trials He refines your soul—
Grants joy and calm though billows roll;
He holds you up by His strong hand,
And guides you to the "Promised Land"!

KETURAH C. MARTIN

A Consolation

When someone comes face to face with a heap of life's insurmountable shatters, it is a wonderful consolation to know that Jesus specializes in everything that to us seems impossible! He has an ear that can hear everything that needs to be said or exposed, and His arm is big enough to save, help, and heal everything that is brought to Him.

Though many individuals attempt all sorts of solutions to try to fix their shattered life, or more commonly to bury it all, yet Jesus remains the only True Solution to a full redemption out of the painful dust and ashes of abuse's destructions. It is a complete waste of time, energy, and life-span to attempt to bury the abuse, hurt, and aftermath of what one has survived in the deadly throes of abuse. The *burial method* of dealing with pain, abuse, sin, or any other negative thing, benefits only one individual; and that is Satan himself. It keeps everything unexposed and in darkness just the way he likes the conditions to be when he works in them. There in the darkness he creates all kinds of unseen footholds and binding strongholds in his unsuspecting captive.

The following are some of the lies Satan tries to inject into the mind and heart of his hapless captives:

- ❖ "I can deal with this all by myself."
- ❖ "God has rejected me and hates me for being so bad and dirty."
- ❖ "Nobody will love or respect me if they know what happened."
- ❖ "If everything is shoved into the closet it will go away eventually."
- ❖ "I am too black and worthless for Jesus to even look at."
- ❖ "It would be better to kill myself than to ever tell."
- ❖ "Nobody would ever be willing to help someone so filthy."
- ❖ "I am too worthless and detestable to receive help or hope."

PRAYER: Lord, I renounce the lie and the instigator behind it, that _____, and I ask that You break that lie and cleanse me from every stronghold that Satan has attempted to create through it. I choose to embrace Your truth, Lord, and I choose to accept the help, cleansing and healing that Jesus alone can bring to me. Amen.

"I Will Cleanse Every Stain"

As loose-sliding shale in an avalanche goes
With speed and momentum, which many don't know—
Just so one is buried 'neath filth, shame, and night
When someone defiles and destroys virgin rights.
Debauched and dishonored, devoid of all choice,
Polluted so vilely when none heard our voice,
When one's inner being is torn down to shreds—
On heart, mind, and body in filth someone treads.
All worth was stripped off to the dark, naked core,
And seems it will never be seen anymore;
There is no esteem, or respect for oneself—
Just filthy and broken—exposed on life's shelf.
The gusty wind whips up the memories so clear,
The filth, guilt, and anguish then pierce like a spear;
The rocks of dark filth jutting up everywhere,
Wreak havoc and pain in a life torn so bare.
Those sharp stones of shame pierce the heart and the feet,
And cause that one longs to make hasty retreat;
Defilement's huge boulders now barricade me,
Obscuring my vision—just foulness I see.
The muck of black grime all these boulders surrounds,
And nothing I see that is stabilized ground;
The limitless guilt now erupts from the muck,
Midst slime-ridden filth, where I'm hopelessly stuck.
Then Jesus comes nigh. Oh, dear soul, hear Him say,
"My Child, I have come to help show you the way;
I give you My hand, so by faith hold on tight—
I'll bear you away from filth's boulders and night.
I specialize, Child, in impossible things:
To heal broken hearts, and remove shameful stings,
Delivering captives from quagmires of grime,
Restore to them cleansing, in place of vile slime.
So yield Me each boulder, your heart's shattered pain—
In love through My blood I will cleanse every stain;
In My righteousness I'll re-clothe you, My Child:
For I have redeemed you from all that's defiled!"

KETURAH C. MARTIN

By Faith Hold On Tight

Viewing the landscape ahead, eight-year-old Alice shuddered fearfully as she saw immense boulders and rocks everywhere. She felt so alone and had no one to talk to and nowhere to go with all the dark shadows around her. If only she wouldn't be so filthy and bad inside, maybe someone would love her just a teeny-weeny bit. Tearfully she glanced about the field of boulders again, wishing there would be some way for her to reach that spot way over on the other side of the valley where the sun was shining so brightly. But she could not see beyond the huge rocks all round her, and everything felt hopeless, both inside her and all around.

As the tears ran in rivers down her cheeks, Alice sat down in the shade of a big rock to rest awhile.

Suddenly she was startled when someone touched her shoulder in a gentle manner. Looking around, she saw Jesus was right beside her, offering His hand to her with a love light shining in His eyes.

"I have seen your heart's cry and have come to rescue you and show you the way out of all these rocks which would hinder your journey. I want to hold your hand and bear you away beyond all the obstacles which the enemy uses to hinder you in the journey to freedom and joy. You are My child, and it is I Who can cleanse you from all the shame and filthy things you feel, which were not your fault. I have a clean white robe that I desire to clothe you with for your journey, and I have healing oil for your tattered heart. Will you allow Me to help you, Child?"

Oh Jesus, can You truly make it so I don't feel all yucky and dirty inside? Do You care enough to help me past all these boulders and the hard knocks that they give me? I am so scared of being hurt again so it is hard to trust anyone. Jesus, if You can love me just a teeny bit, please help me to get out of all these dark places to feel the sunshine. Please hold my hand, Jesus, and help me.

PRAYER: Jesus, I am so afraid, but I want to accept Your help and cleansing. Please help me not to be scared. I give You my hand and my heart so You can help me. And please can You make my body to be clean, Jesus? Amen.

The Path Of Least Resistance

The path of least resistance is the route which many choose:
For human nature bends us, if unchecked, that we will lose;
Though thorny situations are avoided on this road—
Devoid also are roses, as one's inner growth is slowed.
The crushed and hurting pilgrims are avoided on this trail—
They cry for help, midst anguish, yet it's all to no avail:
For none will leave their comfort zone, none care to understand—
Abstaining from the shattered lives—they heed not God's command.
The trail of least resistance will close up their hearts and ears,
To shut out cries of dying souls, despite their pleas and tears;
Here folks will wear their blinders, dark, that they for sure can't see
Reality of wounded hearts, outside "their zone" must be.
The path of least resistance by one common folk is walked,
The livid skeptic here doth tread beside the coward, locked—
They stand on deck of Judgment's Ship, immobilized by fear—
Refuse the lifeline to cast forth—afraid folks see or hear.
The road of least resistance will heed not the traps of death—
Dares not oppose the items dark which squelch the Spirit's breath,
But each man to himself is left to do what he may choose,
Despite the snares that Satan laid, despite that they will lose.
The path of least resistance, many think will make life calm,
Yet God said, "Bind up broken hearts and bring them healing balm"
Now how can peace surround the soul who turns from God's own Word?
Who represent their comfort zone, while God's love stays unheard?
How can we join the Pharisee with Levite priests of old?
Who held their skirts as they passed by survivors, wounded, cold?
Their bubble of self-righteousness, protecting at all costs,
As one lay bruised and bleeding, while dying lone and lost.
Before the Father can we stand in garments, spotless, white,
If we the brokenhearted shun, abhorring their pained plight?
Afraid to get our hands in dirt, nor walk with them a mile,
But rather from a distance view and judgments, harsh, compile.
We too could be in those same shoes—been beat and left to die,
And just the same, in anguished plight, been shunned despite our cry;
If Jesus we would represent—belong to God above,
All comfort zones we must forsake and live agape love!

KETURAH C. MARTIN

Which Path Will You Choose?

The path of least resistance is the one that is most frequently travelled both by the survivors of abuse and also those who should be involved to minister to them as Jesus would. The perpetrators also will take this path unless they are cast into prison or are overpowered by the Spirit of God in such a way that they truly long to make 180-degree turnaround by the power of Jesus Christ and take action. It is our duty to pray for this turnaround to take place that Jesus may be glorified in the transformation that only He can perform.

Often the survivors are just longing for a safe person and place to find a haven where they can feel protected, validated, and receive some hope and help. However, when God's people turn a deaf ear, a blind eye, a closed mind, and/or a cold heart toward these souls in need, they are taking the path of least resistance which is most inviting to their personal comfort zone. Consequently the mission of Jesus *to heal the brokenhearted* is brought to a screeching stop as His own people back away from being used as His hands, feet, and mouth. When God's people refuse to care, validate, or assist the abused, trafficked and brokenhearted, they stand accountable before God for misrepresenting the love, compassion, and potential healing of Jesus Christ.

The path of least resistance for the survivor will usually mean that everything of the abuse, aftereffects and unspeakable pain is buried away and hushed up. Often there are threats involved to keep it thus. However, when a survivor takes this route, those things that are buried begin to fester, rot, and reek until the putrid effects of it are writhing and frothing everywhere. Then relationships quake and shatter, and life continues to get more unsettled, painful, and utterly unbearable as time goes on. Eventually the individual can be destroyed from the inside out, or remain as a bitter, puckered shell of contempt filled with sugarless lemon juice while living the rest of their time as a cripple.

Jesus has the full solution to complete restoration and transformation, no matter what in life you have encountered or endured!

PRAYER: Jesus, I choose to take the path You have laid out and provided. I choose Your healing and desire to lead others to Your healing touch of love, regardless what others say or think, and alone for Your glory. Amen.

Jesus Loves Me

Jesus opened up my box,
Which had taken many knocks;
He took out the dirty rocks,
And the ugly shame that mocks.

Tenderly He touched my pain—
Wiped away my tears again:
Far away He took it all—
Near His cross it all did fall.

Jesus loves me, this I know,
'Cause His actions told me so;
He took me from darkest night,
To the day so clean and bright!

Now He walks with me each day,
With His light shows me the way—
He will always hold my hand,
Leading to a heav'nly land!

PRAYER: Thank-You Jesus for loving me enough to die in my place. Thanks Lord that You have the power to take away all the yucky stuff that hurts so bad inside and makes me dirty. Please make me clean and give me a white robe. Give me a job, Jesus in Your service so I can tell everyone I meet that *You love them!* Amen.

KETURAH C. MARTIN

Truth Of Jesus' Love

Love is sometimes a confusing matter to those who are on their journey to healing, because often the ones who hurt them also spoke words of love, or stood in the place where God meant for them to love unconditionally. Love as they know it is very scary, unsettling, and filled with all kinds of confusion.

It is also very disconcerting to survive domestic violence where one hears words of both love and hate while being so muddled together in the muck of lust that love becomes a filthy thing of utter destruction.

It may take a while to process the concept of Jesus' love while sorting through all those things which defined *love* previously.

When survivors experience the love of Jesus in action through His sincere children, it becomes much easier to understand God's love. But if they are avoided, condemned, and invalidated, the love of God is represented in a way that drives them away in terror and increased self-hate.

Truths about the Love of Jesus:

- The love of Jesus is so strong for you that He died in your place so you don't have to die.
- Jesus' love never slanders or degrades you.
- The love of Jesus never hurts you.
- Jesus' love makes you feel safe and is not scary.
- There is no dirt or filth in Jesus' love.
- The love of Jesus lives and gives sacrificially.
- Jesus' love does not get mad.
- The love of Jesus never forces or shoves you around.
- There is never any fear or threats in Jesus' love.
- The love of Jesus never seeks to gratify self at the expense of others.
- Jesus' love always seeks what is the very best for you.
- The love of Jesus carries you in His arms when you need help, love, and protection.

Cont.

PRAYER: Help me, Jesus, to trust and understand Your love. Help me to know and experience for sure how it is different from the false loves that I have known. I renounce every attempt of Satan to confuse me, and I claim the truth of Your love and blood over his lies. I choose to forgive and release to You the one who portrayed love in the enemy's definition rather than Your way. I choose to accept the love You had for me when You died on the cross for my sin, and I ask You to teach me how to love as You do, Jesus. Amen.

Be Assured God Is There

The Lord is almighty in knowledge and strength—
He has full control over each life at length:
He plans out the details of each soul He made,
And loves them so much that their ransom He paid!

His love is unsearchable, grace is untold,
And all His creation He daily enfolds
Within His control and His kind, loving care—
Wherever you are, be assured God is there.

Oft times we face circumstance, painful or sad,
And know not why we must face anguish this bad;
Of each situation the Lord has control,
Allowing those things which will build up your soul.

He understands fully just what you can bear,
And through every trial has offered to share
Your burden or heartache, your pain, grief, or loss,
And grants grace abundant for every dark cross.

God sees your life picture from start to the end—
Allows only things which will beautiful blend;
Commit to Him fully the pained paths you've trod,
And rest in the arms of your merciful God!

Don't ever despair midst adversity wild,
But hear God's soft whisper, "I love thee, My Child;
I never will fail thee, but walk by thy side,
And I will preserve thee, for whom Christ has died!"

Devoid Of Choice – No Voice

Written as a voice for the unborn

It started one day with a plan in God's heart
Before earth's foundation had yet seen its start,
He chose me back then to be part of His plan—
My Father who holds the whole world in His hand.

God knew me before I had ever been formed
Within my mom's womb—meant to be safe and warm,
Each intricate part of my body, soul, mind
Was lovingly shaped by a Father so kind.

The Lord God of life fashioned more every day
Of me, His creation, in His unique way—
From nothing He made a minute heart to beat,
And as time went on He then fashioned my feet.

Those first twenty weeks God had formed me in love,
Enfolding me safely like wings on a dove—
So safe and secure in my own mommy's womb,
I knew naught of anything close to the tomb.

I heard my mom's heartbeat so constantly throb,
But then felt abandoned and soon to be robbed
Upon that dark day that would shatter my world
When death and hell's demon's attack was unfurled.

So tiny and vulnerable—having no voice
They made me death's target with never a choice—
The agent of satan approached me to kill
By dark brutal torture—abortion's death bill.

Cont.

KETURAH C. MARTIN

Barbarous cold tools soon I felt on my arm
With pinching and pulling midst agony's harm,
I could not cry out, to speak up or e'en weep
As death ravaged near, where one's life rates as cheap.

But…Jesus drew near to my pained, bleeding side
And bore me above, in His bosom to hide,
He gently enfolded me close to His heart
And whispered, "I've loved you, My Child, from the start!"

My Jesus is Love and He died to bring life—
He rose from the grave and redeems from death's strife—
Christ advocates always for life, Oh so small,
And saves each of them, for He's Lord over all!

You Carried Me Through

"Though pain has engulfed me for most of my life,
Amid dark affliction, abuse, and death's knife,
Yet, Jesus, I thank You that many are spared,
And that You preserved me because You have cared.

My Lord, I do thank You that few understand
The anguish unlimited through my life fanned:
For this shows me, Lord, 'they have not known such pain'—
That they have been spared from dark agony's strain!

I thank You that many the filth do not know
Of lust-driven marriage, abuse, and dread woe,
Who can't comprehend the destruction and shame:
For this tells me, Lord, 'they know marriage-love's name.'

How empty and shallow I know I would be,
Had I never suffered those things come to me;
And, Lord, You can see the full picture, I know—
You have my life planned and the right way will show!

I praise You for teaching me, Lord, how to feel
The pain of the hurting, and thus help them heal;
Though suffering's school may be dark, pained, and grim,
Yet, Lord, strength divine has o'erflowed from Your brim!

I thank You for salvaging me from dark death,
Preserving my life when no more I had breath—
Midst pain without limits—when naught I can do,
Within Your own arms You have carried me through!"

KETURAH C. MARTIN

A Message For The Abuser

Many times, those who are travelling the road to healing and restoration face severe battles as the enemy attempts continually to create strongholds of bitterness, unforgiveness, and hatred toward the ones who were used as tools to abuse them. Just one little seed of bitter malice that the enemy can get wedged into the heart and mind can create a poisonous tree big enough to produce murder.

The battle may be even more intense when the perpetrator was a father or husband, for these men were ordained by God to portray the love of God the Father to a child and the love of Jesus Christ to the wife. Until these men and their destructions and misrepresentations are specifically released into the hand of God and His control, our healing is greatly impeded, and potential destruction is pending.

The following is a letter through which you who have faced domestic violence can join me in choosing to release our husbands into the hand and control of God.

To my husband _____,

This is just a short note whereby, with God's help, I choose to forgive and release you into the hand of the Lord for all the ways the enemy tried to destroy me through you. I choose to put into the hand of Jesus all the verbal destructions, false accusations, and deliberate attempts to degrade me to my children and to God's people. By God's grace, I choose to forgive and release all the physical and verbal beatings on my children that were ultimately directed to my heart, and I request the healing touch of Jesus in their lives, my life, and in your life also. I choose to release to Jesus all the violence, filth, and absolute control that shackled me in unseen chains. I claim the blood of Jesus to break every chain and fetter and to loosen my heart to love as Jesus did. I choose to believe that the love of Jesus for the church is so strong that He never hurt her, but He rather gave Himself completely to death so she could live.

Cont.

I choose with God's help to look at you through the eyes of Jesus, and I place within His care the hurting little boy which He helps me to see. I pray God's touch of love on your heart and ask for Him to bring healing and salvation to that little boy who is trapped in a man's body and longing for a touch of love.

Your wife, _____

PRAYER: The Lord bless thee and keep thee: the Lord make His face to shine upon thee, and be gracious unto thee: the Lord lift up His countenance upon thee and give thee peace. Amen.

KETURAH C. MARTIN

Forgiveness Is The Only Way

A grudge may start out very small,
But oh, so soon its bitter gall
Expands and eats its way throughout
The heart and mind with captious shout.

A grudge is like a poison weed,
So dangerous, casting yet more seeds:
The seeds of malice, hate, and wrath
Become large trees that block one's path.

A grudge through Jesus must be brought
To Calvary, forgiveness sought:
For if I can't forgive a grudge,
Then God Himself will be my Judge.

"My Child, again, you must forgive:
For with a grudge I cannot live,
Nor can I keep your heart's house clean
When malice rules as king and queen.

If you forgiveness want from Me,
Forthcoming it must be from thee
Toward each of your fellowmen—
Forgive and then forgive again.

Dear Child, forgive each soul today—
Forgiving is the only way
To have a life unmarred by sin;
Forgive that heaven you may win!"

PRAYER: Lord, I choose to forgive and release to You, every individual who has hurt me. Please take back all the ground the enemy stole through my bitterness, and I yield that ground to Your control. Replace all the unforgiveness with Your divine love and make me an instrument of Your love. Amen

"Father, Forgive Them"

Jesus is the best Example of *choosing to forgive* abusers of anyone in the entire history of the world. Because He went through abuse to a far greater extent than anyone else before or after Him, He understands every situation perfectly and is qualified to assist everyone.

Jesus not only suffered abuse from one person or a handful of people, He suffered and died because of the sin of the whole world and every single individual in it. He gave His life as a Supreme Sacrifice for every person He ever did or would create throughout time, so they could choose to be free from sin and the devil through this prepaid ransom He made for all.

When Jesus chose to forgive, He was enduring far more than the very worst abuse and death that we can truly fathom. In addition, He was also carrying the weight of the sins for the entire population of mankind from the beginning of time until the end of time when eternity will begin. He did not even have the support of His Father, although it was God's plan that He die in the place of humans. Because God could not look at sin, therefore He could not look on Jesus while He was carrying the sins of all mankind.

As Jesus hung on the cross, choosing to forgive, the whole world forsook Him as His Father also turned His face away. Jesus hung there *forgiving* while experiencing a state of unfathomed abuse, complete rejection, and unavoidable death.

Jesus' death was the ultimate hope for us as humans, and He completed what He came to do when He arose from the dead on the third day to live forevermore! If Jesus had not taken power over death, sin, and Satan by arising from the dead, our faith would be in vain. Now, because He is alive, He is at the right hand of God making intercession for us and being our Advocate in every situation. He is also alive to walk with us through every suffering we face and to bring healing to every abuse, as well as be our Savior from sin and a lost eternity.

PRAYER: Thank You, Jesus, for showing me how to choose forgiveness. Thank You for dying in my place so that I can be free from sin and healed through Your salvation and Your name. Amen.

KETURAH C. MARTIN

The Rainbow In Each Tear

The path to healing may be rough,
The journey upward grim and tough,
But don't despair or lose your hope:
For God alone views life's full scope.

He sees the boulders looming high
And hears the pain of every cry;
He knows emerging anguish near
And gently saves each falling tear.

Despite obstructions in the way
The Lord will guide you night and day:
For He can use each painful thorn
To help you grow and life adorn.

He knows that terror oft creeps near,
But sees the rainbow in each tear,
Yet when Christ leads to higher ground
Divine protection will surround.

God knows that peace can follow pain,
That in each tear there will be gain;
He holds our life within His hand
And guides us to His promised land!

So yield yourself to His control—
Your body, heart, the mind and soul:
For God alone can see what's best,
And He will lead to perfect rest!

Jesus Meets The Brokenhearted

How does Jesus actually respond to the brokenhearted individuals He comes across? Is there any time He ever bypassed any sick, abused, or broken people He encountered? Does the Scripture indicate that Jesus ever attempted to get someone to just leave so He could do His own things?

Long before Jesus came to this earth, it was predicted how He would respond to the brokenhearted. In fact the Bible specifically mentions that Jesus came to heal the brokenhearted (Isa. 61:1-3)!

It has always been an immense encouragement to know that one of the reasons Jesus came was for the purpose of bringing healing to anyone and everyone who would accept it from Him. That is 100 percent proof that Jesus Christ cares about those who are shattered, abused, and/or rejected, or whatever the cause for a broken heart! In addition to healing, Jesus has also come to bring freedom to the captives and to open the prison doors of those who are bound! He truly cares about all those in any sort of trouble! The fact that Jesus also came with the intentions of giving *beauty in exchange for the ashes* is an anchor of hope for the survivor to hang onto when the dirty ashes are all that can be seen. The Bible also relays that part of Jesus' mission is to give out the garment of praise in place of the spirit of heaviness. His intention and desire is to transform all these brokenhearted individuals, abuse survivors, prisoners, and captives into trees of righteousness bearing the touch and fruit of the Lord!

We have a glorious future and hope before us as we embrace *the gift of healing* that Jesus brought when He came to earth 2000 years ago. Never accept any lie of Satan which would question the truth of what Jesus has to offer. There may be people who claim they belong to God but do not represent His love and compassion to the broken and abused as Jesus would. That does not discredit what Christ has to offer you, but only disqualifies them from being His ambassadors to administer the love of Jesus.

PRAYER: Lord Jesus, I choose to accept Your great love offer, to heal my broken heart and all the shatters that the abuse left me in. I bring myself to You and ask You to begin the work within. Please walk with me through all the pain of dealing with it. Please restore me, Jesus. Amen.

I the Lord Gather Thee

"My Child, do come closer and rest in My arms:
For I am thy Refuge and Shield from alarms;
Though trials are crushing and life's filled with pain—
My Child, don't despair yet: for all is not vain.

Though grieved and forsaken, I've called thee My Child,
Though you've been refused, so abused, and defiled,
With mercies so great, I the Lord gather thee—
My kindness eternal surrounding shall be.

Oh, thou so afflicted and with tempest tossed,
Although without comfort amid your pained loss,
Should none understand all thy agonized heart—
Yet I will perform all that in thee I start.

Thy house and foundation I lay with fair stones,
With Me in full charge, Child, you're never alone—
Though some speak together against thy pained cause,
Yet I know all things and these dark words will pause.

No weapon against thee shall prosper, My Child—
Each tongue be condemned which speaks judgments so wild:
For this from the Lord shall thy heritage be,
And all of thy righteousness, Child, is from Me.

Commit all thy circumstance, Child, to My hand:
For I am thy God and in full understand;
In floods of great waters I'll bring thee safe through:
For things thought impossible I can still do!"

Renouncing Lies Resulting From Rejection

The rejection and misunderstanding experienced from God's people due to their lack of knowledge was damaging and potentially life-altering. The resulting lies of the enemy had to be addressed.

"Thank You, Lord, for helping me see through Your eyes. Lord, I also want to bring You the lie that 'I Am A Repulsion To You And Your People.' Can You teach me Your truth and how to see it all through Your eyes?"

"My Child, you are looking at yourself through lenses that have been smeared with the shame, filth, repulsion, and pain of your experiences, so it all becomes distorted. I see past the damage, agony, and the projected filth and shame to your heart, which I designed for My use and glory when it is cleansed and healed by Jesus. I have bought you with a price, chosen you, and called you by name—You are Mine! My thoughts for you are more in number than the sands of the sea."

"Lord, if I am not shameful, why have so many of Your people and preachers avoided, shunned, and warned their people against me, while condemning me for surviving all the past abuses of a lifetime?"

"My people are destroyed for lack of knowledge, and those who have rejected, shunned, and condemned you did so with lack of knowledge. They did not look through My eyes and see the wounded little girl so lost, alone, bleeding, and dying for whom I have a plan, or they would have encircled you with My love, help, and understanding. Instead, human reasoning marred their vision and created a fear to relate to you as 'My Child' or to accept what they couldn't understand. Consequently, it became easier to condemn and reject you rather than reverse their reasoning and seek My love, counsel, and understanding. Those people who do not accept, support, understand, and walk with you, I want you to leave to Me, always choosing to release and forgive them."

"Lord, I yield these lies to Your control and ask for Your forgiveness for even considering them. I ask that You would take back all the ground given to Satan through hanging onto them, and I yield that ground to Your control and truth. I choose to forgive and release all those who have shunned, rejected, and condemned me into Your hand, and I am willing to pay the emotional pain and consequences they have caused me. Please bring me healing, Jesus. Amen."

Love In Action

The great sea of life is vaster than withal we sail our boat,
Thus through eyes of Christ our Master let us view each soul afloat:
For His eyes of love are searching for the lost and sinking souls
Who in foaming waves are lurching with no lifeline, hope, or goals.

Let us view their soul's deep value—not the chains that have them bound,
Knowing Christ can make all things new in each lamb which He has found;
With the Savior throw out lifelines, as redeemed fishers of man:
For we're instruments in last times—to be used in God's great plan!

Go and walk beside the brother who is struggling in the way,
Doing daily for another just as Jesus did each day;
Lend a hand to lift the fallen, guide them to the Savior's side,
And though other things are "calling" may eternal things preside.

"My dear children, I remind thee that so much you have received,
And I ask that ye give freely as the needy are relieved:
For when faith is put in action and My love is lived in full,
Then the Gospel has more traction as more souls to Me are pulled."

When you view the brokenhearted, or see downtrod cast aside—
When from loved ones some are parted, then remember Christ Who died:
Look at each soul only, always through the eyes of our dear Lord,
His love minister for His praise: for no less can we afford!

For to live the love of Jesus to the souls out on life's sea—
Though inconvenience squeeze us yet to Him let's faithful be:
For on us the Lord is counting to represent Him always true—
And His promises keep mounting of all His grace to see us through!

PRAYER: "Lord Jesus, I ask You to never waste my pain, but use it as means to understand and empathize with the brokenhearted around me. Guide me to those on life's sea whom You want to touch with Your love and redemption for the glory of Jesus. Amen."

Offering Love And Safety

"I shall not die, but live and proclaim the works of the Lord." This is one of the verses I have clung to in some of my darkest nights. For fifteen years I had an active scar tissue on the mood center of my brain, which caused massive twenty-hour depressive episodes with every seizure that came. Consequently, due to experiencing three to twenty seizures daily, I was overcome with such an intense depression, 24/7, that the suicidal thoughts it produced were a continual threat for years. I wanted nothing to do with death, but the horrible thing mercilessly engulfed me. Additionally, I was severely programmed to commit suicide by two specific perpetrators. Suicide is not something that is instigated by God, neither does He condone medical assistance in dying. It is also something that most people do not want to acknowledge or discuss. However, because it is an unwanted reality, it must be addressed so that more individuals can be escorted by love and validation out of the pit of hopelessness.

Often survivors are engulfed in unfathomed despair and hopelessness due to the extreme agony and aftereffects of the horror they carry. When there is no safe place to go and no safe person to talk to, everything within only grows more putrid and desperately hopeless. If the people who should be safe, supportive, and helpful, such as *medical personnel, Christians, and clergymen*, are not, then the risk of drastic escape becomes more potentially prominent.

It is *not* the job of the Church, its leaders, or the laypersons to judge and condemn the survivor when suicidal tendencies are prominent. Nor is it in anyone's place to withdraw from and/or avoid these hurting individuals, pretending that everything is just fine. It is the responsibility of God's people to live the love of Jesus to the wounded and hopeless, just as Christ did. Ignorance is no excuse, for it is possible to exemplify the love of Jesus regardless of what one doesn't know about abuse or its aftereffects. (See Hosea 4:6 and Ezekiel 34:1-16.)

The enemy is very jubilant when God's so-called *people* reject the wounded or live in willful pretense and ignorance around the needs present. Satan at that point injects more lies and poison to help persuade one *to just end it all since they're so hopeless and worthless, even to God's people.*

PRAYER: Jesus, please help me to live Your love to all the broken people You lead me to. Give me wisdom and willingness to be Your hands and feet. Amen.

Hope And Healing After Rape

Hark, list to the message of truth that I bring—
Old, young, and all others, my song you can sing:
Praise God, I can shout from the mountain tops high,
Exalting my Lord, Who did not let me die!

Abused and degraded, downtrod in the grime,
No friend, hope, or help in the midst of vile crime;
Dear friend, I assure you that Jesus was there—

Had absent He been, I'd have died in despair!
Enfolding me close, He ensured life and breath,
And carried me through what was worse than dark death;
"Life never was meant to be shamed and defiled,
Indeed, I still love you, despite all, My Child.
Now give to Me fully, each boulder of pain—
Give up the black filth and the shameful disdain;

And, Child, do remember that I specialize:
From ruined trashed rubble, to make a great prize
That's fashioned and purified through grace divine—
Engraved in My hand as a treasure that's Mine;
Remember, I too, faced abuse on the cross—

Resigned to the suffering to save you from dross.
And now I stand waiting to transform your life—
Perfect to the fullest, amid shame's vile strife;
Each scar, wound, and damage which pierced through your core,

Fulfilling My purpose, as healing I pour
Inside your pained tatters, which ooze filthy shame,
Life's mountains of pain I remove through My name;
There's no foe or filth which My plan can assail—
Hope, help, and blest healing with Me will prevail!"

No Limits To His Compassion

It is not uncommon for survivors of abuse to feel and believe that they are too bad and destroyed to ever be fixed or clean again. Even the thought of God looking down and accepting and loving them cannot in the least be fathomed. Their terrified hearts cry out in agony and hopelessness as they flounder along, sometimes moment by moment, in utter despair.

But harken, my friend! I am alive today with abundant hope and healing because of the bigness of God to fix and heal everything. He loves and accepts the bruised, broken, trafficked, and abused, regardless of how dark or evil everything was. Jesus will never cast you away because of what was done to you, as some of the bad men try to say. It was Jesus Who stood beside you to keep you alive and He made it so the pain and damage was not any worse.

Though it feels as though you have been reduced to a heap of rubble and ashes, yet I come to tell that there is abundant hope for you to be transformed into a vessel of honor through Jesus Christ.

Clear away the rubble . . .

- I renounce the lie that I am too trashed to find healing.
- I renounce the lie that God cannot love someone this worthless.
- I renounce the lie that I am too dirty to be fixed, healed, or accepted.
- I renounce all Satan's suggestions, schemes, and threats, and I claim the blood of Jesus over them.
- I acknowledge that God never makes junk, and that He can restore trashed ruins into something valuable.
- I acknowledge that Jesus loves me and wants to bring me complete healing.
- I acknowledge that no depth of abuse and shame can separate me from the love of Jesus.
- I acknowledge that one drop of Jesus' blood is far more powerful than our enemy Satan, all his demons, kingdoms, and agendas put together; and through Christ my Savior I shall conquer and win through the victory He has already won over the enemy!

The Weaver's Design

"Your life is a picture that if I may weave,
Will shine with Christ's beauty, but you must believe;
Surrender the pieces and patches that be—
The dolorous segments, just yield all to Me.
Child, bring Me your tatters of agonized pain,
Your remnants of anguish and grief-laden strain,
The rags of affliction now garbing your soul—
Come cast them on Me, Child—let Me take control.
Your bruised, wounded heart that's all mangled and torn,
Can still be restored and with Jesus adorned:
Who gave up His life, all your sins gladly bore—
No shreds are too painful that He can't restore,
By power divine, moved in love's matchless grace—
There's healing at Calv'ry for all you have faced:
For out of the ashes and rends of deep pain,
Thy Lord creates beauty with infinite gain.
The strands of dark sorrow, when given to Me,
Shine forth as pure gold in your life tapestry;
The suffering tatters in luster will shine
When used in the weaving of My hand divine!
The rags of stained filth which were cast upon you,
Will glimmer in cleansing with vesture so new!
While rends of deep anguish, when yielded they be,
Will manifest beauty created by Me!
I see your life picture before it's begun—
Its beauty, eternal, I know ere it's done;
Through Jesus, pain's damage is fully erased—
Each piece, scrap, and fragment is touched by My grace!
My Child, I delight to make known within thee,
My power and glory that others may see
A picture that's woven in love's grace divine,
Which patterns hurt souls to the Weaver's design!"

The Weaver's Loom

In a room where one would observe the weaver busy at his loom, what all could be learned? A weaver's loom is a device that is used to weave cloth into various textures, designs, and for multiple uses, such as rugs, materials, linens, etc. There are handlooms, inkle looms, and the larger looms. Some of the first hand looms were hung from a tree while working with them; others are large enough to fill an entire room.

A weaver works with all shapes, sizes, and lengths of various types of threads and materials. It is noteworthy to consider that much of the material with which he works consists of small shreds, various tatters, and skinny threads to make something worthwhile and beautiful. He also blends together the dark ugly strands with those of glimmering gold to create outstanding designs in his workmanship.

It is little wonder that God can do likewise with the shatters and dreadful things in our life experience. He has far more expertise in weaving something beautiful out of the unpleasant shatters than any weaver in the entire history of the world. God tenderly takes the dirty, obnoxious strands of horror that we cannot even bear to think about into His hand. There He washes them clean and sparkling, after which He begins weaving them with the golden cords of His love. Because He can already see, before it's finished, just how He wants our life picture to be, He knows exactly which tatter of anguish to use with each silver thread of His grace. The pieces we thought were black and ugly begin to look picturesque even from the underside of our life's weaving, which is all we can see with our human eyes. Those painful items soaked in blood and tears, when taken into His hand, become uniquely gorgeous as they are intermingled with the purple and gold of His tender love and healing. As we watch the Lord weaving with loving effort and forethought, suddenly the pain of the past does not seem so deplorable if God can indeed use it to make something beautiful and worthwhile! What joy to see our ashes turn into something beautiful!

PRAYER: Lord, I give You all the tatters, strands, and rags of my broken life. I ask You to weave something beautiful for Your glory out of everything submitted into Your hand. Thank You, Jesus, for making this possible. Amen.

OCTOBER 1
READING: REVELATION 21:3-7

Beauty For Ashes

There buried in ashes with shame, filth, and night,
Enshrouded with hopelessness, hiding all light:
So downtrod I lay in the gathering gloom—
Devoid of all value, naught left but dark doom.

Then Jesus came digging through ashes and dust—
"To look for my ruins" He thought was *a must;*
He saw my captivity 'neath all the shame,
And lovingly sought my stained life to reclaim.

Then reaching beneath the dark ashes and grime—
Not heeding the filth that was putrid and prime,
He picked up my heart that was broken and torn:
Poured oil in the wounds that were bleeding and sore.

Midst solace and comfort He bound up my wounds—
Retrieving me wholly from rubbles and ruins;
The garment of praise He then wrapped around me,
In place of the heaviness one used to see!

He cleansed me and freed me from filth's shameful night—
Gave beauty for ashes as all was made bright;
With His righteousness He then clothed me through love—
Restoring true value for His praise above!

No ash pile is bigger than His love and grace:
For He can repair the most broken-down place;
My Jesus is willing and able to bring
From out of the ashes, a clean heart that sings!

OCTOBER 2

READING: ISAIAH 61:3-7

We Can't Hide The Ashes

Many times during our healing journey, it literally feels as though we are buried in ashes of shame and filth. Jesus does indeed give beauty for ashes when we bring Him our filth, pain, and shame. He delights in turning cesspools of shame into rivers of joy; reeking, stark filth into fragrant, bright blooms; writhing, dark pain into peaceful assurance; and black, shattered trust into full faith in His merciful love and presence!

When we choose to yield these adverse experiences and all their aftereffects into the hand of Jesus Christ, the potential of what He in turn can do is beyond what we can imagine. It will never work to attempt to hide the agonizing hurts, abuses, grief, and/or rejections that we have faced. Satan loves to wreak havoc in the dark of the closet when we seek to hide or ignore it all. Consequently, many individuals anguish through life as emotionally and spiritually crippled, not realizing that Jesus the Great Physician is just waiting and yearning to turn their ashes, pain, and rags into tools. With these tools, He can produce a vessel of honour that is cleansed in His blood, healed by His touch, empowered by His resurrection, clothed in His righteousness, and in-filled with His Holy Presence.

Crippled, alone, and dying for years and decades, I was crying and longing after God. When the Lord's timing was right, He answered my cry more fully than I could have ever hoped for, despite a life of shattered dreams! He can restore the years which the locusts have eaten! Praise be to Jesus!

PRAYER: Jesus, I ask that You would take all the dark, dirty ashes, pain, and horrors out of the closet. I bring it all to Your light, truth, and love, where You can bring hope and healing through the power of Your blood. Please do not allow the enemy to keep anything hidden, and, Jesus, I need Your help to bear the pain of all You bring out to the light. Amen.

But Jesus Stepped In!

As just a small child she was dumped in the cold
Rejected, abandoned, amid pain untold;
Her pained heart was cast with neglect in a ditch—
All trampled and bruised, and made darker than pitch;
Yet never was "love" poured like oil in the heart,
But rather, dark arrows pierced through as a dart.
This little girl trudged in the slough of despair
For years all alone and with no one to care—
With no soul to share with—not one place to turn,
Rejection's pained fires continued to burn.
But there was a Hand so divine and unseen—
Preserving His Child with a loving eye, keen.

She longed for a mother's embrace of the heart,
And wept in lone anguish each time night did start;
For nothing she knew of the kindling of "love"—
Just heartbroken pain and rejection's dread shove.

Yet was it the sustenance of the Most High
Who saw the torn heart and did not let her die?
Amid abuse quicksand, did He hold her up
Despite writhing anguish dispersed in her cup?
Oh, how her heart cried for just one in the land
To help fix her heart and in full understand,
Yet most veered away from the heart-shreds of pain—
The heart-bleeding wounds many held in disdain.
But Jesus stepped in to bring help to the end,
Who midst pain's dark waters did not flee or bend;
He brought complete freedom to depths none could sound,
Oh thank You, my Jesus, for love that abounds!

Bringing Shambles To Jesus

When Jesus steps in to make a difference in someone's life and to bring restoration to shambles of pain and shame, He does a complete job of love. He can restore the years that the locusts have eaten, even when all looks hopeless. His heart is just bursting with compassion for every torn heart and life out there and is waiting with open arms to receive each one into His love and healing.

In my journey, I realized that for years I had believed a lie which is a common one Satan uses to cripple pained survivors.

"Lord, for years I have believed that I'm too debased and contaminated to be of value to You, but I want to reject the lie and ask that You show me the truth from Your viewpoint."

"I, the Lord, have created you with a specific purpose and plan in mind. There are many people who have abused, rejected, and totally crushed you in body, mind, and emotions, against My love and perfect will, but I have preserved you! This has left you feeling so filthy, used, degraded, and below human that from your standpoint, you cannot see that I can still transform you into a vessel for My divine will and work."

"Lord, will You teach me how You see it all?"

"My power, grace, and love is beyond limits, and there is no life that is too trashed for Me to fix, heal, and use for My glory, if you let Me. The filth and destruction man has wrought upon you can be transformed by My hand into something more beautiful than you can fathom, which I can use in My kingdom to exalt My name through Christ Jesus. The filth, shame, destruction, and contamination you feel and suffer are not really yours, but they belong to the perpetrators and the instigator, Satan, who sought to destroy both you and My plan for you. It is through Jesus Christ and all He has done for you that I can cleanse, heal, and restore 100 percent of all the pain, defilement, bondage, and damage. Then I will sanctify you as a vessel of honour ready for the Master's work and glory. You, Child, are Mine!"

PRAYER: Jesus, I too want to bring You the lie that, _____ and I ask You to teach me Your truth. I renounce this lie by the blood of Jesus and desire that You bring healing to me in every area of my life. Amen.

I Came To The Garden With You

"Lord Jesus, I come to the garden with You,
To give You my will, as my strength You renew:
For You've gone before me when You yielded all—
You know my heart's cry, Lord, before I yet call.

Affliction's dark waters I don't understand,
But, Jesus, I know that Your love holds my hand;
Your ways are much higher than mine could e'er be—
Each step in my future You perfectly see.

I kneel in the garden and yield to Your hand
Each breath of my life that is measured like sand;
I yield You each flower of fragrance so sweet,
And, Lord, every thorn I lay too at Your feet.

Lord, here at the brook in life's garden I share
My heart, so afflicted, with Thee Who dost care;
I yield up my will that it may flow with Thine,
Requesting that Thy will be done, Lord—not mine.

Lord, please be the Gardener of my heart's soil,
And dig up the weeds that would round my heart coil,
Plant deep in my heart all Your seeds of true love—
And lavishtly water with grace from above."

My Lord and I walk the steep ridge hand in hand,
He brings me to heights where I then understand:
That when my will, yielded, with His flows as one,
His grace is outpoured and His will shall be done!

In The Garden With Jesus

When Jesus went to the Garden of Gethsemane, He went specifically to give up His will and the human part of Himself to God. He wanted to be alone with His Father before yielding Himself into the hands of evil men who would brutally abuse Him and then murder Him at the site of crucifixion. He desired to gain the strength He needed from His Heavenly Father, knowing that His hour to face death for all of mankind was nearly upon Him.

As Jesus went a little way off from the three chosen disciples, He fell on the ground in extreme sorrow and heaviness. Coming before the Father, Jesus pled for Him to *take this cup away before I drink it.* Then in total submission to His Father's will He added, *Nevertheless, not My will, but Thine be done.*

The devil was also there in the garden to fight against Jesus, doing everything he could to defeat Him. But the enemy is not nearly as powerful as the Son of God!

The unfathomable distress that Jesus experienced in the garden affected the physical, emotional, and spiritual parts of Him as the whole world was put on His shoulders and the choice at hand. Then Jesus began to sweat as it were great drops of blood as he prayed in agony in the garden. A third time He prayed and gave up His will into the Father's hand, and then the soldiers came to transport Him to judgment and death.

Jesus showed us the importance of giving up our will to accept the will and work of God. Through it, He became a faithful High Priest Who is able to save us all to the uttermost and can share in our sufferings because He understands completely.

It is very important in our healing journey to surrender to God our will, the past and pain, and all the lies and inroads that Satan has tried to make in our times of vulnerability. Jesus, in His love escorts us step by step, breaks every bondage/lie, takes back ground from the enemy, and builds a foundation anchored on His truth.

PRAYER: Dear Father in heaven, I choose to surrender my will to You and ask that You help my will to be totally lost in Your will. I choose to open my life of agony so You can begin Your touch of love and healing within. Take everything ugly and painful and please make it into something for Your glory. Amen.

KETURAH C. MARTIN

Jesus Frees From The Past

It matters not, friend, what your past doth all hold—
In arms of acceptance the Lord would enfold
You close to His breast in His undying love,
And seeks to bring freedom and light from above!

Just kneel at the cross in surrender sincere,
Where Jesus awaits you—in love He draws near,
Desiring to cleanse, free, and heal all your past,
Regardless what burdens on Him you will cast.

Though sin-stains seem blacker than others' you know,
And chains of dark bondage each day seem to grow,
The blood of my Jesus sufficient abounds,
Forgiving all past life—brings cleansing profound!

The blood of Christ Jesus brings freedom from past—
No anguishing cloud over you can it cast:
For healing and cleansing in Christ is complete,
Thus arms of the past cannot drag back defeat!

Because of Christ's vict'ry o'er sin, death, and hell,
Our past has been conquered by pow'r naught can quell:
For freedom, perfected in Jesus is found—
The shackles of past life cannot keep us bound!

The presence of Jesus with us now abides,
With past all behind us, we stand justified;
He's cleansed and restored us—so lavishly healed:
As purified vessels, for His glory sealed!

The Worst Past Is For Jesus!

Many times there are individuals who believe that their past is way too horrible, defiled, evil, and excruciating for Jesus to even be willing to look at. But one thing I was often reminded of by one of God's agents when this belief came up with me was the thief on the cross beside Jesus. The thief had lived a wicked life and deserved the punishment he was getting. He knew what he deserved, but just before he died he addressed Jesus.

"Lord, remember me when thou art come into Thy kingdom," he said.

Jesus replied in love, "Today shalt thou be with me in paradise."

Today that man is with Jesus in glory because he was humble enough to recognize Jesus as *Lord* and to ask for His help.

This short story has always made it very obvious that with Jesus there is no respect of persons. There is nobody that is too bad for Jesus to love, forgive, cleanse, or bring freedom to.

Jesus' love has no measure. His grace has no limits. His mercy is unfathomed. And His forgiveness moves things as far away as the east is from the west. (See Psalm 103:12.)

He died for all, and His arm is not shortened that it cannot save, but is outstretched to all, regardless of where they find themselves or what is their experience. Even the dark world of the occultic realm and all the ritualistic things therein are not too hard for Jesus to take care of completely while He enfolds you in His arms of love with loads of freedom to give out. Without His freedom, love, and healing in these things, I would not be alive to tell the story of hope! Praise God for His unspeakable gift of love and hope from all the realm of darkness!

The death of Jesus on the cross was fully sufficient for all our sin, needs, abuses, and pain. He has all power in heaven and in earth and there is nothing too hard for Him to heal, restore, fix, forgive, and/or transform!

PRAYER: Jesus, I choose to believe that You have all power and love to fix my trashed life and make it into something of worth. I claim Your blood over all my past, sin, and abuse, and I ask You to heal me and make me an ambassador for You, with my past wiped clean through Your blood, Jesus. Amen.

Stop! And Hear The SRA Survivors

A Victim's Cry . . .

> "Will somebody listen? Can anyone hear?
> Oh, for a safe heart that could feel my pained tears!
> Why can no one validate all I've been through,
> And many believe not the death waves that blew.
>
> When I speak the truth of what happened to me,
> It's mostly discounted as *absurdity;*
> Please send someone, Jesus, with love's open heart,
> Who will understand all the things I impart.
>
> No soul comprehends how the death threats do loom,
> If I dare expose all the filth, pain, and doom,
> Yet when I risk all and will dare to speak up,
> Dark doubt and rejection is hurled in my cup!
>
> Can nobody realize my dangerous spot?
> Know not they that I will face death if I'm caught
> Exposing the coven and deadly deeds there?
> Will someone grant safety, believe, and just care?
>
> Oh, please just believe all the filth, shame, and night,
> The rituals gruesome, midst blood-flowing rites;
> So many are suff'ring and dying in pain,
> Midst horrors that none will believe could e'er rain."

(continued later . . .)

PRAYER: "Jesus, I come to You on behalf of all the suffering and traumatized children/survivors around the world. Surround them with Your Presence and eternal love, Jesus. By the power of Your blood, Lord, bind every power of evil that is attempting to steal, kill and destroy them. I commit each lamb into Your power and control, and ask that You bring each one to freedom, life and healing in You. Amen."

I Hear Your Pained Cry

For the SRA Survivors . . .

This is a note of acknowledgment from the author addressed to all of you out there who have experienced the atrocities of Satanic Ritual Abuse and its aftermath. I understand and validate the terror of what is daily faced about *never speaking, and the threats involved.* I understand the unspeakableness of all that happened, which few can comprehend unless they have been there. The invisible lines and unseen fences and everything they hold, I acknowledge and lay before the Lord Who knows it all.

I validate your survival and commend you for your will to live when it would have been much easier to die. I stand beside you emotionally as you endeavor to wade through the insurmountable inner agony, whose true depths observers have no way of understanding.

Most of all I praise and thank Jesus for standing right there in the darkness, pain, and terror, ensuring your survival of the unspeakable evil and horror that was around you. Even though you may not have seen or felt Him near, He was there because He loved you, and you are alive.

You are precious in the sight of Jesus, the Son of God, Who was made the Supreme Sacrifice once for all to free you and all others from the grip of satanic evil. You may not know Him yet, but He knows and loves you far beyond all human comprehension. He had all the details of your existence written in His book before they were even fashioned in the womb (Psalm 139:15, 16).

Though your life may feel completely wasted and destroyed, I must share that there is abundant hope, help, and healing available because of Jesus and His love for you.

The following prayer I pray on Your behalf:

PRAYER: Lord Jesus, I bring _____ to You and ask that You would enfold her in Your arms of love and give her a place of safety near Your heart. I claim the blood of Jesus over _____ and every experience of pain and darkness she has endured. In the name of Jesus, I bind every evil power, ritual, and chain that would bind or destroy _____ . Pour out Your continual strength on _____ and lead her gently by the hand into complete healing and freedom. Hear her cry, Oh Lord, and attend unto her prayer, in Jesus' name. Amen.

Stop! And Hear the SRA Survivors

Conclusion of the Matter . . .

We must stop and hear the survivors of pain,
Regardless how gruesome the horrors sustained:
For Satan the world's disbelief doth expect—
And schemes, that our doubts on the victim reflect.

We can't let the enemy hide 'neath our doubt,
But we must believe what he's truly about:
To steal and to kill—to destroy is his name
And evil is boundless where he plays his game.

We cannot pretend that these things happen not,
Nor turn a blind eye to the ones who are caught,
But we must accept these survivors of pain—
Accredit the horrors and wounds they've sustained.

They need a safe haven and heart that will hear,
Someone who will validate each pain and fear,
A soul confidential, who lives out God's love,
Is what they must have to be touched from above.

Do not judge or scorn them in this their dire strait:
For hurt upon hurt will just add to their fate;
Leap not in with judgment but in love draw near,
And represent Jesus—just listen and hear

For we are the instruments God seeks to use,
To pour out His healing on all those abused;
Through doubt and neglect we can't let Jesus down:
For He's won the vict'ry o'er evil profound!

*Inasmuch as ye have done it unto one of the least of
these, My brethren, ye have done it unto Me.*
—Jesus

OCTOBER 12
READING: MATTHEW 28:18-20 AND 1 JOHN 4:4

A Plea To God's Children

Brothers and sisters in Christ the world over, I implore you in the name of Jesus to open your hearts, ears, and minds to the cries of the needy, abused and hurting.

The label *Satanic Ritual Abuse* needs not cause alarm or strike terror to your heart. It need never cause you to shut your mind or close your willingness to assist in love someone who is trapped in these death talons. You never need to avoid them with skirts lifted high as you pass by on the other side of the road.

We are the hands, feet, mouth, and representation of Jesus Christ. As children of God and joint-heirs with Jesus, we have nothing to fear from Satan, his demons, or anything occultic when we are armed with the Lord!

We've got the power over every demonic force and over Satan himself, through the blood of Jesus. Why do we cower, brethren, when all of heaven is backing us, the Spirit of God is within us, Jesus is leading us, and all of God's angels are around us? With all these in their places, there is no room left for Satan to be anywhere but under us, because of Jesus! We have the power available to us if we but take it, and we never need to fear or make excuse. God is calling us to reach out to all broken men/women and minister to their needs. Because Satan is 100 percent defeated, we must proceed as though we do in fact believe it. The source of Satanic Ritual Abuse and all its aftereffects is defeated through the blood of Jesus. Christ's lambs who may be caught in it against their will need love, safety, and assistance to get out of the clutches of death. They need to know the power of the only blood that counts. But how shall they know if nobody is willing to stand up to Satan? Why should we quail before a defeated and doomed devil?

We cannot let Jesus down, but must rise in His power! After all, He has invested into our life, redemption, and eternity! He is counting on us to represent His unconditional love to everyone and every need. That means He will also give the grace to do it.

PRAYER: Lord, I confess and renounce every excuse I have ever used to avoid addressing the enemy on this level of the occult. I claim the blood of Jesus over Satan, every demon of hell, and over every occultic activity. I claim the protection from evil that is mine through the blood of Jesus. Lord, please give me Your wisdom and guidance to willingly be used by You in every way You direct. I announce that Satan is defeated, and I have no cause for fear. Amen.

KETURAH C. MARTIN

His Work Of Grace

What marvelous grace has come down from above,
When God sent the Gift of His infinite love!
For we were all trapped in the darkness of sin,
And destined to die in our lost state therein.

But God's love divine has prevailed and has won—
His riches and grace He sent down through His Son:
For someone must pay for the sin of all man,
And Jesus was willing to fill God's great plan!

The Lord laid on Jesus the sin of mankind—
Made Him to be "sin" for the doomed and the blind;
He gave up His lifeblood to rescue my soul:
For He paid death's penalty and full parole!

Because of the price which my Jesus has paid,
I now have a hope which can nevermore fade:
For all of my old life has passed far away,
When with His shed blood Christ has washed me today!

Through Christ my Redeemer I now can begin
A life that's transformed and all empty of sin;
A vessel of honor I am by His grace:
Since He became "sin" for the whole human race.

And now when His Father looks down upon me,
The righteousness only of Christ doth He see:
For His work of grace is stamped deep on my heart,
And from this new life I must never depart!

OCTOBER 14
READING: 2 CORINTHIANS 1:9, 10 AND JOHN 3:16-18

Salvation

This diagram is meant to help explain the timeline of the history which pertains to why mankind needed the Savior, Jesus Christ, to pay their ransom from sin. If Jesus had not been willing to die in our place so Satan would be 100 percent defeated, then we would not be able to escape from the clutches of the evil one. When we accept the sacrifice Jesus made on our behalf and ask Him to apply it to our lives and the sin therein, then we are given power which is far greater than any scrap of empowerment which Satan can ever claim to offer. We are also given power through Jesus over all the power of Satan, and he cannot touch us when Jesus dwells within.

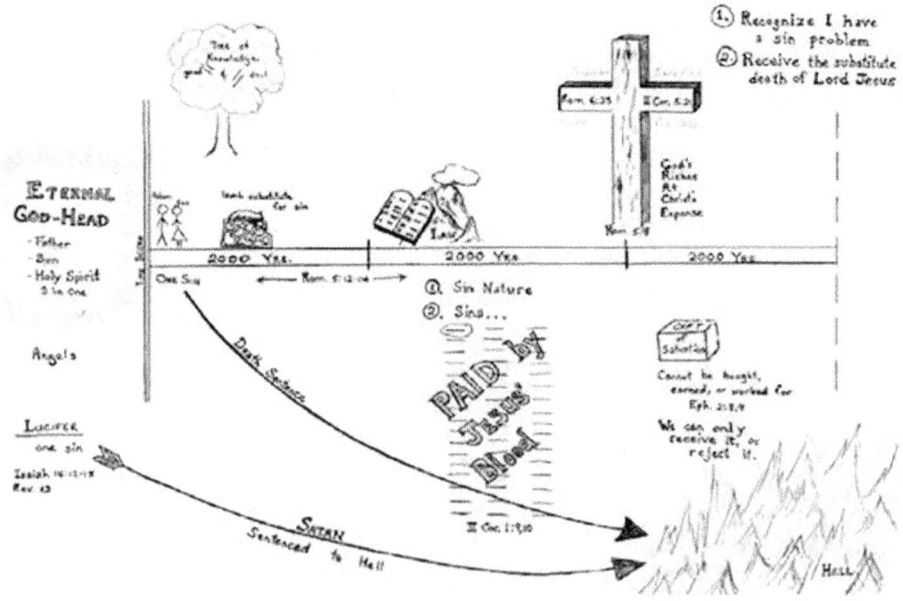

PRAYER: Lord Jesus, I want to accept Your gift of salvation so I can be rescued from Satan and be free to serve You. I renounce in the name of Jesus every agenda, lie, and chain of the enemy that would deter me from truth and salvation. Thank You for dying for me, and I ask You to forgive all my sin and wash me clean in your Supreme Sacrifice. Fill me, Jesus, with Your Presence and Your power. Amen.

KETURAH C. MARTIN

Thy Heart I Now Hold

"My Child, do come near Me—thy heart I now hold,
And close to My breast, I My Child do enfold:
For I see thy life from beginning to end,
And grace for each moment I daily extend.

Thy tears and thy heartache, I see, My dear Child—
I understand fully the tempest so wild;
Midst darkest affliction when night lingers on,
My Child, don't despair, for I bring thee My dawn!

Midst misunderstandings, relentless and grim,
Which those in dark ignorance have spilled o'er your brim,
Don't ever give up, nor grow bitter at them:
For I've chosen thee for My own diadem.

Adversity's waters shall not destroy thee:
For I have all power—thy God still shall be,
And I know just what you are able to bear—
My grace all-sufficient I freely do share!

The dark persecutions and anguish untold,
My Child, can be used to produce finest gold:
For I cannot bless their inflictions of pain,
But if you yield all to Me, I shall bring gain.

Surrender the pain and oppressions that be,
And choose to forgive all who work against Me;
Each pained situation commit to My hand:
For I am thy God and in full understand!

I see thy heart bleeding, deprived, and so torn,
And comprehend fully affliction's pained thorn;
Though only the underside, dark, can you see—
Thy Lord is creating true beauty in thee!"

What Does God Say And Think?

For years, Carol was engulfed with inexpressible agony within due to all the rejection and misunderstanding from the majority of people around her who could not fathom the depth of her suffering.

However, God very graciously provided an agent of mercy whom He used. The pair He chose was open to understanding from the heart Carol's plight of excruciating aftereffects of the prior years of abuse.

It was through this avenue that some very wonderful truths were gained which helped to set Carol free from the lack of knowledge and misunderstanding around her. She learned, after many tears and heartache, that the most important thing is not what others think, perceive, or understand about you. What really counts is this: *What does God have to say about the matter?* Did God see all that happened in the abuses? Then He knows the truth, whether anyone else chooses to accept those facts or not. Ultimately, it is God before Whom we will all stand, and if the truth is not known and accepted before that, then it will all be manifested at that time. These truths and many others were brought out repeatedly as Carol learned to apply them more aptly all the time. Even in the face of severe and painful rejection or slander, it is ultimately God Who is the One Who knows and accepts the truth regardless of any other.

The following are some truths Carol learned while working through rejection:

- What God knows and thinks is most important.
- The truth will always stand regardless of what is believed by others.
- God understands you completely, even when others may not.
- What others think or propagate about you does not really matter if it is not true. You will need to choose to forgive and release them and the effects so the enemy doesn't create bitterness, and so you remain free before God.
- God has not rejected you, even though many who can't understand have.

Prayer: Lord Jesus, I thank You for understanding and loving me, even though some cannot. I choose to forgive and release to You those who have judged and rejected me. I ask that You would bring forth the truth and glorify Yourself. Please fill me with the love of Jesus toward all who have said or thought wrongly about my experience, and I give it all to You. Amen.

Our Lives Are In Your Hand

"Dear Lord, we can't see what may lie up ahead,
The path still not trod is untold and unsaid;
We know not if sorrow around the next bend,
Will send us to You, that Your grace You may lend.

We know not what blessings You're ready to pour
On us, from Your loving and bountiful store;
Adversities coming, dear Lord, we can't see—
Know not if dark trial our portion shall be.

But this we're assured, Lord, that You will be there,
To walk right beside us and each burden share;
That our path uncharted, by You is well-planned:
For our life and future is stored in Your hand!

When watery depths we are called to go through,
You'll walk close and guide us as strength You renew;
When through raging fire our pathway may lead,
Our hand You still hold and no flames can succeed!

Our life is well planned and secured in Your hand—
Each week, day, and moment You have fully planned;
To You we surrender the future, complete—
With You in control, every need You will meet!"

For You Lord can see all that lies up ahead,
And know all about every step we shall tread—
Please feed us Your grace and with strength lead us on
Until we meet You in the new heaven's dawn!

A Bigger Hand

Often in life, for all people, there are situations and circumstances which are unpleasant, and situations one would like to change. This is an even greater reality when one is dealing additionally with a shattered life of agony.

It is very important to always remember that there is a bigger hand holding all the pieces of our broken life. When one's life is falling apart at the seams, or some type of abuse is shredding one's heart, God is there with His hand to preserve His child and to catch every piece that falls. God will never let even one piece that He is holding fall or be lost, for His love for you is incomprehensible.

The hand of God is big enough to hold the mountains of agony that may be crushing you at this very moment. His hand is also big enough to lift those mountains and set you free. The scattered pieces of our agonized heart and life can all be gathered up by this hand divine that is so much bigger than anything we could ever experience!

Below are promises God gave me while I was bringing Him some of the painful pieces of my life:

- I have chosen to preserve your life for My glory.
- I have chosen to use the rejections and pain to prepare you for service when you release it to Me.
- I have chosen you to understand and empathize with the rejected and brokenhearted.
- I have chosen to give you beauty for ashes, the oil of joy for the years of tears, and a song of praise for the spirit of heaviness, pain, and rejection.
- I have chosen to turn Satan's attempts at your soul's destruction into My project of transforming the broken, pained, and dirty shatters he wreaked in your life into a cleansed and beautiful vessel through which to pour My love on the heartbroken.
- You are of value to Me, and My thoughts toward you are more in number than the sands of the sea.
- I will complete the work I have begun in you and will never let you go.

My Great Debt To Repay

My gracious Redeemer my ransom has paid,
While buried in scum, the full payment He made;
He chose to show mercy as ruined I lay—
Death's "penalty" paid while igniting hope's ray!

He chose to descend to the depths of my pit,
Where chained in captivity, there I did sit:
Extending His love to me, wretched and bound,
And rescued my soul from that squalor profound!

My Jesus decided to save me from sin—
In love brought me cleansing for foulness within:
His blood's mighty power washed whiter than snow—
He chose to release me from past, sin, and woe!

Christ chose to forgive me for sin-stains so vast—
From the east to the west, so far they are cast:
God's "sea of forgetfulness" swallowed them up,
Because Jesus drank in my place death's dark cup!

My Savior, in love, chose to break every chain,
Which bound me as captive to Satan's ruined gain,
And all Satan's wardens who guarded my soul
Christ vanquished and judged under His great control!

There's naught I can do, my great debt to repay,
For my dear Redeemer, Who rescued today,
Who chose to include me as His own joint-heir:
Reserving a place in His glory to share!

"Lord, I am resolved to now give You my 'All'
I choose to surrender complete at Your call:
My heart, mind, and body, my talents and time—
You've paid for them all, Lord, and they are all Thine!"

"I will restore the years that the locusts have eaten, and will revive that which Satan thought he had beaten. I am the Lord!"
"The trials yielded to My hand will become treasures in the sand!"

The Heavenly Father
February 13, 2012

Treasures

I always thought it would be so wonderful to dig through the sand dunes and find a big heap of treasures! Wow! But how much greater is the fact that God can take all our yielded pain, tatters, and trials and transform them into treasures with eternal value! He can even take the years that were eaten up by the anguish of abuse and rejection and restore those years. What a wonderful and loving God we have Who cares about all our lost or stolen treasures and can make it all better than before! Thank You, Jesus!

Thank God For The Pain

Dear soul, are you burdened with loads of deep pain
Which cut the heart's core, despite sunshine or rain?
Does heart-throbbing anguish consume all your ways,
As clouds of dark past shadow each of your days?

Take time to thank God for this agony sore,
Which surges within and oft spills out the door:
For pain is an indicator of great need—
A blessing disguised that with Christ we must heed.

For Jesus is waiting, e'en now by your side
To help you resolve all the things you may hide;
He longs that you bring Him your dark agony,
So that He can heal you and set your heart free.

Have you ever felt that not one understands?
Or faced condemnation from various hands?
Friend, do not despair although this is your plight:
For Christ understands, and for thee He doth fight!

Come bring Him your pain, the rejection and tears,
So He can transform them to blessings and cheers:
For they are but tools that the Lord seeks to use—
When given to Him you will bloom and not lose.

Thank God for the pain, which He uses to build
The vessel He's chosen, redeemed, and then filled;
Praise God for these tools that help us understand
The bruised and the hurting throughout this His land.

Thank God for the pain which doth indicate need,
For Jesus the One Who brings healing indeed:
For sufferings dark that teach us to reach out—
Can turn into blessings with never a doubt!

OCTOBER 22
READING: 1 THESSALONIANS 5:16-18

Thanksgiving

Offering thanksgiving is a very effective tool with which to combat the negatives that the enemy tries to inject into our mind. When our heart and mind is filled with praise and thanksgiving, there is not much room left for the enemy to get in his agenda yet.

When we choose to go against our human tendency and specifically thank God for the pain in our life, that really goes against all Satan had hoped to gain. The pain and shatters which the enemy instigated to bring some level of destruction now become a thanksgiving item! This is terrible in his books, but to God, it is as sweet-smelling incense which glorifies Him!

To look at physical, emotional, or spiritual pain as something *formidable and terrible* will only give the enemy opportunity to pull a fast one over on us as he injects poisonous thinking into the mind.

But if our pain can be placed completely into the big hand of God and we allow Him to give us some of His vision about how to view it, that is when miracles can begin to happen. When God has our pain in His hand, it is He Who can reverse every evil intent the enemy planned to use it for. In God's hand, it becomes tools that build, strengthen, and shape our soul, character, and whatever plan the Lord has for us to be used for in His life work for us.

Reasons To Thank God for The Pain:
- The Bible commands thanksgiving for everything.
- Pain becomes a blessed tool in God's hand when our wills and attitudes are surrendered to His will and healing hand.
- The devil's defeat is spelled more clearly in our thanksgiving.
- Pain is an indicator of some need in us, and we need to thank God that He is the One Who shows and can fill this need.
- Pain gives us understanding and empathy for those in agony and need.
- Pain, like pruning, can help cause us to bloom and grow.
- Except the Lord build the house, they labour in vain that build it.

PRAYER: Lord, I choose to thank You for allowing this pain, even though I cannot understand how it could benefit. I surrender the hows and whys to You and ask that You would transform this pain into something worthy. Amen.

Beneath God's Wing

Beneath the Great Almighty's wing
I am secure, and I can sing;
No evil there can touch my soul:
For I am safe in His control.

No hurtful word can scar my heart,
Though it aim at me like a dart:
For I am safe within God's hand,
Who holds me up and helps me stand.

God knows when I have done my best,
Despite what others may attest;
Content with Him I shall abide:
For by God's grace I'm justified!

Should those around not understand—
Hurl hurt at me while in His hand,
In peace I rest, for my heart knows
My Lord takes all those lashing blows.

He pilots me through stormy seas—
Refreshes me in peaceful breeze;
He is my Shelter in the storm,
And in His care I'm safe and warm!

He guides me on to heaven's shore,
Where storms and pain come near no more;
In heaven comes eternal rest,
As I'm enfolded to His breast!

OCTOBER 24
READING: JOHN 11:11-44

Resurrection And Victory

Jesus, the Son of God, was a man Who suffered abuse which surpasses what we can fathom. *He was despised and rejected of men; a man of sorrows and acquainted with grief.*

In the beginning of time, God said that *the penalty for sin is death.* Jesus did not have to come to this earth to live and then die in the place of all mankind as He bore their death penalty. But Jesus chose to be made *the sin offering* (even though He never sinned) for all people because of His unfathomed love to us all. He chose to face abuse, persecution, and death so He could make a way possible for us to reconnect with a holy and just God. Because of all He suffered triumphantly in abuse, rejection, and death, now He is fully able to succor and assist all those who come to Him, and He understands perfectly.

After Jesus had been crucified at the hand of the chief priests and the Roman soldiers, He was laid in the grave over the Sabbath.

Early on the first day of the week, an angel came and rolled back the stone at the mouth of the grave so the whole world could see that Jesus was no longer lying dead within. He had taken power and authority over death, sin, and the grave and conquered them forever! Praise God! Because of His triumphant resurrection, we can also be recipients of victorious power through Jesus to rise above sin, defeat, eternal death, and every stronghold that the enemy attempts to ingrain within through abuse, or any other method.

Through Jesus Christ we have access to all the riches in glory to meet our every need. We can also have the confidence that through the love, mercy, and power of Christ we can have complete healing and divine restoration from every degree of abuse we may have encountered. Jesus, Who suffered it all before us, can restore the most broken life; and He specializes in things thought impossible!

PRAYER: Thank You, Jesus, for taking the death penalty for me. Thank You for understanding the writhing agony of rejection and abuse, even though so many of Your people try to deny its reality. I choose to place my shatters of pain into Your hand of love and power, and ask that You bring the restoration and healing which alone is possible through You. Amen.

KETURAH C. MARTIN

Rags Or Riches?

When coming up out of the horrors, pain, filth, and devastations of abuse, there are so many crossroads of decision to make in a world of shattered trust. One of the first decisions one has to look at is whether they are going to choose rags above riches or vice versa. There is nothing substantial we can do in our own strength to escape the insurmountible pain and shambles of shameful worthlessness that are engulfing us after our agonizing experience.

Therefore, we must make a conscious choice whether we will limp along in a crippled fashion with loads of agony and/or burdensome filth, or whether we are going to come to Jesus Christ Who is the only One that can truly help us right down to the naked depths of the heart's core. Jesus is a Counsellor Who not only hears us out, but also understands completely and goes beyond suggesting how to deal with the aftereffects. He does deal with them in a 100 percent thorough manner if we but allow Him to. Jesus came to bind up the brokenhearted; to open prisons for those in bondage, proclaiming liberty; to give out beauty for ashes and the oil of joy for mourning, along with a garment of praise for the spirit of heaviness. In addition to these things, He also bring cleansing for all the lies, strongholds, and influence injected within, along with any wrong we may have committed before, during, or after our shattering experience (Romans 3:23).

Then comes the joyous experience of being clothed in the robes of Jesus' righteousness where we can be hidden in Him Who is our Rock, Refuge, Redeemer, and Reliable Friend. Because of the power of His blood, love, and resurrection, we can begin life anew with Him to guide us. However, it is up to us to make that conscious choice and begin the healing journey with Him.

PRAYER: Jesus, I choose to come to You for my healing, and I ask that You teach me step by step the path You want me to take so that You can do Your healing work in my life. I choose the riches You have to offer instead of all my filthy rags. I choose You to be Lord of my life and all its tatters. I long to be clean and hidden safely in You, Jesus. Amen.

"Fear Not, I've Called Thee"

"Fear not, My Child, for Mine thou art—
I've called thee and thy way I chart;
Since I in love redeemed thy soul,
I safely guide though billows roll.

For thou art precious in my sight,
And I have loved thee day and night;
My chosen witness, Child, are ye—
For My own glory formed I thee.

When through the waters thou pass through,
Whose waves may dash with pain anew:
Yet I the Lord will be with thee—
Grant grace each step, thy strength will be.

And when the rivers overflow—
Submerging grief thy heart doth know:
Thy hand in Mine, I lead thee on,
Through all the tempest, to the dawn.

When thou must walk through fire's flame,
Remember, thee I've called by name:
Through fire I walk hand in hand
With thee, My Child, as I have planned.

Each step of life I walk beside
Thee, Child, and with thee will abide;
Despite what comes I hold thy hand—
'Twill bring thee to the promised land!"

Facing The Dark, Fearful Things

God is always faithful to bring out anything that is hidden so that His children can experience true freedom and healing rather than being crippled through that which is buried.

Whenever something is exposed, He also promises to walk with us every step with the grace, strength, and wisdom to resolve it; or He may lead us to someone He can use as His ambassador through whom the Lord will assist us. The Lord brought me a lot of assurance, direction, and courage during these painful times of following through with Him when He exposed a need for His touch.

"Lord, thank You for showing me all that You have and for reminding me 'not to keep anything hidden.' But, Lord, I am so afraid that complete openness will result in rejection as it did before, and everything about this subject is so vile, repulsive, and terrifying. So many people want to shove all this type of stuff under the carpet and leave it unresolved."

"The barriers, mountains, and walls surrounding you pertaining to these issues are impossible to scale on your own, but with Me, all things are possible."

"Jesus, it feels as though I am literally drowning in the excruciating filth, unlimited pain, and ceaseless shame, which is too deep to even verbalize to You or anyone else."

"Do not despair, My Child, and don't ever lose hope, for I will complete the work and transformation in you that I have begun. I see and understand your heart in this matter. You may need some outside help to address these atrocities committed against you and all the aftereffects of the devastation. My child, do not allow the enemy to plant doubts in you about what My power, blood, and love can do to transform these experiences into something of beauty which glorifies My name."

"Lord, can You show us where in this endless internal mess and filthy pain that one should begin?"

"I will not fail or forsake you, but will lead you step by step to freedom and healing. My Spirit also guides those through whom I work on your behalf. Remember, though I understand your agonized state, yet I see what Jesus has done for you and the plan I have for the vessel I am restoring. I the Lord look on this eternal work rather than at the vile destructions which the enemy has wrought against you! I AM the Lord, and I delight in giving beauty for ashes, a song of joy for mourning, and My own garment of righteousness for you to wear!"

PTSD Is Not Sin

There may be individuals out there who, if they do not understand some things about abuse and its aftermath, default to the mentality that *the whole thing is just a sin issue.* This is very detrimental to the progress of the survivor in the healing journey, and, in short, is a convenient path of judgment.

There may be many folks who cannot comprehend the agonizing throes of physical and emotional suffering one encounters when plagued for years with post-traumatic stress. This does not discount the reality of it.

Though this is not a diagnostic definition, yet it is important to define this phenomenon in order to identify with those suffering and to help all others to better understand.

Post-Traumatic Stress Disorder may develop when a person has been exposed to a traumatic event during which the following were present: the person witnessed, experienced, or was confronted with a happening that involved actual or threatened death; serious injury/abuse; or a threat to the physical integrity of self or another, involving intense fear, helplessness and/or horror.

The traumatic event is persistently re-experienced without warning when a flashback may trigger the memories of the occurrence. Then the body will automatically begin to physically and emotionally re-experience (as though happening currently) the specific parts of the abuse/traumata as it relives the same type of terror, pain, and helpless horror as at the original scene.

This does not mean that the individual is having wrong thoughts or is rehashing the past, etc. Rather, it means that when trauma and abuse remain unresolved, there is far greater potential for the body to continue reliving the horrors retained within it. It must be pointed out that all PTSD symptoms of my experiences have completely diminished in all the areas of abuse or trauma which have been fully addressed and had healing brought to by Jesus. There is abundant hope available for everyone who so suffers, and there is healing outside of *the band-aid solution* of pharmaceuticals! I was mercifully brought out of the most horrible and terrifying PTSD pit where my body was in a nearly constant state of physical distress beyond comprehension as it relived the countless brutalities of abuse crimes. Thanks be to Jesus!

PRAYER: Jesus, I thank You for bringing Your great love, mercy, and healing! Lord, please guide me daily to my heavenly goal. Amen.

OCTOBER 29
READING: ISAIAH 63:9 AND PSALM 17:6-9

With Thy Lord You Shall Soar!

My Child, do come closer and rest in My arms,
Though life's filled with trials and many alarms:
For I am thy Lord and I hold full control
Of each situation that comes to thy soul.

I see, My dear Child, what you're able to bear,
Allowing no more, because I really care;
And, Child, be assured that what I call you through
Comes in the same package as grace rich and true!

My strength is made perfect in your weakest hour,
As you are endued with My grace and full pow'r;
When you feel engulfed with the dark trials, sore—
Just rest in My arms as I bear you to shore.

For when you are weak and just cannot go on,
I never will fail you, but bring you a dawn;
On wings as an eagle I'll bear you to Me,
That calm above tempest you safely shall be!

There, Child, with thy Lord, you shall soar far above
The dark, heavy trials on wings of My love:
For with Me beside you, My peace reigns supreme
Despite all the tempest, though fearful it seems.

And there I will teach you to fly through the storm,
Although you may flutter as wing muscles form;
Yet I can fly faster than, Child, you can fall,
And I will be there to bear you above all!

PRAYER: Lord, please help me to trust You even when it feels like I'm falling and everything is out of control. I ask You to take full control of my life, healing and future for Your glory. Amen.

OCTOBER 30
READING: MARK 9:17-29 AND EPHESIANS 6:10-12

Fast And Pray Today!

Today is a day in which Christians everywhere should be fasting and praying on behalf of all those in captivity whom Satan is gearing up to use on his biggest holiday of the year—*Hallowed Eve*. To remain in ignorance or denial does not stop the reality.

Every year, children and adults die in the name of Satan on this day he claims for his own glory. Jesus taught us about the necessity of prayer and fasting when it comes to taking authority over the power and demons of darkness. We cannot afford to remain passively idle when individuals are dying!

POINTS TO REMEMBER . . .

- ❖ Jesus has the power, love, and mercy to break completely every fetter for such prisoners of the devil, for nothing is too hard for our Lord!
- ❖ We need to respect the power of Satan but not fear it or him, because *greater is He that is in us than he that is in the world.*
- ❖ We must always view the prisoners of Satan through the eyes of Jesus and extend His love and hope to them. We may be the only gospel they will ever know, and but for God's grace, there too we could be.
- ❖ It is a known fact in the circles of Satanism that *when Christians are praying specifically and claiming the blood of Jesus over their activities, Satan's power is bound and the rituals, curses, and suchlike are impeded.*
- ❖ Every fetter of occultic bondage the blood of Jesus can utterly destroy.
- ❖ Jesus has won the victory over Satan and all his schemes; therefore we don't fight for victory, but from the victory Christ has won. We claim the victory through the blood and name of Jesus that causes the enemy to flee in defeat!
- ❖ There are many books, potions, games, activities, and holidays available today that if we engage in will automatically open us up to the enemy's deception and open the door to his strongholds.
- ❖ Jesus loves all those bound in occultic fetters just as much as *the upstanding church member.* We are no better than any of them.

Cont.

KETURAH C. MARTIN

Prayer: Lord, I claim the power of the blood of Jesus over every person and medium that is being used as a tool in the hand of Satan. I claim Your blood, power, protection, and everlasting presence over each individual who is trapped and being brutally used in the name of Satan. Lord, please surround each captive child with the Angel of Your Presence and save them in the name of Jesus from the atrocities of the devil. I claim Your blood and power, Lord Jesus, over all satanic activities, in Your name! Amen.

The Devil's Holiday

How can folks so blatantly tamper with fire?
And play with the devil which costs them so dire;
They put Satan's toys into innocent hands—
His holiday celebrate on peer's demand.
But Halloween only doth celebrate death,
Where Satan midst rituals takes blood and breath.
The year's darkest day is on Halloween night,
When innocent victims are bound in death's plight—
Just hear children crying in pain, blood, and fear,
As death's bloody sacrifice looms ever near.
As lambs to the slaughter they give up their life,
While Satan wreaks havoc in blood-flowing strife;
His pawns would believe that "true power they gain,
As death swirls around them midst demons and chains."
Perversions run rampant in Satan's vile name,
While innocent victims are used, crushed, and shamed—
Their bodies defiled and hearts shattered in pain,
As at their expense Satan plots ruthless gain.
Beam forth hope and help for survivors in need,
That all works of darkness be vanquished indeed!
The devil would have us to idly sit by,
To shut ears and hearts to the victims' pained cry,
To discount the truth of his horror-filled deeds,
So that his deceptions and deaths can proceed.
We must just be willing to hear them all out,
With never a judgment, a harsh word, or doubt:
For they need a place that is safe, filled with love,
So that they by Christ can be healed from above.

(This poem is included as a voice for those who can never speak again and as a warning and a plea to all who yet live. I validate all who know of what I speak and encourage you to continue on your healing journey.)

Cont.

PRAYER: Jesus, I claim Your blood over every place Satan is worshiped tonight. Bind the powers of evil, Jesus, and set the captives free! I claim healing for every shattered, dying victim; I claim Your Presence and light to guide them to truth and divine healing. I bind every demon of hell and claim the blood of Jesus on all the captives that must be set free in His name. Amen.

In Your Presence Of Love

"My Lord, when You call me to heaven above,
Where I shall delight in Your presence of love,
Oh, how my heart yearns to behold Your dear face
And thank You in person for Your wondrous grace!

When heaven's bright portals I enter at last—
The things of the earth shall forever be past,
And then I shall run into Jesus' strong arms—
Be clasped to His bosom, now free from all harms.

One glimpse of Your face, oh my Lord, will repay
The pain, grief, and heartache I felt in earth's day;
Oh, just to behold my Redeemer Who died,
And now has reserved me a place near His side!

To rest in the arms which have carried me through,
And feel the embrace of my Saviour so true,
Oh, that will make all of earth's trials as naught,
When over the river in Your arms I'm brought!

Then down streets of gold I forever shall sing
The glories and praise of my Saviour and King,
With angels and saints who have gone on before—
We'll worship Christ Jesus—in triumph adore!

All pain, death, and sickness will vanish for aye,
And life everlasting will shine forth each day,
In heaven's bright clime where no foe can assail,
But sweet, endless vict'ry with Jesus prevails!"

KETURAH C. MARTIN

NOVEMBER 2
READING: PSALM 118:15-17 AND 2 TIMOTHY 1:7

Safe And Secure

"Behold, I send an Angel before thee, to keep thee in the way, and to bring thee into the place which I have prepared."

There are many uncertainties and precarious situations and feelings that individuals face while traveling the road to healing. This is very common after coming through alive all that they have. Safety is often a prominent issue as terror of the perpetrator is intermingled with possible death threats, etc.

Never discredit or scorn the fear that survivors may deal with, sometimes on a 24/7 basis. In some cases, especially where fleeing satanic covens, curses, cues, and commissions, there can be a very real threat to one's life as the leaders attempt to keep all their activities in total darkness, even if it means death to some.

The Lord understands perfectly all the threats and/or terror you may be facing. In His foresight, He has already sent His angel before you to keep you, guide you, and bring you to a place of safety, security, and healing.

To go through the healing process with the Lord Jesus is such a comfort, because we know that He Himself has already walked this road and has all the strength we need. He also is the One Who holds our complete healing in His hand. He is just waiting to walk with us step by step through the dark valleys along the way. Jesus is well aware that the enemy also lurks around on *the pathway to healing* and hoping to do anything possible to stop or obstruct our progress. Satan does not want anyone to expose the truth about how he operates in deception and fear. Jesus is willing to walk this journey with us so He can fight our battles against Satan for us.

When God bears us above the storm on wings as an eagle, He also teaches us to fly by relying on Him in every fearful situation. God can fly faster than we can ever fall, and He swoops in under us to break the fall when He sees that we need His help. Walking or flying the healing road with God is the safest and surest way we will ever reach our goal.

PRAYER: Lord, I ask for Your protection from all evil and harm. I ask that You would lead and be in charge of my healing journey. I renounce Satan's attempts to hinder healing, and I claim the blood of Jesus over my life and future. Amen.

Nails And Hammer

Have you spat upon the Master,
With the scoffers of that day?
As they cried out, "Crucify Him"—
Christ rejecting all the way.

Are you holding, friend, the hammer
Which was used on Calv'ry's hill
As the cruel nails were pounded,
Causing sinless blood to spill?

Are there nails within your pocket
That today you seek to hide,
Which will pierce the hand of Jesus,
Wounding Him at eventide?

Have you constantly surrendered
As you die each day to sin?
Have you given all to Jesus
Or does self still reign within?

Friend, if self retains a portion
Of the throne within our heart,
Then we're pounding nails with hammers
—Wounding Jesus from the start.

For His finished work on Calv'ry
And His resurrective pow'r
Is all scoffed and disregarded,
Should self reign for just an hour.

Yield your "All" unto the Savior—
Choose full cleansing in His flood:
Nails and hammer now surrender,
Claiming vict'ry through His blood!

KETURAH C. MARTIN

By His Stripes We Are Healed

As we traverse along in our journey, God does not usually show us everything that needs His healing touch all at one time. It is more common that He, in His mercy and knowledge of how much we can bear, only shows us step by step what He desires for us to bring to Jesus for healing. God's faithfulness is beyond our comprehension!

Sometimes when the inner agony is too great, an individual may be tempted to conceal the items of pain from those in a helping position. This, I know from experience, looks so appealing, and even more so if one is not understood. However, God was faithful to bring the buried need to my attention and lovingly waited for me to respond to what He had shown. Of course, He did not force me, but my entire progress was hindered until I was willing to go to places buried so deep that 97 percent of potential helpers could not bear to attempt the chore of trying to understand or validate the painful need.

When things are deliberately buried or kept buried, that is when we need to question whether we are holding the nails or hammer that helped put Jesus on the cross.

What Jesus did on the cross was sufficient to go to every level of pain, the most gruesome sin, and the most trashed life and bring about a transformation. The agonizing tidbits of our life that may be hidden are never too disgusting, fearful, or destroyed for Jesus. Because of His death and suffering on the cross, and also all the stripes He bore before death, Jesus holds full healing for every person in the entire world from creation to the end of time.

The healing one could attain from any level of medicine or psychology is only a drop in the bucket compared to what Jesus has done in my life—and is just longing to do for anyone who wants to experience the same fullness of joy and healing.

PRAYER: Search me, Oh God, and know my heart; try me and know my thoughts, and see if there is anything hidden inside that You want addressed and brought to Jesus for healing. I acknowledge that what Jesus suffered for me is sufficient to take care of any level of healing that is needed, and I accept that in His name. Amen.

Where God Leads, He Feeds

The Lord may lead to rivers wide,
And ask that you would cross the tide;
How dark and angry are the waves,
But He'll cross with you and will save.

God never leads you to a place
Where you'll require added grace,
Except He plans to hold your hand—
Midst grief and anguish, help you stand.

And when God leads to mountains high—
The path ascends up in the sky:
Dear soul, be glad for your own Guide
Who's walked before, and now beside:

For He will climb each step with you,
And breath by breath will strength renew;
He holds your hand and guides your feet—
Your every need will fully meet!

And should your path through fire lead,
Know God is with you there indeed:
He quenches all the painful flames—
Gives grace and glorifies His name.

When drifting on affliction's sea,
One's bark is tossed so hopelessly,
Yet Jesus walks the sea with you,
Controlling waves, remaining true!

Wherever God His children leads,
Sufficient grace He also feeds:
For He's begun a work in you,
And He will safely see you through!

KETURAH C. MARTIN

NOVEMBER 6
READING: ROMANS 11:33-36

God Makes A Way

Did you ever think about the fact that God has amazing eyesight, far better than our finite minds can even begin to grasp? He could see our life picture from start to finish long before we were even born. He could also see and discern what things we would encounter in our life and just how He could make a way for us through it. When I consider it all, how could I ever dream of wanting anyone else to be in charge of my life journey, including my healing? There is no one else Who could be so equipped to escort us through the rivers, over the mountains, around the pitfalls in enemy territory, or even through the fire, fog, or hurricane.

When the children of Israel were penned in from behind by the Egyptians, with rock walls on both sides of them and a sea in front, God made a way for them also. He commanded them all to start marching into the sea, and as Moses lifted his rod over the waters, they parted asunder until there was a dry path all the way through. God not only led them through the sea in a visible way but also protected them from the enemy behind them. He placed a great cloud between them, which was darkness to the foe but a source of light to His people.

This is also how God desires to help those who have been wounded and abused. Often the enemy is crouching somewhere seeking to destroy them, but God is ready to assist with him also. Regardless of what kind of battles there are to fight against Satan, the Lord is right there to do it for you. In fact, Jesus has already won the battle over Satan—it's just that the enemy is too stupid to give up on us and continually fights God, Who has all power.

God is willing to walk with us to healing, whether it is through flood, storm, and fire or over insurmountable mountains. His grace is without limits, His love is deeper than the deepest ocean, His understanding is infinite, His power is measureless, and His healing touch is matchlessly profound!

There's nothing my God cannot do, except fail!

PRAYER: Lord, I choose to have You as my General to fight all the battles against Satan. I thank You for all the healing You are bringing me, and I ask that You continue all the work that You have started for Your glory! Amen.

"You Now Can Go Free"

One day, God in love began working on me,
That He might reveal His great mercy so free;
He tenderly washed all the wounds in my heart,
And brought healing hope where before were pained darts.

The past, though so tattered, I laid at His feet,
Desiring to houseclean, so full and complete;
His Spirit then prompted to make my wrongs right,
With my fellowmen, in the past's lonely night.

Imploring the Savior for His strength divine,
We went hand in hand where His Spirit did shine:
I asked for forgiveness as God had made plain,
But lo, what was happening? What is this pain?

"I will not forgive you, just be on your way!"
These words I hear uttered in anguishing sway:
My numbed heart cries out midst rejection so bold,
And I feel abandoned—left out in the cold.

But hark, hear the Savior, Who stands by my side:
"My Child, take new courage—with you I abide—
Because you obeyed Me, you now can go free,
And this man's refusal his own hurt shall be.

My Child, just release him right into My hand,
Along with the darts that you don't understand:
For you've done your part and the rest is for Me—
So leap and rejoice, Child, You're totally free!"

KETURAH C. MARTIN

NOVEMBER **8**

READING: PSALM 59

Following, No Matter What

There are times in the healing path that will not be easy, although, in reality, none of it is easy. Rather it is a very difficult road, but wonderfully worth it in the end! Don't ever give up no matter how hard, painful, or lonely it may be. There were only a handful of truly devoted people in my life (especially the first years), who did not join the multitudes in their pressure and denial attitude *to just give up the healing and pretend it is all fine.*

I must ensure that anyone out there embarking on the healing journey knows positively that, no matter what agony you go through before you get to the finish line, *It will be worth it all!* Don't ever allow the enemy or anyone else he would use to tell you *to just forget it all,* or *to get on with your life and forget the past.*

When God may ask you to do a hard thing, such as making a wrong right, just go in His strength and see what great things He will do for you. If for any reason someone may receive you in a wrong way and disregard the job you were sent by God to do, don't allow Satan the satisfaction of causing you to feel devastated. Rather, you have every reason to rejoice, be at peace, and leap for joy (Luke 6:22, 23), because you faithfully followed what the Lord required of you. In such cases, it becomes vitally important to release the person, their words, and the pain it caused all into the hand of Jesus as you choose to forgive them. Once that step is done, you are free before God, regardless of what is said around you, as long as your heart stays clear before Him.

At the end of the day, it is the word of God that counts and what He thinks of you that matters. When He has commanded and you have obeyed, that is enough to have *a peace* about, even if someone else does not see as God did and attempts to create *pieces.*

PRAYER: Lord, I choose to follow through on the journey to healing, regardless of how others may respond to what You show me. I renounce every attempt of Satan to hinder the work You want to do, and I claim the blood and power of Jesus on my life and the healing He is doing. I choose to forgive and release anyone who may be used by the enemy to discourage me and I surrender them into Your hand to deal with. Amen.

Thistles In The Heart's Garden

Come, dear soul, let us ponder beneath God's true light
The condition our heart's in, despite painful night;
Did abuse's stark anguish produce seeds of hate,
Which was nurtured, not knowing the enemy's bait?
For 'tis Satan who offered those dark seeds so grim,
Which when planted will bind without mercy to him;
And he seeks to ensure that you never forgive,
So that he may have reign in your heart, and there live.
Are there flourishing thistles deep rooted within,
Which have neatly been hilled with the vomit of sin?
Do the briars of bitterness tangle your heart
With their roots piercing through you as poisonous darts?
Do you water these thorns with malicious intent
As upon your offender revenge you would vent—
Desiring to see that he soon is brought low—
That he pay a great price for the pain he bestowed?
The dear Savior's forgiveness within your own heart,
Will be measured by depths of release you impart:
For the Lord will forgive us just as we forgive
So our choice can squelch wholly our freedom to live.
Friend, the Master of Gardeners stands by your gate
And will aid in your choice to root out weeds of fate;
But it's you who must choose, despite thorn-nurtured soil
To forgive your abuser, though flesh would recoil.
When you choose to forgive and your heart's garden bare
To the Gardener, Jesus, the soil He'll prepare:
For the Lord understands how and where the roots grow
And it's Jesus alone Who the weeds can o'erthrow!
Just go down to the cross and in willingness pay
For the consequent damage of what came your way;
Then release the offender complete in God's hand,
As the Savior brings cleansing throughout your heart's land.
Oh, the glorious freedom which then floods your soul—
All the thistles demolished with Christ in control;
With offenders released to His power divine—
The forgiveness and healing of Christ is now mine!

The Thorn Of Bitterness

The thorn of bitterness starts out as just a small seed that Satan successfully plants within the mind at an opportune moment. When one faces anything unjust, including abuse, the entire human nature rises up in defense. It is at this point that the enemy may try to introduce his dose of poison, which comes in the form of one seed in the mind. Just because a thought zooms through our mind does not mean it is planted or even a thought we own, but rather that Satan is attempting to get us to receive it and make it our own. It is our choice to either immediately renounce the seed he brings, or to take it up and look at it, feel it, and ultimately plant it.

The seed of bitterness once planted can potentially grow faster than any other seed one could plant. After the seed has sprouted and roots are spreading, they nearly go wild as they reach out in every direction with poisonous arms. Of course, it is all underground in the heart and mind where it cannot be seen with the naked eye. The roots are relentless as they endeavor to entangle deeper and deeper, leaving trails of poison as they go.

Once the roots are spreading unseen within, it isn't long before it becomes obvious to observers that there is a bitterness tree growing within an individual. The track of poison it leaves comes out in words, attitudes, and also actions. Soon, if left unchecked, it will poison one to such a degree that the personality will be marred to a point where others may find it difficult to relate with them. The poison of bitterness is like mixing two chemicals together that will potentially eat up whatever they are put to until it is disintegrated to nothing.

Bitterness is the devil's tool of destruction and will eat one up from the inside out. It has no convenient stopping point and will take the power of God to truly reverse it. Every root Satan has fertilized will have to be dug up and the ground reclaimed for Jesus if victory is to be gained. Engaging in bitterness is like cutting one's own throat or taking measures to sever their own lifeline. It leaves one uselessly crippled for as long as they choose to wallow in its venom.

PRAYER: Lord, I choose to forgive and release _____ for _____, causing me to feel _____. I ask that You would take back all the ground Satan gained through my bitterness, and I yield that ground to Your control. I renounce all thoughts and implants of bitterness and I choose Your love, Jesus. Amen.

Abundant Life!

My Savior died on Calvary,
That He might give new life to me;
That through the precious blood He spilt
He might forgive my sin and guilt.

When Jesus rose up from the dead,
He conquered death, now lives instead;
Abundant life He gives to me—
Because He lives, He makes me free!

Each hour with strength I am endued
That fullest life might be renewed;
Christ stands by me to battle sin—
Gives resurrective pow'r within.

Fullness of joy He gives each day—
Imparts a song when dark the way,
Amid calamities and care
He gives true joy as life He shares!

The peace of Christ by far exceeds
The calmest scene our mind's eye reads:
This tranquil river in my soul
Guides me to my eternal goal!

Abundant life will be complete
When I may kneel at Jesus' feet:
Sing praise for His salvation, true—
For giving me a life that's new!

KETURAH C. MARTIN

Appointment With Death

The Bible says, "It is appointed unto men once to die, but after this the judgment." We are all appointed to die at some point and then face eternity. Jesus made it possible that we do not need to fear death if we accept the provisions He made when He died in our place at Calvary (John 3:16-18; 1 John 1:9).

Some people have an additional appointment with death, created by perpetrators of evil. It is very scary to have this kind of death looming over one's head and chorusing throughout their body, mind, and soul. This was the lot I faced for years, though the core of it all was not understood at first.

At this time I want to commend and validate all of you who may have been severely brainwashed to commit suicide or some other deadly deed. God has a tremendous plan for you to fill because He has ensured that you are still alive today! I commend all of you who, when there was only a thread left between you and death, chose to hang on just a second longer and then another one. You are also commended for any time you ever dared to reach a hand out to touch a glimmer of fleeting hope, despite the unseen prison bars around you. Just that move alone took tremendous courage, especially with that monster of death's appointment leering at you from the shadows.

Most of all, I need to praise God and shout from the mountain tops that *Jesus Christ is the Giver and Sustainer of life!* It was Jesus Who kept you and me alive against innumerable obstacles designed by the enemy to ensure destruction!

Let the sighing of the prisoner come before Thee; according to the greatness of Thy power preserve Thou those that are appointed to die.

Jesus, Who secured abundant life for all of us, is the One Who also has the power over death and every appointment of death. Jesus holds the keys of hell and of death, and He has defeated every attempt of Satan against you and me! We are alive and free to serve the One Who broke the appointment of death for us. Now He is waiting to bring you complete healing and restoration also.

Prayer: Jesus, I thank You for preserving my life despite the pit of horror and pain. I renounce every appointment and programming of death, and ask You Lord to break and abolish it all by the blood of Jesus. I choose to accept the life You have to offer me, and I ask that I might have life more abundantly. Please bring me to complete healing for Your glory. Amen.

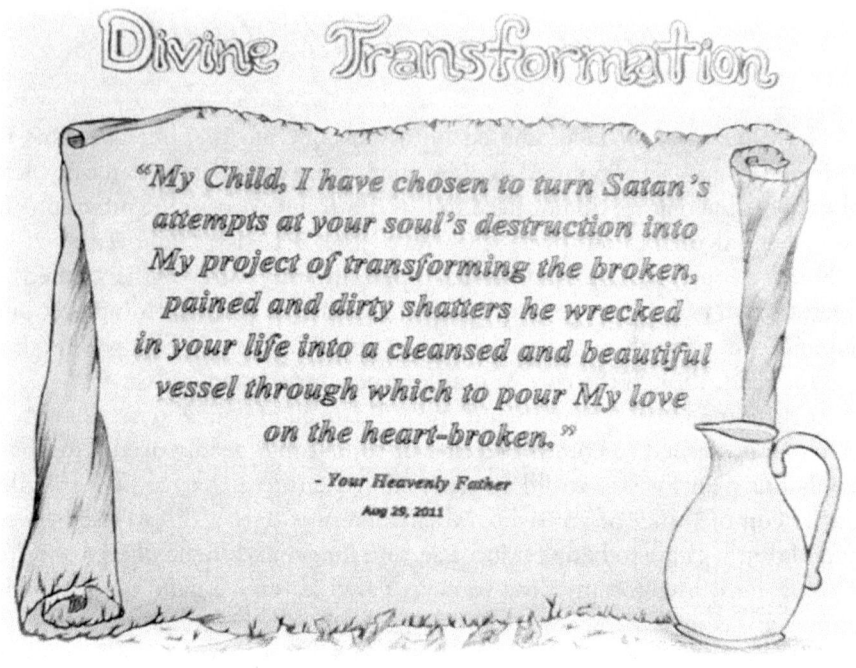

Divine Transformation

"My Child, I have chosen to turn Satan's attempts at your soul's destruction into My project of transforming the broken, pained and dirty shatters he wrecked in your life into a cleansed and beautiful vessel through which to pour My love on the heart-broken."

- Your Heavenly Father
Aug 29, 2011

Shattered Pieces

When the Lord picks up the shattered pieces of one's life, He is not at a loss to know what to do with them: He only waits for your permission to do what He yearns to do. A life trashed by abuse, trafficking and violence is not a write-off in God's books. Rather, to Him it is a golden opportunity to make known to the world what miracles of love and power He can perform in the broken pieces which He now holds in His hand. Here is an opportunity to make a vessel of honour, which ultimately He can use to pour out His love on many others. There is always hope wherever there is life, so don't ever despair about how many pieces it seems your life is in. Jesus specializes in the things that seem impossible to us and is glorified in restoring broken pieces.

PRAYER: Jesus, I give all the broken pieces to You for restoration. Amen.

"Turn Not Ye Again"

"How turn ye again, My beloved, My prize?
Why hearken ye now to the enemy's lies?
The lies and deceptions with which he will snare
Will bind you in bondage again, unawares.

My Child, I'm your God and from you have not strayed,
But near to your side I so long to have stayed,
Yet when My dear children look left or turn right,
They oft walk away to the darkness of night.

When Satan doth knock, My dear Child, at your door,
Ask Jesus to answer—send Him on before:
For if you attempt to face Satan alone,
You surely may falter, to danger be prone.

My dearly beloved, stay close to My side,
And feed on My Word, which is daily thy Guide:
For if ye will never let go of My hand,
My Presence and power will cause thee to stand.

Turn not ye again to the left or the right,
Where beggarly bondage would darken thy night:
Thine eyes must be focused on Jesus each day—
Through Him you will conquer each mile of the way!

Though Satan may try all thy faith to destroy,
Yet still you remain as My prize and My joy;
I'll never forsake you, but walk by thy side,
Where you shall know vict'ry as near you abide!"

Renouncing Lies

Countless times, the enemy of our soul tries to make inroads so he can derail our progress and healing. Doubts, lies, and bitterness are some of his prominent tools. Often, the time when we are bringing the anguishing pain to Jesus for resolution is when the enemy fights the hardest. If he succeeds in planting any deceptive suggestion or lie in our mind or heart, it must be rooted out in order to avoid obstruction or derailment.

The following are some lies we do well to renounce so our healing isn't impeded:

- I renounce the lie that God had no plan or purpose in my birth or existence.
- ➤ I acknowledge that God knew me before I was formed in the womb (Jeremiah 1:5) and created me for a valuable purpose.
- I renounce the lie that God cannot love someone that is as despicable, bad, and useless as I.
- ➤ I acknowledge that God is love, and because of His love, He sent Jesus to die in my place so He could save me and heal me.
- I renounce Satan's lie which promotes my pain as being too intense for God to be able to completely heal, thus limiting His power.
- ➤ I acknowledge that Jesus came to heal the brokenhearted, and nothing is too hard or painful for Him to heal completely.
- I renounce the lie that I am too worthless to ever be accepted by God or people.
- ➤ I acknowledge that my value before God is so great He sent Jesus to die for me, and it is the value in His eyes which truly counts.
- I renounce the lie Satan brings that the healing process is too painful and that I should just give up and get on with life.
- ➤ I acknowledge that I shall conquer in the name of the Lord and shall cross the healing finish line regardless of pain, opposition, or misunderstanding.

PRAYER: Lord Jesus, I choose to confess and renounce the lie that _____, and I embrace Your truth that _____ . I ask that You would take back all the ground Satan gained in me through believing or entertaining this lie, and I yield that ground to Your control. I ask You to replace all lies with Your truth. Amen.

KETURAH C. MARTIN

NOVEMBER 16
READING: JOSHUA 24:15

At The Crossroads

The Heavenly Father your life fully planned,
Each breath and each day He now holds in His hands;
From start unto finish your life He doth see—
Is shaping and molding for what you could be.
But, friend, it is you, at the crossroads must choose—
Your destiny's end—will you win or now lose?
Our Lord made provision—our ransom debt paid,
Yet, here at the crossroads, on you choice is laid.
He gave heaven's Best for the sin of mankind—
Christ died in our place with our future in mind;
He purchased salvation in love none can rate:
For our Supreme God is far greater than great!
My friend, at the crossroads, which way will you take?
Your ticket to heav'n, which Christ paid, is at stake;
He opened the way to His Father above,
And here at the crossroads He beckons in love!
He longs to restore you in love as you are,
Despite any sin, any shame, wounds, or scars:
For He at the cross can restore and make new—
The things thought impossible, Jesus can do!
He'll walk by your side on the road to the cross,
And there fully cleanse all your past, sin, and dross;
He then will re-clothe you in His robes of white:
For by His shed blood He dispels death and night!
The world offers pleasure, deception, and doom,
Where Satan's recruiting binds captives in gloom,
Concealing their fate in his sly, wicked schemes,
And binds them in chains worse than any wild dreams.
God's plan for your life may in fullness proceed,
When you at the crossroads choose Christ for your needs:
His arms are outstretched and His grace is today—
It's here at the crossroads that you choose the way!

"God will never allow the fire to be one degree

"Do not jump from the soup into the fire."

"Wait I say on the Lord."

hotter than it needs to be for the purifying."

Fire And Purifying

There may be times when people feel as if they are just keeping afloat in a soup-pot of pain, misunderstanding, and/or rejection. There are sudden urges to just jump ship and try to leap around the fire. Satan is doing everything possible to obstruct your healing. Don't give him the satisfaction that he's looking for when he attempts to get you to throw in the towel and give up. Often God is allowing our outward circumstance to be used to purify us within even though it is uncomfortable. He is in full control of how hot the fire gets and how long one is there. The results are worth the extra pain when the purified gold in our life is brought forth in the hand of God, and Christ is glorified.

PRAYER: Lord, I choose to allow You to purify my heart and soul. Please give me strength and courage despite the heat. I release to You all those who do not understand or support the work You're doing. Help me to never give up. Amen.

NOVEMBER 18
READING: LUKE 24:13-32 AND 1 CORINTHIANS 15:33

Communication

Communication is a skill that takes true efforts and a will;
It takes much practice day by day to talk to others in right ways.

Communication must be clear—be understood by those who hear;
One's actions go with what they say, will help or hinder in some way.

We often will communicate in unknown language none can rate:
For just a look can volumes speak, portrays the bad side or the meek.

Assertive we must learn to be, our thoughts and feelings speak more free;
To others bring our thoughts across—provoke no anger, cause no loss.

Assumptive words must never be allowed to pass our lips so free,
Our speech must glorify God's name, that we on Him may not bring shame.

And if we don't communicate, a mixed up life will be our fate:
For our emotions get suppressed—rage on inside, won't let one rest.

Before we judge another soul, let's walk a mile within their role,
That we may see through Jesus' eyes the truth of all their needs and cries.

Let's strive to talk direct and calm, to speak our feelings, lessen qualms,
Communicate with confidence, with firmness kind and making sense.

May Jesus govern every word so He is pleased with all that's heard:
Each word let's fill with love divine, that Jesus through our words may shine!

PRAYER: Let the words of my mouth and the meditation of my heart be acceptable
in Thy sight, Oh Lord, my Strength and my Redeemer. Amen.

Communicating

Everyone is different when it comes to their survival and communicating about it. For many, everything is kept secret due to the shame and pain or because of death threats involved. Often there is terror of rejection, condemnation, and/or lack of protection if anyone knows the agony suffered. Safety and confidentiality are also issues which help determine one's ability to dare to share or communicate their feelings and experiences.

Sometimes the perpetrator has implanted such a degree of brainwashing against talking, which may be intermingled with threats, that the individual wouldn't dare cross the line, which outsiders usually cannot even detect. Brainwashing, threats, and programming ingrained in the survivor can create immense barriers that are unseen and rarely understood by the observer or those in helping positions. All the unseen fences and invisible lines have a marked impact on the ability to share the atrocities which are crushing one within.

It is very important for the present and future well-being of survivors that they find a safe, trusted, and confidential individual to be able to share with at some point. It has been statistically noted that when these life-shattering experiences of agony are concealed or deliberately buried, the person carrying that load is far more susceptible to sickness, depression, and the deadly poisons of bitterness and hatred.

Many victims and survivors are ultimately caught in the clutches of suicide and/or desperations such as drugs and alcohol, which the outsider cannot understand because of the core issues that are buried and unknown to anyone. To be on the brink of suicide does not mean that the individual doing a balancing act there is doomed and evil. Rather it is an indication that there are serious pain issues of the heart that need to be understood, validated, and addressed in love—not judgment. It is the responsibility of God's people to make a safe place where survivors can share in confidential safety.

PRAYER: Dear Jesus, it is really scary to think of telling this stuff to anyone. Maybe You could teach me how to tell it to You, because I know You wouldn't blab it around to others and judge me for this pain I cannot bear. Please help me, Jesus, and bring healing. Amen.

"I have chosen, rescued and
restored you for a purpose.
My Child, go out and tell
those broken in pain, abuse
& bondage that there is hope in
Jesus to be completely free
from all the chains, lies & demons
of the enemy. Share the truth
that the power of just one drop
of Jesus' blood is more powerful
than all the kingdoms & demons
of the enemy put together.
I, the Lord, am still on the throne!"
- Your Heavenly Father

A Joint-Heir With Jesus

"My Child, I long for you to feel safe enough to come near unto Me and share your load of pain and shame. I never meant that My children would have to carry such a load. Through Jesus I am offering you the opportunity to become a joint-heir with Him in My kingdom when I adopt you as My very own child. The pain, filth, and abuse you have endured can be transformed into gems of great worth when yielded to My hand. As My own child you will be an equal heir with Jesus Christ and share together all the riches in glory for all eternity. And remember that *I will never fail you!*"—Your Heavenly Father

My Lord Has A Plan!

Through storm clouds of trouble, midst anguish and pain,
My Lord has a plan of most infinite gain:
Though I, amid trial, may not understand—
Each circumstance, pained, He doth hold in His hand.

He blends the dark strands of deep anguish untold
In His skilful weaving, with skeins of bright gold—
Though only the underside dark can I see,
Yet He the full picture doth view perfectly.

He sees the frayed edges, by circumstance worn,
Where dark tribulation has tattered and torn,
Yet each pained experience He can still use
To weave the full picture just as He shall choose.

He sees all the knots which in hardship were tied,
Where faith and a prayer with dark death did collide;
My Lord knows the tatters of life rent and torn,
Which He by His grace can repair and adorn.

It may be that I can't in full comprehend
Why dark strands of anguish He weaves in the blend,
Yet if I but trust and leave all in His hand,
He graciously works on the purpose He's planned.

Although in this life I may not fully know
Why God allowed dark tribulation and woe,
But this I'm assured, "My God knows what is best—
His purpose, in time, He will make manifest."

"I yield, Lord, each heartache and tatter of pain,
And ask that with it You make beauty and gain—
That for Your own purpose You may then acquire
A vessel of honour, perfected by fire!"

KETURAH C. MARTIN

The Lord Makes It Plain

Repeatedly in my healing journey, I was told by well-meaning people that I was just supposed to forgive, forget, and get on with life. In agony of heart, I finally brought this expectation and judgment to God to find answers.

"Lord, it feels as though nobody can see or understand that there is anguishing pain there. Instead, they think that 'all I need to do is to forget the past and put it behind me.' When I was told these things, Lord, where did You fit into this picture; and how do You feel about it all?"

"Even as these words and thoughts were being brought out, I, the Lord, was looking into the depths of your wounded heart while searching for someone to stand in the gap through which I could minister to reach the pain and items buried far below what eye could see or mind could understand."

"Jesus, is it possible to forget an agonizing past when the pain is surging night and day in bloody tatters, and one cannot see to even go on?"

"When My children are wounded, abused, and destroyed as you were, it cannot be truly forgotten or put aside until it is exposed and brought to Me for healing, cleansing, and restoration."

"Then why do Your people so often insist that it all be cast behind, whether healed and resolved or not?"

"Only I, the Lord, can see the depth of pain and damage of My wounded children. My people who are human cannot see or know this depth. When they do not rely totally on My understanding, love, and insight, they will attempt to force the wounded ones through a coerced healing process rather than waiting on My timing or specifically seeking My will and ways."

"Lord, how do You want a damaged and pained individual to respond to those who are pressuring the completion of healing when the inner agony feels worse than death and the obstacles are everywhere?"

"They need to cry unto Me, and I will answer them and show them great and mighty things which they know not. They also must surrender the people, the pressure, and the lack of understanding into My hand, as they abstain from all the bitterness bait put out by the enemy. I will not leave My wounded children to writhe and die alone in agony, but I, the Lord, will raise up someone to stand in the gap to be used by Me to bring healing and hope to them."

Thank-You Lord, for showing me Your viewpoint, and for assuring me of Your undying love.

"I Will Perfect That Which Concerneth Thee"

"What doest thou here, in the cave of despair?
Why weep ye and writhe midst thy anguish and care?
My Child, know ye not that I'm with thee alway—
Despite all the heartache which clouds up thy day?
Come out of the darkness and bask in My light:
For I will not leave thee in this thy dark night;
I understand fully thy life of pained loss,
But I can refine thee midst agony's cross.
I know every tatter within thy pained heart,
The ravaged destruction I've seen from the start,
But all is not lost—My dear Child, I've a plan—
Yet ye must submit all your pain to My hand.
For when it's surrendered to My divine will,
As ye wait before Me, so yielded and still,
Then I can begin all these dark strands to weave,
Creating true beauty—but ye must believe.
My Child, ye have purpose and value to Me
And I perfect daily that which concerns thee;
Thy life, though destroyed and reduced to a heap,
Is still in My hand, and My child I will keep!
So, Child, don't despair midst thy trial and cross:
For nothing you yield to Me will be a loss—
From ashes and ruins a vessel I make
That's worthy to pour out My praise for My sake.
Because of the plan that I've laid out for thee,
Which cannot be stopped by thy soul's enemy,
Uncover thy face and My great love behold:
For I have preserved thee as fire-tried gold.
Entrust to My hands all thy pain, shame, and past,
Thy mountains of anguish upon Me now cast:
Thy God doth restore thee to life of new heights,
And I'll work through thee to bring wounded hearts light!"

Knots, Blotches, And Threads

Looking critically at the back of the quilt top that was supposedly meant to portray my life story, I was aghast at the sight I beheld. Already in my mind I had labelled the quilt as a worthless scrap of useless shreds tied together with dirty threads and rotted twine. Here and there I saw blotches of big black smears, beside which were some ugly knots and ragged holes. The frayed and tattered edges were unfinished and in sad need of some kind of help. Despairingly, I cast the apparatus into the corner, hoping to never again have to look at it. It seemed to have nearly ruined my day!

However, the next day Jesus came walking into the room carrying the discarded quilt top over His arm. As He approached, I looked at what He carried with consternation and severe misgivings.

"My Child," He spoke gently as He drew near me. "You must not cast away the masterpiece I have begun and have laboured so hard over. You don't appear to appreciate what you see here, but you must look through My eyes at what I have restored and created. You can only see the underside of all the shreds, tatters, and painful shatters of the life pieces brought to Me for healing. When it is held up to the eternal light of My love, then you will see the full picture more clearly and understand every knot, scrap, thread, and tatter that I wove together with My undying love. I will complete the work I have started in you and finish the masterpiece I have begun. The scheming foe that created shreds of agony and abuse for destruction will cringe in utter defeat when he sees My transformation."

"Teach me, Lord, to see all the work You do through Your eyes and in the light of Your countenance," I replied to His explanation.

PRAYER: Dear Lord, I acknowledge that Your ways and thoughts are higher than mine. Even though I cannot see the full picture as You do, I choose to continually trust it all into Your divine hand. I ask that You make all the knots, threads, and scraps into something that can extol the love of Jesus. Amen.

NOVEMBER 25
READING: 2 KINGS 6:8-17

Hope For The Ritually Abused

We plead your mercy, Lord, be used on all those ritually abused,
Who have survived the horrors past—in Satan's realm they have been cast.
The perpetrators of this crime are sold to Satan, filled with grime,
Who seek to shatter hope and trust of victims: for this is a 'must.'
A broken trust in God and man—to sense from God eternal ban:
Midst torturous rituals, bloody crime, extolling Satan all the time.
Diverse abuses heap and pile on helpless victims, feeling vile:
Abuses here of every brand, in cruelty dealt by forceful hands.
Most oft essential to survive—that mind and body stay alive,
The victim's mind will block the deeds of bloody horror, threats, and creeds.
These memories locked 'neath lock and key, dissociated oft may be
From knowledge of the victim's mind, but side effects are undefined.
Midst Satan's rituals cruelty rules—the victims forced through brutal schools:
They're brainwashed thoroughly each day—in suicide's dark programs lay.
"You may not speak to anyone of what you've seen or here's been done:
For you'll be locked up as 'insane,' and I will kill you—not in vain!"
In chains of bondage, hopeless bound, so bruised and broken, hopeless found:
These battered victims long for aid—of worth divested—helpless made.
So many folks don't understand the broken lives throughout this land,
Proclaim these things can happen not, bypassing pain abuse hath wrought.
"Each broken piece of all your heart, which writhes in anguish from the start;
The surging terror, should you tell; the hopeless guilt, which ceaseless swells:
Christ Jesus understands it all and waits to answer every call;
Though shattered, lone, and left to die, He knows and hears your feeble cry!
There's hope in Christ, oh broken heart: for God hath loved you from the start—
Your anguished bondage, pain, and strife, Christ Jesus heals and brings new life!
The life that's marred and broken worst, e'en though it seems has been accursed,
Can be repaired by Christ above—there's naught too hard for His great love!"

Special Message from Jesus: "My Child, I invite you to bring Me all your pain, abuse and chains. I have conquered in full the enemy, Satan who destroyed you. Therefore I can perform a complete transformation in you, turning what he intended for destruction into eternal riches in glory through My blood and resurrection."

KETURAH C. MARTIN

No Limits To God's Love

"Greater is He that is in you than he that is in the world."

There are no limits whatsoever to what depths of darkness, pain, and horror that God's love can reach. There is no individual trapped in occultic bondage, rituals, and terror to whom He does not extend His love, grace, and mercy. Jesus gave His life so that *Whosoever believes in Him should not perish but have everlasting life.* He also said clearly that *He that cometh to Me I will in no wise cast out.* Jesus is actually waiting with open arms of love to receive even those who would be leading out in satanic rituals and bloodshed. He desires to reveal to them the power of the Supreme Sacrifice He made.

It seems that it may be quite advisable that God's people periodically get their spiritual vision tested *at Jesus' Optometry.* Here He can assist them to unconditionally view every individual through the eyes and perspective of how He sees them. He also would give divine wisdom and insight to always separate the person from the problem. We must never write off anyone as beyond hope, regardless of where they are in life.

As children of God, we never need to fear anyone, even though they are practicing occultic rituals and are into Satanism. The only difference between them and a born again believer is that the believer *is a sinner saved by grace, and the Satanist is a sinner needing salvation by God's grace!* Of course, we must put on the full armour of God and stay continually under the protection and power of the blood of Jesus, for then Satan cannot touch us. We must also respect the fact that the enemy is more powerful than we are on our own strength, but with the Holy Spirit within us and Jesus walking beside us, the devil and his attempts against us are all in vain. Who but the children of God are equipped with sufficient power to go in and assist those who are crying out for hope, help, and deliverance as the deadly chains of horror drag them to doom? We are responsible and accountable before God to be armoured and willing to be His messenger even to those in occultic bondage. Satan flees when he sees the blood of Jesus applied to our door-posts. But he also makes every attempt to implant fear and intimidate us about going on his turf to rescue the crying captives he has concealed there. What are we going to do about it? Sweep it under the carpet? Or rise up in the power of Jesus and live out His love through the power of His blood and resurrection life?

Rejection's Reflection

This heart-burning question was finally brought to God after years of being turned out in the cold, seemingly due to a life of abuse and its after effects.

"Jesus, can You show me why it has always seemed that I have been a waste of space, unwanted or without value, in the churches that call themselves by Your name?"

"I have usually had at least one person who made attempts to befriend and accept you. But when some of them began to understand that the inner wounds and life-destructive abuses were far deeper than they could comprehend, the enemy sowed all kinds of fears, lies, and misgivings in them. He sought to devise a way to ensure that you would become destitute and alone while trapped with an abusive husband. However, you must always choose to forgive and release these individuals, leaders, and churches to Me so that Satan never gains any footholds in your life as he so desperately is seeking to do. He continually tries to engraft roots of bitterness within to defile you. He is defeated through the power of My blood, and I the Lord will continue to fight and conquer the enemy for you, but you must wear the armour I've provided!"

"Jesus, I choose to renounce the lies that I am worthless to God and man and that I deserve rejection. I choose to embrace the finished work of Christ on the cross to heal my heart from all the pain of rejection, to cleanse me from the lies of Satan, and to forgive me for believing them. I choose to forgive and release those who call themselves Your children but have misrepresented You, causing me to feel confused, betrayed, rejected, and disillusioned about Who You are. I am willing to pay the emotional pain and consequences they have caused me, Lord. I ask You, Lord, to please take back all the ground which I gave to the enemy, or which he has stolen, and I pray that You would take complete control of these grounds and my life. I request Your Spirit's presence, power, and prompting in my life that He may guide me into all truth, fill me with Your love, and guide me so that Satan cannot regain any grounds: for I yield it all to You. I pray Your blessing on all those who have hurt, rejected, or misunderstood me."

"I have graven you upon the palms of My hands—You are Mine!"

"I have graven You
upon the palms
of My hands –
You are Mine!"

Your Father in Heaven

Engraved On His Hands

To be graven upon the hands of God is really an amazing fact when one considers it. To reflect that God would think of us in such a way that He would even take the time to write us on His hand is very encouraging on our daily journey. What do you suppose God thinks whenever He looks at His hand where we are engraved? I believe He views His child with love-light in His eye as He meditates on all the things He wants to do through us to touch another life and glorify His Son Jesus at the same time. He rejoices in the plan He put into place through the death and resurrection of His Jesus, through Whom mankind can have an active and living relationship with their Creator.

PRAYER: Thank You, God, for thinking on my low estate and making it possible that I can be Your child and walk daily holding Your hand! Amen.

Imprisoned In The Jail of My Mind

"My mind, Lord, is tied into dark, deadly knots
Where daily I'm strangled in slippery thoughts,
Seems never will stop, but will race wildly on—
My heart's crying out for some peace and a dawn.
It feels I'm imprisoned within my own mind
Where chains of the devil do shackle and grind;
Lord Jesus, please free all my heart, mind and soul
And of ev'ry thought, Lord, please take full control.

The lies of the enemy strewn all about
Are randomly growing as trees of dark doubt,
He fights day and night to ensure I am bound—
Attempting each moment to steal yet more ground.
I feel so alone in the mind's prison grim
Where chaos and anguish spill over the brim,
A cell of stark solitude—lonely and drear,
Where thoughts always scream, yet with nobody near.

I long to be free, Lord, from fetters and chains
Of dark, grimy thoughts which infuse my own brain,
I choose to surrender the mind's battlefield—
Each pain, loss and heartache to Your hand I yield.
Lord, be my sole Vision, my Help and my Hope,
And stop my descent down this slippery slope,
Break each chain and fetter—each thought by Your blood
And stop the insanity of this dark flood.

Lord Jesus, I bring You the tatters and strands
Of my broken life, which so few understand,
Each shatter of anguish and shard of deep pain—
I give them to You, Lord, so You can bring gain!
For out of the ashes of agony great
The tools of deep suffering no longer spell 'fate'
For when it's all yielded to Your hand and will,
You bring restoration and say 'Peace be still!'"

KETURAH C. MARTIN

Understanding—Not Judging

There are certain depths of inner excruciation that very few people can comprehend, unless, of course, they have been there. The Lord was very gracious to me and sent two doctors who understood to some degree this depth of agony.

When one experiences the ravages of daily and repeated abuses for years, then in order to survive, it is all subconsciously pushed into a closet. Here it continues to pile up until it is so compacted and immense that often God will mercifully allow the emotions to go into a comatose state for a period of time. However, He is also very gracious to bring it all back to light and to the emotional level of feeling again, in His time. As our Creator, God knows that we cannot be healthy (physically, spiritually, emotionally) when these horrendous effects of abuse and horror are stuffed away and beginning to rot. He is always right beside you when the time is right for you to feel again, and walks alongside those who must go through this experience. God alone can heal this depth of anguish so that one may move on after it is dealt with.

Many individuals who live in unspeakable emotional excruciation are limited to very few coping skills that they know about. Many of them have no safe person with whom they may share or have a confidential outlet. As a result, they resort to slashing or inflicting any type of physical distress on themselves that can be imagined. Often for this they are judged, condemned, rejected, and cast out in anger by the very people who should be their greatest source of support. When such is the response, hopeless despair may escalate to suicidal proportions. Even though it is not *a good* way to relieve the inner agony temporarily, yet I do commend these survivors for their desire to hang on to life a bit longer. It is not our place to judge or accuse them of looking for attention, etc. Rather, it is our job to come alongside them and offer a safe place to share. Do not preach at them, but just be a gentle presence there. Never overreact or panic, for those things only increase the self-hate and inner pain to greater dimensions. Validating their pain and survival is one of the most important things to do in the critical moments, for in most cases, there are no other words or expressions for this depth of agony.

Please note: This author does not propagate this method of pain release as a good thing, but rather seeks to help people understand and be supportive when it is that bad.

Preserved By God

It is rarely possible for the one suffering to see that there could possibly be any good outcome to the unspeakable pain and destruction they experience. However, after being miraculously delivered from death itself on several occasions, it became very clear that the hand of God was indeed preserving me. There were even policemen and doctors who in tears accredited my survival to the hand of God! Many times a few of God's faithful agents reminded me in the darkest of night that the Lord was preserving my life for a purpose which only He knew. Later, Christ made it very clear that He would never waste my pain if I would place it all in His hand. After understanding better that the pain can be reversed and used for good and for God's glory, it was no longer a bitter thorn, but a tool in the hand of Jesus Christ, the Great Physician! Thank You, Jesus!

God Holds The Storm

At first a sapling's weak and small,
But through the years grows strong and tall,
Yet it must suffer hardships long
Before it grows mature and strong.

It takes the years of sun and rain
For it to grow and strength to gain;
Those rainy days can be so drear,
But soon will come the sun's bright cheer.

It takes the howling storms that blow,
And then to stand midst winter snow:
It takes the wind that whips and bends—
On all these hardships, growth depends.

Our life is like a growing tree,
And often storms our lot may be:
For with no storms we can't grow strong,
Cannot withstand what comes along.

Within His hand, God holds life's storms,
Decides what comes, and in what forms;
Life's storming fury He controls—
Allows what's best to build our souls!

Though we don't understand the pain,
God has a purpose for some gain;
Amid life's tempest gives us peace,
And leads to heav'n where storms will cease!

DECEMBER 3
READING: EPHESIANS 4:24-27 AND 2 CORINTHIANS 6:17, 18

Anger Transference

Note: **God prompted this page for survivors of dad-abuse, and in no way does it reflect on author's father.**

Desperately, Ruthann struggled to get safely hidden under the calves' overflowing hay manger as an angry voice drew nearer. Her nine-year-old mind could not understand why a daddy would always be looking for her and wanting to hurt her with words and actions. Daily and hourly, she went over it in her mind, trying to decipher what wrong she had done that made her to be so bad in Daddy's eyes. Finally, after coming to no logical explanation, she concluded that *It just would never be possible to be loved or accepted by him. She was too bad and yucky and dirty to ever be anything special or wanted.*

"Ruthann!" yelled the angry voice nearby as the little girl quivered in terror. As he violently yanked her from under the manger, her eyes were brimming with tears as her heart pounded relentlessly in terror. Without any further words, she was horrendously used and beaten, still having no idea what wrong she had committed.

"Now get into the house and help your mother," he roared as he yanked Ruthann to her feet. "And don't you go telling anyone what kind of horrible things you were doing out here, or it will be a lot worse for you!" he yelled after her.

It is scenarios such as this one that lay the ground in a child for future devastation when they may desire to serve God but can only see Him as the image portrayed by their earthly father. The same anger, terror, and shame that were always linked with their dad are suddenly transferred to the Heavenly Father. Most sincere seekers do not want it to be thus, but the whole process is often so subconscious that it is engulfing at times, as rage and fear may burst out in an unleashed fashion.

Anger is an emotion, just as are love, hate, or fear. Usually it hits a person suddenly, without any planning. What one decides in the first five to ten seconds to do with the anger determines whether it becomes wrong. We can either bring it to God and seek His help and direction, or else wallow around in these feelings, feeding them further until they grow into a monster whose teeth will bite far harder than we ever could have imagined.

PRAYER: Lord, help me to see You and Your love for Who You really are. I choose to release Dad into Your hand. Please help me, Jesus! Amen.

KETURAH C. MARTIN

DECEMBER 4
READING: REVELATION 21:7 AND ROMANS 8:14-18

A Heavenly Father's Love

How can one possibly get out of the anger fangs that are a carryover from the life-altering abuses perpetrated by a father? Is there any way the yearning heart can connect to the loving Father in heaven Who is 100 percent different from an abusive father?

The following form letter (**which doesn't in any way depict author's father**) is designed to be used by anyone seeking to find freedom from the jaws of father-rage and to pursue a living and loving relationship with the Heavenly Father.

To Dad,

This letter is just to tell you that my life has been devastated due to not receiving a true perspective of God as my Father because of how I was treated by you, my blood father. The verbal lashings produced fear to speak to God. The physical beatings made Him look scary and violent. The filth and sexual abuse portrayed that I'm too filthy and unacceptable for Him and that He is standing over me as a judge for being so dirty. The rejection and absolute control made it feel as though a Heavenly Father cannot be trusted. And the way you always hurt my mom with your words and actions while you said that you loved her made me very scared of love. That means if God is love, He will hurt me.

Dad, I want you to know that I choose to forgive and release you, with all your abusive words and actions, into the hand of Jesus. I choose to release to Christ all the false perceptions of God that you portrayed, and I renounce them all with His power. I choose to forgive and release the false love you displayed to my mother, and I claim the divine love of Jesus to be my guide for love. I choose to forgive and release all the filth and sexual perversions you committed against me, which produced a shameful fear of a Heavenly Father.

Cont.

Dad, I release you into the hand of the Lord for Him to deal with, and I ask Him to grant you a suitable blessing today. I reclaim my life through Jesus as God designed it should be. Every generational sin and stronghold created through the abuses, I renounce and claim the blood of Jesus over, so that they will not dictate my future. I request Jesus to take back all the ground Satan gained in me through the abuses and I yield that ground to His control. May God bless and keep you and show you the true love of Himself.

—Your Son/Daughter

KETURAH C. MARTIN

In the Trafficker's Trenches

Though down in the traffickers' trenches I'm called,
Where many a soul is abused, raped, and mauled—
The sinister alleys breathe hopeless despair,
But yet I know fully My God is still there!
The trafficking web winds around the whole world
Where sin so nefarious travels unfurled;
The agents of Satan by demons controlled—
Exploit and destroy in a heartless greed, cold.
Past gutters of terror where predators wait
To capture the innocent – spell out their fate,
The traffickers, evil, seek out helpless lives
With threats, drugs and lies, or perchance guns and knives.
They force in the vulnerable, homeless and sad,
With violence uncouth – so deprived and ill-clad—
To hold as a captive, to sell and resell,
While feeding lust's greed in a dark, filthy hell.
The "madams" lay bait to deceive and beguile,
Attempting to lure hapless victims awhile
And when the trap snaps amid danger and loss,
The innocent suffer beneath a vile cross.
The lust-driven pimp will pursue fleeing girls
As death threats and greed after them he still hurls
The deafening curses ring out through the night—
Foul message in texts are sent out to affright.
The freedom of choice does the Lord give so free—
Though souls pursue evil, yet still He will be
Close by every victim to shield from the worst
And carries them through all the filth that's accursed.
My Jesus walks with me and leads me each stride,
To walk with the trafficked, the wounded and tied,
Though demons of hell may assail me around—
My Jesus has won! And His vict'ry abounds!
One drop of His blood scatters demons of night,
Breaks fetters and chains as the pimps all take flight;
Though slavery runs rampant God sets these girls free,
For Christ died—now lives—and proclaims Victory!

The Slavery of Trafficking

The Lord's heart is wrung in anguish as He views how the world has become a massive cesspool of filthy corruption with the atrocities of nefarious greed, perpetrated by traffickers, pimps and johns. The state of the worldwide slavery/trafficking at the expense of the innocent is at its greatest peak of evil, likely in history. But the Lord knows and is keeping the record of a just God, who will recompense justice on all those who choose to perpetrate evil against the innocent and vulnerable.

Though the majority of the average people have no clue to what depth of wickedness and destruction the children are being destroyed, yet the Heavenly Father sees it all, knowing every detail. When His little ones are being sold as cattle to the vilest of the vile who choose to destroy their innocent purchase, God does step in. Though it may seem like God is just letting bad things happen, He actually sends His angels to stand between His child and the demons of hell that are working through evil and disgusting men. Should God remove His Presence or that of His angels, the children being used for sex slavery, child sacrifice, adrenochrome, and organ harvesting would die immediately. It is the Lord alone who saves their lives amid insufferable trauma; or in His great love will take them directly to His bosom of love in glory—forever free from evil predators, demonic forces, and vile traffickers.

Jesus said, "Whoever offends/hurts one of these little ones that believe in Me, it would be better for him that a millstone be hanged around his neck and he be drowned in the depth of the sea." This means that the punishment from God for hurting and destroying His children is going to be far worse than to be drowned in the depth of the sea under the weight of a massive millstone.

Whether one may be in the trenches of filth, threats and terror as a lamb trying to escape brutal slavery, or as God's ambassador to help rescue the innocent—the Heavenly Father is loving, helping and guiding you to safety, hope and healing. He has an eternal plan for your life that was planned before your birth. No matter how agonizing and terrifying it may get, yet the Lord holds you in the palm of His hand as He guides you to a better tomorrow, and grace sufficient to complete His calling for you. Grab His outstretched hand and hang on, whether you see Him or not. He will never leave or forsake you!

PRAYER: Lord Jesus, I entrust my life, the anguishing tatters and all my future into Your Almighty hand for Divine protection, for Your ultimate healing, and for complete cleansing. I ask You to restore the years that the locusts have eaten and transform me and my pain into the likeness of You, Jesus. Amen.

Light From The Morning Star

He came as an Infant to Bethlehem's stall,
That night long ago, as the angels did call—
Their loud Hallelujahs rang out through the sky:
Announcing the Christ-Child, sent down from on high.

He came to the world in its darkness and night,
To be our Redeemer—become the world's Light;
The people in darkness a great Light have seen—
In death's blackest shadows so long they have been.

Up Calvary's hill did this Prince of Peace trod,
Fulfilling redemption as planned out by God:
For He paid our ransom through death on the tree—
Arose in great triumph that we can be free!

The love, life, and light from the Bright Morning Star
Still penetrates darkness, though near or afar—
Illuminates wholly, each life where it shines,
Thus hope springs alive and dark death no more dines.

Now "Glory to God!" with the angels we sing,
For sending His Son and for light He did bring;
From bondage and darkness He truly sets free—
"We bring now ourselves, Lord, as gifts for just Thee!"

PRAYER: Lord, thank You for loving me and all mankind enough to send Your only Son to pay the death penalty that we deserve for sin. Thank You for making freedom through salvation in Christ possible for whoever will come and receive the Great Gift You have provided. Lord, I want to receive Your Gift, Jesus. Amen.

Where Was God?

When a child is suffering affliction of body and also enduring the anguish, filth, and shame of repeated rape, where is God? When there is not a soul in the world that is safe to confide in and the death threats are lurking around every corner, where is God?

In such dire situations, the enemy would like us to believe that "I am too bad and dirty for God to care," and "I do not deserve to be helped." Be most assured that Satan is a liar and the *father of lies,* and it is most detrimental to linger even a fleeting moment over the suggestions he attempts to weave into one's agonizing circumstance. We must consciously choose to reject the lies and suggestions he subtly tries to inject and, even in our darkest night, to cry out to God for His truth and light.

To be abused and molested is never God's divine plan. However, because man was created with the power of choice, God does not force a perpetrator of such crimes to do that which is right. As a result, many innocent victims suffer horrendously and often all alone—but God . . .

We can be positively assured that, when someone is suffering through the anguishing throes of abuse and/or defilement, God is right there holding His child in His arms to safely preserve the life that He created for a purpose and for His glory. Should God withdraw Himself from the suffering victim at such a time as this, her fate would be death. It is the Angel of His Presence Who is sustaining and preserving for a divine purpose that God alone knows. "For the oppression of the poor, for the sighing of the needy, now will I arise, saith the Lord; I will set him in safety from him that puffeth at him" (Psalm 12:5).

PRAYER: Lord Jesus, I acknowledge that You are the Source of my life and survival, and I thank You for standing beside me throughout everything. I choose to renounce all Satan's lies, and I ask You to take back all the ground He gained through them. I surrender that ground to Your control. Jesus, please teach me Your truth and surround me with Your light, hope, and Presence and bring me to healing. Amen.

Christmas Joy

C is for Christ Child, in Bethlehem born,
H is for Holy night, stars did adorn.
R is Redemption, for which cause Christ came;
I for the Inn—'twas no room for His name.
S is the Star that showed men in their day,
T the Three wise men brought gifts on their way.
M is for Mary of such humble worth,
A is for Angels proclaiming His birth!
S is for Stable, accepting our King,

J is for Jesus, salvation He brings!
O is for Others—God's love to them show;
Y answers "Yes" when salvation we know!

Jesus Is the Reason for the Season!

PRAYER: Lord Jesus, I thank You for coming to this earth to save me through Your birth, death and resurrection. I want to receive Your love and salvation, and ask You to forgive me for all the wrong things I have done. Please wash my heart, body and mind with Your blood and make me a new creature in Christ. Through Jesus I want to be a child of God the Father. Amen.

When Life's Plate Runs Over

Just what is it like when one's plate overflows?
When circumstance, harsh, like the wild winter blows?
The burdens of anguish may mount to the sky,
And crushed 'neath the load, someone feels she could die.
The plate may be dripping with heartbroken tears,
And midst abuse violent be heaped up with fears,
The victim is crushed by abuses she bore,
As all of her being was stripped to the core.
The spectators gather, observing her fate
Of limitless pain and abuse none can rate;
So many hurl darts of rejection and doom:
For in their small world the abused find no room.
When life's plates run over midst pain none can know—
When dark situations may blizzard and snow—
Though life seems more frigid than all the far north:
Yet hope's ray of light in its dawn will spring forth!
When plates overflow and life seems all forlorn—
When crushed hearts are bleeding, so tattered and torn,
Yet there is a Father, Who sees the distressed,
And He's fully promised to help the oppressed.
God gathers the fatherless child in His arms,
And near to His heart He doth shield from alarms;
He stands near the broken, abused, and cast out
And offers assistance with never a doubt!
My friend, take fresh courage—don't ever despair,
Despite what you've suffered, the Lord is still there;
The fuller your plate is, the greater God's grace—
He'll carry your load and assist in life's race!
So trust to His hand all the pain in your plate,
The dark situations that no one can rate—
He'll take all the ashes and past filled with pain,
Exchanging it all for eternal, bright gain!

KETURAH C. MARTIN

Exhaustless Grace

It is likely that everyone at some point may feel as if their plate is overflowing or may not know how to deal with a certain portion of their circumstances or experience. Some people cry out God at the onset of their tribulation, and others may wait until they are at the end of their rope. Still others may with great forcefulness abstain from ever crying out to the only One Who can truly offer the help and strength they need.

Those who have outlived their abuse will usually have a lot more on their plate to cope with than the average person, and more than what meets the eye. However, for anyone desiring to live a productive life subsequent to abuse, there is a vital truth that should always be considered. *Despite how full and overflowing your plate may be with the aftermath of abuse and all your current circumstances, the Lord's grace and strength can never be exhausted or run dry!* Why should we limp along with horrendous burdens that were never meant for us to bear when the Lord Himself is waiting to carry for us? He is willing and able not only to carry it all, but also to assist you in resolving all the painful things that are being packed around until there is nothing left to pack!

To think of going to the painful site where it seems one's life has been destroyed is never an appealing option. Rather, it holds quite a portion of terror, a mountainous heap of agony, and possibly a great flood of filthy waters all around it. In our feeble minds, it just doesn't seem like a possibility. That's when Jesus draws near to assure you that the grace He will bestow through this journey by far supercedes every degree of agony, filth, or terror one can imagine. The grace and strength Jesus imparts in the healing journey is exhaustless and beyond all measure! His grace is well-known to expand by leaps and bounds when the need and the pain increase, and one of the best things about Jesus being in charge of one's healing is that He will never walk out on you, but will always complete the work He has begun!

PRAYER: Lord Jesus, I ask that You could empower me with the amount of grace and strength that is needed to deal with all the stuff I've been packing around. I renounce every lie of Satan that says *it's not worth it* and claim Your blood over all his suggestions. I choose Your life and healing, Jesus! Amen.

Pros And Cons Of Healing

Often people like to weigh the pros and cons about some issue before making a decision. God has preserved my life so many times against all obstacles and has shown Himself strong on my behalf in my healing. Because of this, I feel compelled to let all the hurting individuals out there know that there is abundant hope for your situation when you allow and invite Him to be involved. To this end, I have created a list of the pros and cons when looking at the subject from the opposite end of where you may be. What are the disadvantages and the advantages of pursuing healing for abuse?

Disadvantages
- I'm afraid I will be killed if I tell.
- There is nobody that cares to understand.
- To trust anyone is not possible.
- I'm afraid of feeling the pain and shame.
- The carpet covering it all will be disturbed and someone might see.
- I'm afraid I will be rejected and disowned.

Advantages
- ✓ Complete freedom is possible through Jesus.
- ✓ The agonizing load can be healed and disposed of.
- ✓ There is nothing too hard for God to heal.
- ✓ Satan is defeated and I can claim the victory that's mine in Jesus.
- ✓ I need not remain a cripple the rest of my life.
- ✓ The enemy has no right to use my pain or past to control me.
- ✓ There is sufficient grace and help available through Jesus.
- ✓ I can be an heir with King Jesus instead of a slave to the devil.
- ✓ The past does not need to dictate my future.
- ✓ There is unspeakable joy and freedom just waiting to enfold me!

PRAYER: Jesus, I don't know what I'm waiting for, but it is so scary. I choose to renounce every fear that Satan is trying to inject and claim the blood of Jesus over every obstruction to healing. I believe, Lord, that You are willing and able to bring me freedom, healing, and joy, and I choose to accept all that You are waiting to bestow through Your love. Amen.

Jesus Walks The Streets At Christmas

'Twas days before Christmas in Vancouver's core
Where folks of all age groups from many stores pour;
So many were laden with bundles so great—
Engulfed with big plans midst the year's festive state.

Then Jesus was seen walking down Granville Street,
Observing each face of the throngs He did meet:
Some faces were grief-stricken, some grown so hard,
So many were heartbroken, pain-filled, and scarred.

The Master's heart yearned o'er the beggarly poor,
The orphans and homeless—no love or food sure;
He glanced at the rich, who in scorn passed them by,
Not heeding their need or their pained, desperate cry.

He looked at their packages jostling along—
Saw thousands of dollars which could have brought song:
"If only more hearts could be burdened to care,
Denying their 'wants' and with needy to share."

And in the town square, Christ a group there beheld,
Where His birth and purpose was totally quelled:
For there in stark counterfeit Santa Claus sat,
Obstructing the view of the Son God begat.

His heart throbbed with pain as dark Calv'ry He saw,
Where He gave His life in such agony raw,
Yet here in the city scant place could He find,
Where He was received as the Savior Divine.

Though many have kept Him in mangers of hay,
Just how does He rate in your own life today?
His miracle-birth paved the way to the cross,
Where He died—now lives, to redeem from death's loss.

Beware Of The Father Of Lies

The enemy of our soul is as a roaring lion, seeking to devour whoever he can get his clutches on. Satan is very crafty and does not necessarily always pounce on his prey and immediately devour them in a few big, juicy bites. Rather, as "the father of lies," he will subtly get his potential prey side-tracked. He does this by what may seem to be simply "stopping to look" at something he points out to observe, a thought, rationalization, or theological alternative, etc. However, one can be sure he will always have some type of trap hidden that will spring without warning. Once the trap is sprung, he will very often drag his prey into his hidden lair where he can gnaw at them spiritually in a more deliberate fashion. He craftily feeds them some juicy lies and tantalizing influence that most usually hold some fleshly appeal and desensitizes them as they are numbing out spiritually. (See 1 John 2:15, 16.)

The devil's destructions against his prey very often begins with injections of camouflaged poisons into the mind where he attempts to either create a war zone or build a stronghold through his subtle lies, influence, and ultimate deceptions. The Christian's mind is the favourite place where Satan seeks to do battle and gain concealed grounds in a believer. The mind is where the majority of spiritual warfare and potential downfall for all humans begins. If the enemy's initial thought injections are not immediately dealt with through the power, blood, and Word of Jesus, and brought into captivity to the obedience of Christ, he gains a direct advantage as it becomes harder to get rid of him and his persistence. The believer must not take even a moment to attempt to reason or dialogue when the enemy injects thoughts, doubts, attitudes, or sights. To engage in any manner gives him the time he needs to work the poison of what he has just inserted. As soon as the injected poison begins to spread, it also starts to grow or magnify until life-sucking doubts are casting deadly shadows in every direction. Doubts are a deadly poison to the child of God and can turn into full-fledged unbelief as Satan is subtly building unseen fortresses in the mind.

PRAYER: Lord, I renounce every attempt of Satan to gain any thought or recognition in my mind and claim the blood of Jesus on him. I claim Your truth and light to infill my heart and mind, leaving no room for the enemy. Amen.

KETURAH C. MARTIN

My God Stands Between

Oh, just for one soul to walk with me a mile—
That someone would care to assist through death's pile;
Is there just one friend who can fathom this pain,
Accredit the anguish and limitless strain?
Although it be many or e'en just a few,
Who understand not all the things I've been through—
Though it be scarce one who in full comprehends,
Yet there remains One Who my case doth defend!

For He has a heart for the fatherless child,
And He saw each act of abuse on us filed;
The woman abandoned, abused, or cast out,
He takes in His arms and defends without doubt.
So therefore my cause I can cast in His care,
Although the majority haven't been there:
When most cannot grasp the destruction unseen—
My God always stands by His love in-between!

When words of dark slander in ignorance are said,
By those who've not lived through the years abuse fed—
The Father's love then intercepts ev'ry word—
When misunderstood, He with strength fully girds.
It's not so important just what people think,
Nor whether they spew out some words that may stink—
Their words, thoughts, and attitudes aren't about me,
But just between them and their Maker they be.

Though misunderstandings cut right to the core,
And salt upon wounds, they so lavishly pour,
Yet "Father, forgive them," with Jesus I'll say:
For they know not truth about what came my way.
I choose to release each of them to God's hand—
Their words, thoughts, and attitudes, and their closed stand:
For God sees the truth and He knows every heart—
He is my Defense and from me will not part!

My Defense Is God

When the Lord is working on behalf of one's healing and restoration, there is nobody who can stop the work He has begun. *For the Lord of hosts hath purposed, and who shall disannul it? And His hand is stretched out, and who shall turn it back?*

Often there may be many people around you, but very few, if any, are open to understanding and getting involved in the healing journey. However, the unwillingness and lack of involvement of others must be left up to God to deal with. It is He Who has begun a good work in you, and He will never let you down. Even if the entire world should refuse to be understanding, supportive, or walk with you on this journey, yet the Lord Jesus can never fail you. It is far better to have the Lord as your defense and guide in the healing process without anyone else to walk alongside you, than to have many friends without the true defense of God at your side!

God knows the whole story of your life, inside and out, but those around may not. Because of this, He is willing to stand between you and anyone who projects words and attitudes of judgment and condemnation about the healing process you are in. God is not a quitter, so you never have to fear that He will drop you or give up on the work when you have a willingness of heart and mind to follow His direction. Remember, it is God's verdict and opinion of you and your needs that really counts, not the restricted view of those around who can only see skin deep!

The Lord is a defense for the defenseless, widow, and the fatherless. No other individual can shield and defend us as God does, for there is no counsel, wisdom, or knowledge that can go against what God is doing or has decreed to happen in our journey.

PRAYER: Lord, I want to thank You for being my Strong Tower and Defense, especially when nobody else could understand. I choose to release to You everyone who has condemned the healing work You are doing in me. Please grant each one of them a touch of Your love and grace today in whatever they may be facing. Teach me to love as You do, Oh Lord. Amen.

My Maker, My Husband

The Lord my Maker, most Divine,
Has planned my life with His design:
By His great hand uniquely made—
A heritage, which none invades.

Though left alone, forsaken, grieved,
Abandoned, sorrowed, and bereaved,
The Lord in mercy gathers me—
His kindness great He lets me see.

For God's my Husband—even mine—
The "Lord of Hosts" His name Divine:
Forsaken and midst grief refused,
He's called me and has not accused.

"From thee My kindness won't depart,
Though tossed, afflicted, pained at heart,
Nor shall My peace be moved from thee:
For I'm thy Lord—My mercy's free!

In righteousness I'll help thee stand,
So far from all oppression's land;
No fear or terror shall come nigh:
For I protect thee from on high!

Thy children shall be taught of Me:
For this My covenant to thee—
So great shall be thy children's peace,
Whose knowledge of Me shall not cease.

With loving arms I gather thee—
A 'Chosen Jewel' made by Me;
My righteousness from thee shall shine:
For I have called thee, thou art Mine!"

The Lord As Husband

Those who have experienced some of the better things in marriage and all that is involved may have difficulty understanding everything contained here. But it is only fair to identify with those who know nothing about what a marriage ordained by God was meant to be. True, every marriage has some bumps and disagreement along the way. And every marriage that is to last takes 110 percent Christ-inspired efforts of love (not lust) from both partners, but that is not what this is about.

God has never designed for marriage to be overrun with divorce and remarriage. In Moses' day, He allowed it because of the hardness of men's hearts. When one is experiencing severe abuse, absolute control, terror, and children being destroyed, God in heaven sees and hears. He actually does more than that according to 1 Corinthians 7:11: "But and if she depart, let her remain unmarried, or be reconciled to her husband: and let not the husband put away his wife." When there is absolutely no way to reconcile and there are lives at stake, God made *an escape route* for the bruised, battered, and bleeding woman and her children to survive and find safety.

This, however, does not give any room or license to divorce, seek revenge, or remarry. "Whosoever putteth away his wife, and marrieth another, committeth adultery: and whosoever marrieth her that is put away from her husband committeth adultery" (Luke 16:18).

When "the escape route" from death is used, the Lord steps in and fills the role of Provider and husband to the grieved and forsaken woman. He will not leave you destitute but will walk every step of the way with you if you ask Him to. He is a Father to the fatherless and supplies in ways one would have never dreamed. But it is mandatory to daily choose to forgive and release your husband into the hand of Jesus and seek to receive His true love. To have true love does not mean you must endanger yourself or your children, but rather that you view the one who hurt you through the eyes of Jesus, seeing the little boy within that is most likely in need of a loving touch from the Master. Spite, hate, and revenge will only be shooting ourselves in the foot while bequeathing ground to the enemy so he can build strongholds within us.

PRAYER: I choose to forgive and release my husband into Your hand, Lord, and ask that You would touch him with Your love. Amen.

Peace On Earth

As shepherds watched their flocks by night,
They suddenly were filled with fright:
The angel of the Lord came down—
God's glory bright shone all around!

To Bethlehem, let us draw near,
As tidings of great joy we hear:
"To you is born a Savior, Child—
The Baby, Jesus, meek and mild!"

"Glory to God!" the heavens rang,
As all the joyful angels sang:
"Good will to men, and peace on earth,
Comes down from heav'n through Jesus' birth!"

Then to the stable, glowing bright
With God's great Gift, His Son of Light,
The shepherds hastened on their way—
Found Jesus in a bed of hay!

And later on, a star shone bright
Which guided wise men through the night:
With frankincense and myrrh and gold,
They sought the King, foretold of old.

Let's hasten now to Christ our King—
In lowly birth, salvation brings:
Peace, mercy, love, He doth impart,
When Christ is born within our heart!

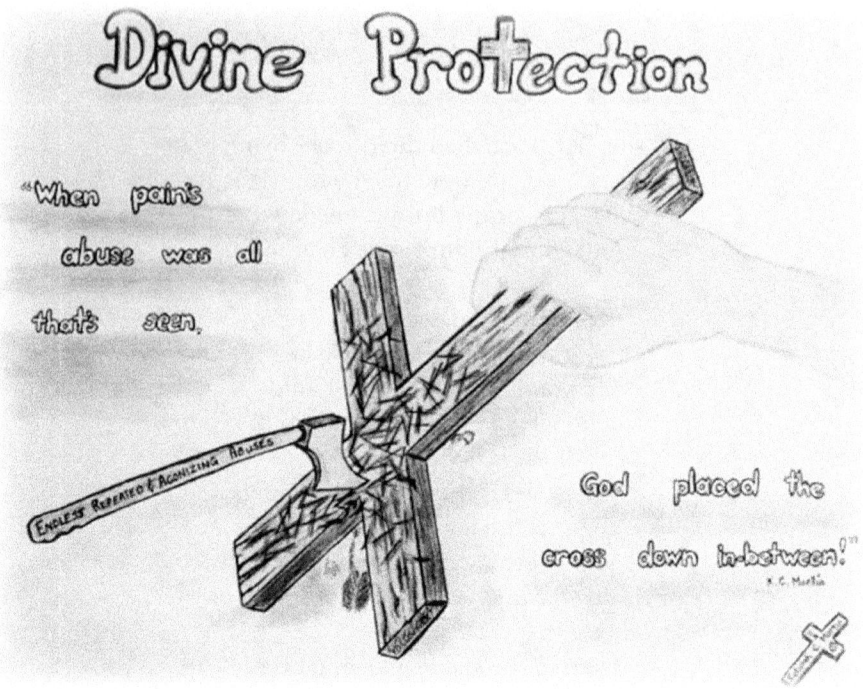

The Cross In-Between

This is a literal picture of what Jesus showed me when I cried out to Him, asking where He was right in the midst of the life-shattering pain. When He responded with this picture, I never again questioned His whereabouts, for I know beyond doubt that *if Jesus had withdrawn the Angel of His Presence, I would not have survived.* What unspeakable love and mercy He truly has shown in these situations!

At the time of writing this book, I tried to put this picture in for December 19—the next page I was doing. However, no matter how hard I tried, it was blocked from that day and always resorted to December 20. Finally I realized that God must want it to be put on my birthday so He can remind me that He has preserved me from the day of birth and has a plan for me! Praise be to God! Hallelujah!

When Jesus Makes New

My Jesus makes new: for a choice He once made,
To taste death for me and sin's penalty paid;
In me a great wonder of grace hath been wrought:
For Christ paid my ransom—my soul He hath bought!

When Jesus makes new, one again can begin
And start with a record that's free from all sin;
The bondage of pain, the deep hurts of the past,
Through healing in Jesus do not need to last.

When Jesus makes new, all the past is behind:
For He fully cleanses from all that would bind;
The deep inner wounds and the anguish of night,
My Jesus can heal as He radiates light.

When Jesus makes new, Satan loses all hold,
And flees from His blood, where before he was bold;
The fetters and chains are cast into the sea,
When Jesus steps in and sets captives all free!

When Jesus makes new, He gives purpose for life,
And dissipates hopelessness, wrapped in dark strife;
He shapes and He molds us for service divine—
Creating clean vessels through whom He can shine.

When Jesus makes new, right beside me walks—
In love holds my hand as together we talk;
He tells of a mansion He's making for me:
For I'm a new creature—in Jesus I'm free!

The Wrecking Of Homes

In warfare of life our sly enemy roams,
Whose specialty lies in the wrecking of homes;
With force he'll attempt to break in courtship's door—
With words, lust, and touches he'll pry and he'll bore:
Dark lies are injected to husband or wife,
Implying some failure, thus leading to strife;
He hammers down trust till in splinters it lies,
And love's bursting bloom will thus wither and die.
He drives forceful wedges that stop and blockade
The discourse of spouses till ruins are made
In daily relating, in attitudes too
Then talking out issues they cannot, won't do.
To wives he will whisper, "You slave in your role—
Submission should never be part of your goal;"
But when she steps out of her God-assigned place,
She hurts her own soul and the home is disgraced.
He brings situations which cause "self" to rise,
Arrayed with abuse which will heed not the cries
Of love's self-denial and sacrifice true,
But slaughters emotions in anguish anew.
The husband might say, "I'm the head, you obey!"
Yet fails to submit to Christ leading the way.
For Satan well knows that mere man will but fail,
And seeks to ensure that God's love won't prevail.
But Christ can build walls that the enemy razed,
Which granted protection in love's bygone days,
He brings restoration to discourse once sweet—
But husband and wife must cast all at His feet.
Die wholly to self is a "must" for each day,
That Jesus as "Lord" may direct all the way:
For when He is given the reins of one's life
He dissipates fully abuse and pained strife.
Oh joyous communion and fellowship sweet,
When Christ as the Leader makes each life complete;
If we but allow Him, He'll fully create
A life, home, and marriage where love rules each gate.

KETURAH C. MARTIN

Paralysis

For anyone, especially survivors of abuse, the enemy often uses two of his most effective tools to create spiritual paralysis in anyone who will give him a fraction of an inch. These deadly tools are doubt and fear. For those who have experienced the fangs of abuse, the doubt about their value and any hope of restoring it runs rampant. The enemy watches for an opportune moment to latch onto these doubts to create total unbelief in what God can do on their behalf.

As soon as the doubts and all that they consist of reach the heart, numbing paralysis begins in earnest to pervade the believer as darkness gradually descends. The Bible says that "whatsoever is not of faith is sin," and sin will always bring darkness and disillusionment. By this time, Satan is gnawing on his captive prey, but often, the paralysis is so severe that his subject cannot feel what is happening internally, or if the doubt has developed into full-blown deception, he would not even know it.

To be spiritually paralyzed by doubt, with the consequent unbelief and deception, can be a very frustrating place to be. This is especially true if the enemy's captives don't realize they have been captured, and, in their head, they want to serve Jesus, yet everywhere are unseen or unknown obstacles that they cannot identify. They may feel disconnected from God yet desire to feel connection and assurance, but it is obvious that there is a barricade which is insurmountable if it cannot even be identified.

The tool of fear that the enemy uses comes from many angles. One of the greatest fears is that of sharing anything that happened due to threats and fear of rejection. This fear is drastically increased when even God's children do not make a safe, non-judging and confidential place for them to share and be supported. Discreditation of their experiences by believers is a method Satan uses to feed the fear in survivors, which keeps them captive. Sometimes there is fear to be in the public or any place where there may be males around due to the abuse that they suffered. Fear paralyzes one into a mode that is too scared to reach out and receive the hope and healing that Jesus offers. Fear can be replaced by the love of Jesus, for perfect love casts out fear.

Prayer: Lord, I renounce all the fears, lies, and doubts with which Satan has bound me. I choose to believe that You can bring me healing and freedom through Jesus! I renounce all fear that You'll reject me, and I claim Your healing. Amen.

To Spread Joy In Giving

He sits in his miserly corner of coins,
With pantry well-stocked and with rich-girded loins;
The bronze, gold, and silver he counts and recounts—
Old Scrooge, Ebenezer, in wealth daily mounts.

The orphans and homeless slink past his rich door,
Afraid that today he will growl out once more,
Despising their beggarly fashions of gloom—
Withholding all substance, pronouncing their doom.

The crippled and blind boys are wholly disdained—
His lofty, self-viewpoints are fully ingrained:
For all of the needy are lower than he,
Deserving of naught in his wealthy degree.

He lavishly gathers the gold to himself,
And others' stark needs he doth perch on the shelf:
From all his abundance no dime can be spared,
For those of less fortune, the sad and impaired.

The downtrod and heartbroken he doth cast out,
Assured they are naught that he need fret about,
He harshly condemns their abused, broken state,
And seeks fading riches, his "joy" to elate.

My friend, let me tell you, "I must not, can't bear
To live as a miser in selfish despair—
While breath in me lingers I must still be used
To lift up the needy, and help the abused.

And when Christ the Master shall bid me arise,
To spread joy and giving, to hear wounded cries,
No sacrifice then is too great while I live—
For them I'd be willing my life e'en to give!"

KETURAH C. MARTIN

The Star of All Hope

Keturah C. Martin

Wendell D. Glick

1. The Lord Jesus Christ was sent down to this earth— Was born in a sta-ble in low-ness of birth; The Babe in the man-ger was sent down to save: For He paid our ran-som from sin and the grave; For He paid our ran-som from sin and the grave;

2. The kind Prince of Peace came to heal bro-ken hearts— To bind up the wounds which were tat-tered a - part; This Je - sus can heal in - sur-mount-a - ble pain. Midst ru - ins, im - pos - si - ble, bring a great gain! Midst ru - ins, im - pos - si - ble, bring a great gain!

3. Though born midst the low - ly, near beasts of the stall, Yet King of all kings, He is Lord ov - er all; He sets cap-tives free and gives sight to the blind, He walks with the down-trod and lends a hand, kind. He walks with the down-trod and lends a hand, kind.

4. As an - gels near Beth - le-hem sang out that night— We too would pro-claim His great love, grace and might: To grief He brings sol - ace and heals ev - 'ry pain- The deep - est of needs He can fill and sus - tain. The deep - est of needs He can fill and sus - tain.

Cont.

Refrain:

(SB) The Star of all hope shin-eth bright-er to - day:____
(AT) The Star of all hope____ shin - eth bright - er to - day:____ For Je - sus our

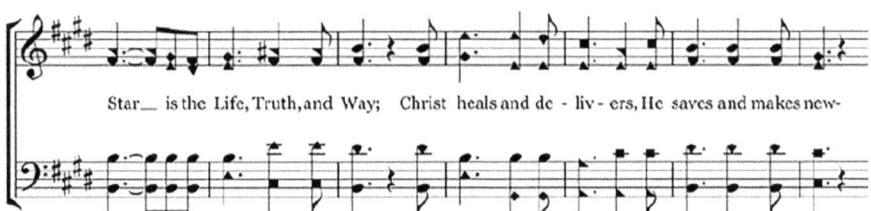

Star__ is the Life, Truth, and Way; Christ heals and de - liv - ers, He saves and makes new-

Those things thought im - pos - si - ble Je - sus can do!____ Those

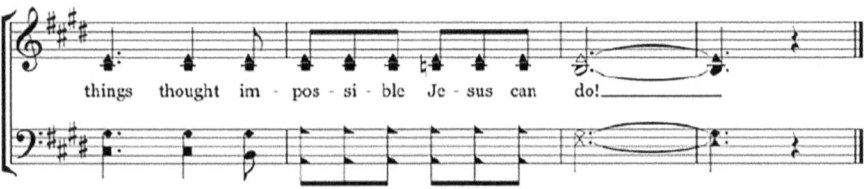

things thought im - pos - si - ble Je - sus can do!____

November 1, 2008

KETURAH C. MARTIN

Prayer And Psalm

Put your name in the blanks

When _____ dwelleth in the secret place of the most High, she shall abide under the shadow of the Almighty. _____ will say of the LORD, He is my refuge and my fortress: my God; in Him will I trust.

Surely He shall deliver me from the snare of the fowler and from the noisome pestilence. He shall cover me with His feathers, and under His wings I will trust: His truth shall be my shield and buckler. _____ shall not be afraid for the terror by night, nor for the arrow that flieth by day, nor for the pestilence that walketh in darkness, nor for the destruction that wasteth at noonday.

A thousand shall fall at my side, and ten thousand at my right hand; but it shall not come nigh me. Only with _____ eyes shall she behold and see the reward of the wicked. Because _____ has made the LORD, which is my refuge, even the most High, her habitation; there shall no evil befall neither shall any plague come nigh her dwelling. For He shall give his angels charge over _____, to keep her in all her ways. They shall bear _____ up in their hands, lest she dash her foot against a stone.

_____ shall tread upon the lion and adder: the young lion and the dragon shall she trample under feet.

Because she hath set her love upon Me, therefore will I deliver her: I will set her on high, because she hath known my name. _____ shall call upon Me, and I will answer her: I will be with her in trouble; I will deliver her, and honour her.

With long life will I satisfy _____ and show her my salvation.

PRAYER: Thank You, Lord, for being so ready to defeat the schemes and attempts of the enemy on my behalf. Thank You, Father, for the secret place under the shadow of Your love where I can rest and abide. I request Your Presence and power throughout this journey for the glory of Jesus. Amen.

DECEMBER 27
READING: JEREMIAH 33:3

God's Telephone Service

Since 1847 to 1922, during which time the telephone was invented by Alexander Graham Bell, the phone service and technology has been always trying to improve on all it has to offer, including its bill. And sad but true, the more people have, the more they want until technology can become a god.

Long before mankind came up with the phone idea, God had His own telephone system in place, which even at this point far exceeds what man has come up with. Not only does He have an excellent telephone service, but He also has thousands of agents who do all their service calls free of charge!

The following are some of the policies of God's telephone service:

- ✓ There are no monthly fees, service charges, or long-distance plans.
- ✓ Before they call, I will answer, and while they are yet speaking, I will hear.
- ✓ God is able to do exceeding abundantly above all that we ask or think.
- ✓ For He shall give his angels charge over thee to keep thee in all thy ways.
- ✓ God shall supply all your need according to His riches in glory by Christ Jesus.
- ✓ Your Father knoweth what things you have need of before you ask Him.
- ✓ Whatever you shall ask in My name, that will I do, that the Father may be glorified in the Son.
- ✓ Your Heavenly Father will give the Holy Spirit to them that ask Him.
- ✓ I will call upon the LORD, Who is worthy to be praised: so shall I be saved from mine enemies.
- ✓ Call upon Me in the day of trouble: I will deliver thee and thou shalt glorify Me.
- ✓ The Lord is good, ready to forgive, and plenteous in mercy unto all them that call upon Him.
- ✓ And all things whatsoever ye shall ask in prayer, believing, ye shall receive.
- ✓ The LORD is nigh unto all them that call upon Him, to all that call upon Him in truth.

PRAYER: Lord, teach me how to effectively use Your telephone service so I can be connected to You, relate to You, and access Your love and grace. Amen.

KETURAH C. MARTIN

Write In Pencil

Our lives are often so filled up with our plans, hopes, and ideas that we become accustomed to navigating our own course and drawing up our own blueprint. However, despite our most genuine attempts, unless the Lord build the city, they labor in vain that build it. We need to be willing to let Him take the wheel and choose our course. After all, He can see through any storm, darkness, or fog just as if it were a clear, sunny day with nothing adverse in the way.

For those who are traveling from survivor's ship to the victor's finish line, it is important to always draw our plans and goals in pencil. This is actually the best suggestion for everyone, especially if Christ is the Captain of their ship. That way the Lord can erase whatever He sees best when He charts our course for us. Because He can see the entire past and future, He can look ahead into the horizon and know what is coming up in our immediate future, as well as the long term. When God sees best to erase our plans and goals, it is because He has something far better in mind to fill that exact spot. We do well to remain versatile and flexible so the Lord can maneuver our ship in any direction He knows to be best, despite the gale or storm that then may be encountered. It is very possible that if your ship is steered into a stormy gale, He knew that something far worse would have been forthcoming in the other direction, so He helped you avoid it.

Sometimes in our healing journey, there are times when nothing makes sense, and we just want to get through the journey in *an instant mashed potatoes* fashion. Instant mashed potatoes and healing do not go together unless there is a miracle just as when Jesus walked the earth. Many people looking on expect it to be thus, but sadly, unless one has walked that road, they usually have no clue what many of the agonizing realities actually are and speak from an idealistic viewpoint. *Forgive and forget* is only 50 percent on God's blueprint for a survivor headed toward ultimate victory. When we insist on drawing the blueprint and doing so in ink, then God cannot work freely in us to bring about complete healing.

PRAYER: Lord, I choose to allow You to be the Captain of my ship, and I ask You to draw the blueprint and chart my course where You see best. I ask that You also do the scheduling so I make the stops that You have planned. Amen.

Emotionally Abused

As she rode home from school, twelve-year-old Laura felt as if her heart was literally being torn into little bloody shreds. She was all confused about what was happening in her seventh-grade world. This was the first year in a new school, but it was supposedly a Christian school, so why did it hurt so badly to go there? Why was she so evil that nobody wanted anything to do with her? And why must she always have those horrid seizures where she would fall down, causing everyone to laugh at her?

As she continued to reflect on her day, she thought back to those two times she had had an epileptic seizure today. Usually after about five seconds of feeling really horrible in her head and chest, she would suddenly not know anything. Then after a while, she would wake up on the floor and see everyone staring at her, whispering to each other, and smirking at her in this detestable plight. Laura, having no one to truly be able to share with or discover what the truth really was about herself, turned all the school abuse and shunning in on herself; and daily her self-hatred grew. The picture of love, God, and Christians became very distorted and confused as this scene was repeated almost daily; and her self-hatred escalated. This is just a real-life example of a case of emotional abuse where the innocent suffer due to ignorance and lack of compassion for something there was no control over.

Many individuals suffering severe emotional pain are never acknowledged and often not understood, because it is a pain which nobody except Jesus can see. When your leg is broken, people and doctors sympathize and bend over backward to help. But emotional distress is so misunderstood that one finds it very difficult to ever expose it or seek help. Often the abused suffer such extreme emotional agony that it would hurt far less to have a limb cut off, yet the pain remains invalidated and they are pressured to just pull up their bootstraps, forgive, and get on with their life. This mentality is a huge hindrance to healing. However, even if the whole world refuses to understand or validate the anguish one is experiencing, yet Jesus Christ never changes. He always understands and remains willing to help and bring healing to every throbbing emotion. He went through extreme emotional abuse also and understands perfectly.

PRAYER: Jesus, can You please make a safe place for me to be when those around do not understand and do things to hurt all the feelings inside me? I choose to forgive and release each one to You, and I ask for a big portion of Your love. Amen.

False Guilt

There are three basic kinds of guilt which mankind experiences. The first one is simply that *All have sinned and come short of the glory of God.* We are all born with the human nature that will sin frequently without divine intervention. Therefore we stand guilty before God until we acknowledge that guilt and accept the gift of salvation, which was purchased by Jesus when He died on the cross in our place.

Another kind of guilt is when one is forced to *face criminal charges* due to having committed some crime or illegal thing. Whether they are willing to acknowledge the wrong or not, in the eyes of the law, they are still guilty.

The third guilt is the one we want to look at a bit so those who are travelling to healing and the finish line can better understand some of the things that are common to face on this journey. *False guilt* is what one feels after being abused in any way, especially if the experience is turned inward in a self-blame mode. Someone suffering from false guilt is usually in a state of inner confusion, self-blame, and/or severe brainwashing from the perpetrator.

- It is false guilt when you feel condemnation for the sexual abuse and/or believe it was your sin (Deuteronomy 22:25-27).
- It is false guilt when the victim accepts the perpetrator's messages that portray blame, sin, and threats on her for the evil he just committed (Ezekiel 18:20).
- When one is engulfed with extreme self-hate and cannot forgive themselves for being used and abused, they are living with the effects of false guilt.
- When a wife feels that she *is too bad to be cherished* by her pornographic husband, she barely exists and is encumbered with false guilt. Those into pornography cannot love their wives beyond a 3 percent level.

PRAYER: Lord, I ask that You would show me what is true guilt and what is the lie of Satan to confuse me and keep me in bondage. If there is anything in me that stands guilty before You, please forgive me and I ask that Your Spirit would reveal that to me. I reject all false guilt in the name of Jesus and claim Your truth. Amen.

DECEMBER 31
READING: 1 CORINTHIANS 2:9 AND JOHN 14:1-3

"I Will Take You By The Hand"

A field of snow all white and clean—
With awe I view its glistening sheen:
No tracks I see, just purest white,
Which glimmers even in the night.

Just so, each morning dawns so clear,
With yet no tracks of dirt or smear;
An opportunity from God
To choose just how it will be trod.

A field of white is each new year,
Which as of yet has no shed tear;
And at the threshold of its door
Stands Christ with all His treasure store.

His offer stands so true and strong,
"I'd love, with you, to walk along;
To be your Guide each day and night,
Your Refuge, Strength, and leading Light.

For every step I have rich grace
To pour on hardships you may face;
My love unending will surround
Your every step in untrod ground.

So at the dawn of this new year,
I welcome you, My Child; come near:
For I will take you by the hand
And lead you to a better land!"

PRAYER: Lord, I thank You for helping me through the past year, and I surrender the new year into Your control so that You can be my Savior, Pilot, Captain and Guide every step of the way. Hold my heart, life and future in Your divine hand throughout the coming year, for Your glory. Amen.

KETURAH C. MARTIN

www.ingramcontent.com/pod-product-compliance
Lightning Source LLC
Chambersburg PA
CBHW070901120626
46546CB00001B/91